61-12546

12-11-61

DAG HAMMARSKJOLD

JOSEPH P. LASH is a star editorial writer and columnist for the New York *Post*. Originally from Morningside Heights in New York City, he graduated from City College of New York and received a master's degree from Columbia University.

His early interests were political, and it did not occur to him to be a journalist until James A. Wechsler of the New York *Post* asked him in 1950 to cover the UN for the *Post*. He has been doing it ever since.

Mr. Lash has had articles published in *Harper's, New Republic*, and the *Progressive*. He also assisted Elliott Roosevelt in editing *F.D.R.: His Personal Letters*.

During World War II, Mr. Lash served in the Army in the Pacific. He is married, has one son, and lives in Greenwich Village.

JOSEPH P. LASH

DAG
HAMMARSKJOLD

Custodian of the

Brushfire Peace

DOUBLEDAY & COMPANY, INC.
Garden City, New York

This book is dedicated to
TWL, JL, ER and JAW
who kept me afloat during the
roughest part of the passage

Library of Congress Catalog Card Number 61–12546

Acknowledgments

In writing this book I have been helped by many UN diplomats and officials. They will recognize their observations and assessments throughout. If the acknowledgments are not more specific, it is only because anonymity is one of the obligations of the diplomatic calling. There are accounts in this book of conversations between Mr. Hammarskjold and various statesmen and diplomats. These were reported to me by second or third parties. Mr. Hammarskjold was a faithful practitioner of quiet diplomacy for whom the rule of discretion was absolute. I had the benefit of several private talks with Mr. Hammarskjold, who agreed to the writing of this book but urged me to keep it as impersonal as possible.

J.P.L.

Contents

1. Custodian of the Brushfire Peace 1
2. Dag Hammarskjold—Who Is He? 7
3. The Swedish Heritage 16
4. An International Priesthood 46
5. Mission to Peking 56
6. Holding the Line in the Middle East 66
7. Back from the Brink 80
8. The Steep Hill of Suez 94
9. Arab "Good Neighbors" 112
10. "Constantly Rebuffed but Never Discouraged" 128
11. Preventive Diplomacy 137
12. The UN and the Cold War 147
13. The UN as a Third Force 164
14. A UN Presence 177
15. Vox Populorum 189
16. The Sources of His "Power" 203
17. The Private Man 213
18. The Congo—Precedent or Fiasco? 223
19. Chairman Khrushchev Pounds the Desk 263
20. One-Man Job 281
    Epilogue 293
    Index 298

1

Custodian of the Brushfire Peace

"KOREA, CHINA, INDONESIA, KASHMIR, PALESTINE, HUNGARY, NORTH AFRICA. THERE ARE FIRES ALL AROUND THE HORIZON, AND THEY ARE NOT FIRES ANNOUNCING PEACE."

June 5, 1958

It was New Year's Eve, 1960. The cluster of UN buildings—the upended slab and truncated hourglass—were shrouded in silence. After the banging of shoes, the pounding of desks, the Niagara of speechmaking, stillness had taken over. The carpeted halls were empty, the lounges deserted, the mimeograph machines at rest.

Even the normally austere thirty-eighth floor seemed more hushed than usual. The gay Fritz Glarner abstractions on opposite walls in the Secretary-General's waiting room could not overcome the feeling that curfew had been sounded for 1960.

Only the Secretary-General and his faithful Achates, Andrew Cordier, their secretaries, a guard and a switchboard operator remained on duty. Some members of the "Congo Club," as those in charge of the Congo operation at UN headquarters were called, had gone home before lunch. The Secretary-General had taken the others—Cordier, Dr. Ralph Bunche, and Heinz Wieschhoff, "one of the world's best people on Africa"—to lunch at the Gripsholm. "Three Americans and a Swede," one of them had commented self-consciously. After lunch Bunche went home and Hammarskjold told Wieschhoff, who was scheduled to leave with him for Africa the day after New Year's, that he should go home too and be on hand for the neighbors who were coming in on New Year's Eve.

Hammarskjold and Cordier remained on duty because of the Congo and Laos. The day before, the UN had got wind of a move by Colonel Mobutu to go after a pro-Lumumba garrison in Kivu Province by way of Ruanda-Urundi, a Belgian-administered trust territory. In a *note verbale,* Hammarskjold had cautioned Belgium that giving Mobutu's forces such transit rights would violate Belgium's obligations as custodian of a trust territory and constitute defiance of the General Assembly resolution against outsiders intervening in the Congo.

If Hammarskjold's most acute concern on New Year's Eve was the reply from Brussels, downstairs, where a few newsmen loitered in the glooming bullpen, the story was Laos. Laotian representative Sisouk Na Champassak was scheduled to come in for another talk with Hammarskjold at five-thirty. He brought alarming news of alleged intervention on behalf of the pro-Communist faction in Laos by the Communist neighbors of the tiny landlocked kingdom. In Washington, U.S. officials were trying to decide whether to have SEATO intervene directly to aid the pro-Western faction. From Peking issued warnings that the U.S. was "at the brink of the precipice." Moscow was calling for a meeting of the Geneva signatories. Sisouk did not ask Hammarskjold for UN assistance. His meetings with the SG, as were those of the other delegations who came in to talk with him about Laos, were designed to keep a safety exit open away from the brink, if that should become advisable.

Reports were also flowing in to Hammarskjold from his own representative in Laos, Edouard Zellweger, a level-headed and experienced Swiss diplomat. This was not the first time that internal Laotian instabilities and external East-West rivalries had threatened international peace and security. A year earlier the SG, at the request of the Laotian Government, had himself taken a hand in stabilization efforts and established a UN presence in Vientiane under an economic hat. But that was when the play of international forces—the Soviet-American thaw, Sino-Soviet disagreements, allied interrelationships—had moved into a balance where all sides were prepared, if not to welcome, at least to acquiesce in the Secretary-General's responding to Laotian requests for help.

At that time Hammarskjold had used the end-of-the-month Security Council luncheon that is given by the outgoing president to present what Council members called a "brilliant" exposition of the Laotian situation. He set forth a policy line of nonalignment, internal reconciliation and economic development that appeared to have universal agreement from everyone.

On New Year's Eve, 1960, the line remained valid. But there was little Hammarskjold could do. The only solution for Laos was its complete neutralization. Unwillingness by both sides to accept this had greatly reduced the effectiveness of the UN technical assistance mission in Laos. Neutralization on the pattern of Austria or Finland would mean strictly hands off on all sides, and none of the powers on New Year's Eve were ready for that.

Hammarskjold was further immobilized by the Soviet attack on him as a lackey of Western imperialism. A new Laotian initiative would undoubtedly arouse Moscow's furious hostility. The attacks he could shrug off, but he could no longer be certain that his intervention would serve a useful purpose. All that Hammarskjold could do in the circumstances was to place himself in a condition of "intensified availability." On New Year's Eve this meant maintaining a "fingertips" knowledge of the forces and personalities stirring up the Laotian cauldron. It meant rearranging African travel plans so that they would permit an immediate return to headquarters.

Sisouk filled in the corporal's guard of reporters who awaited him as he left the elevator. They filed their stories. Oscar Faura, the bluff and helpful Peruvian who was UN press duty officer that weekend, announced the "lid is on" and the newsmen finally departed to their various New Year's Eve celebrations, unaware of other dramas unfolding on the thirty-eighth floor.

At 6 P.M. a cable had come in from Hammarskjold's special representative in the Congo, Rajeshwar Dayal of India, saying that a light plane had flown over Bukavu, the capital of Kivu Province and had dropped pro-Mobutu leaflets. It was of a type that could only have come from an airfield in Ruanda-Urundi. Concurrently radio stations in Usumbura, Katanga, Brazzaville were broadcasting disturbing rumors and reports of troop movements. All tended to confirm UN fears that Colonel Mobutu was about to initiate a military operation against pro-Lumumba Congolese forces from the privileged sanctuary of Belgian-administered Ruanda-Urundi. Hammarskjold had an aide deliver an oral protest to the Belgian delegation.

Later in the evening a new crisis arose. The Cuban delegation delivered a letter, declaring that the U.S. was "about to perpetrate, within a few hours, direct military aggression" against Cuba and asking for "an immediate meeting" of the Security Council. Despite the gravity of the complaint and the Secretary-General's responsibilities in any crisis affecting peace and security, Hammarskjold learned that a great deal had been going on without his being informed. Soviet Deputy Foreign Minister Zorin, who was president of the Council until midnight, and Omar Loutfi, the permanent representative of the United Arab Republic, scheduled to be president during the month of January, had been apprised of the Cuban letter hours before Hammarskjold. At Zorin's urging, Loutfi had agreed to set a meeting for the next day. Wieschhoff was told he had better return to headquarters. A staff member was assigned to call the Council members about a New Year's Day meeting; only junior delegation officials could be located New Year's Eve and could not give consent for a meeting the next day. Meanwhile, the SG's office tried to locate Georgi P. Arkadyev, the Soviet national in charge of the Political Affairs Department. They finally tracked him down at a New Year's Eve party at the offices of the Soviet delegation. Arkadyev was requested to come down to headquarters immediately where the SG and Arkadyev were soon closeted in earnest conversation on the obligations of an international civil servant and the UN chain of command. It was Arkadyev who had failed to inform the SG of the Cuban complaint and set the machinery in motion for a council meeting without apprising him.

The sequel to this story is that the Cuban Foreign Minister, unable to get his meeting on New Year's Day, then urged the beginning of the week; the Western powers wanted the end of the week. They finally compromised on Wednesday, January 4.

There had been no abatement meanwhile in Congo developments. The Belgian delegation informed the Secretary-General an answering message had come in from Brussels to his *note verbale* and would be communicated as soon as it had been decoded. It suggested, somewhat disingenuously, that Brussels had not been privy in advance to the request for transit rights and was not itself overly enthusiastic about the development. The Secretary-General and his aides prepared a second and sharper note to the Belgian Government and a report to the Security Council, which the Secretary-General is obligated to keep informed. All in all, the Secretary-General and his aides did not finish until one-thirty New Year's morning.

Congo, Cuba and Laos was the combination New Year's Eve. It was not an unusual one. When he had assumed office seven years earlier there had been fears that Hammarskjold would not be interested in developing the political potentialities of the office of Secretary-General. Instead, by what some, in tribute to a kind of wizardry in the operation, called a "conjuror's act," Hammarskjold had transformed the few pregnant phrases in the Charter on the Secretary-General's office— and its more numerous silences—into a unique writ in the cause of international peace and security.

Skillful handling of a series of crises in the Middle East, South Asia and Africa, out of which had emerged the concept of a UN presence as the instrument for defusing the crises attending decolonization, had turned the Secretary-General into a custodian of the brushfire peace, helping the new states of Asia and Africa move from colonial subjection to vigorous nationhood without becoming entangled in great power rivalries and without further envenoming those rivalries.

In the course of doing so, this lonely and unassuming civil service aristocrat had become the most famous Swede since Charles XII. But on New Year's Eve for the first time he confessed there was a real danger of overburdening the Secretary-General. He could take it. He had great physical stamina and no family responsibilities. But the Charter did not stipulate that the Secretary-General should also be "unmarried and in superlative health."

On New Year's Eve Hammarskjold felt himself on a sort of steeplechase with problems involving peace or war racing across his desk, with a mass of documents absorbing all his remaining time and none left for the long-term thinking that was indispensable.

Indispensable because a new challenge had arisen that was shaking the UN to its very foundations. In the summer of 1960 when the UN had moved swiftly and competently into the Congo, the role of the UN in a divided world seemed well established. But that was when Africa was united and the big powers were agreed on keeping the Congo out of the cold war.

By year's end, as the SG prepared to leave for Africa, the great powers were quarreling violently; Africa was splitting up into right, left and center nationalisms; the Congo was close to civil war and anarchy; a Soviet drive was on to reduce the Secretary-General's office to impotence.

The UN was being put to a supreme test: not only the future of the Congo but the usefulness, some thought the very existence, of the UN was at stake.

"I am hopeful—that's a professional weakness: hopeful and insistent," Hammarskjold commented to newsmen on his way to Africa. He was replying to a query about his chances of getting Belgium to heed his protests, but it also served to describe the mood in which he approached the larger challenge.

2

Dag Hammarskjold — Who Is He?

In the spacious, rose-carpeted office that houses the U. S. Secretary of State, the telephone rang. It was the end of March 1953, and John Foster Dulles, its new occupant, was conferring with H. Freeman ("Doc") Matthews, Acting Deputy Under-Secretary and formerly in charge of the European desk, and Paul H. Nitze, head of the Policy Planning Committee but about to leave the government.

Dulles listened, put down the receiver and turned to the two men: "That's Cabot Lodge. He tells me they have suggested a fellow by the name of Hammarskjold and Vishinsky has accepted."

"If you can get him, grab him," Doc Matthews commented.

Nitze recalled having dealt with Hammarskjold in 1946 when the Swedish–U.S. trade agreement was renegotiated at Sweden's request. Sweden had run into a foreign exchange crisis and needed relief. He had never seen a better-organized collection of data or a more excellent presentation of a complex problem, Nitze told Dulles.

Dulles' mystification at the name of Hammarskjold did not exceed that of his delegation in New York when French representative Henri Hoppenot first brought up the name and said Vishinsky had indicated he was acceptable. Lodge moved fast. A decision had to be made so promptly he did not have an opportunity to meet with the Latin-American group, as he later explained to complaining diplomats from that group.

When Hoppenot, backed immediately by Sir Gladwyn Jebb, suggested Hammarskjold, members of the U.S. delegation went out to canvass their Scandinavian colleagues asking, "Who is this guy?" They were surprised to learn that "this guy" had just recently been in New York heading the Swedish delegation in the opening weeks of the second part of the Seventh General Assembly. The dossier that was amassed, from Americans who had dealt with him chiefly in Marshall Plan negotiations in Europe, as well as Europeans, showed a Swedish civil service aristocrat, gifted administratively, unobtrusive rather than flamboyant, a brilliant technician, an executant rather than a political leader, and, some feared, a compromiser rather than a fighter.

These qualities, while they left some questions among the Americans, were precisely the ones that recommended Hammarskjold to his British and French sponsors. They had not been enthusiasts of the bold political initiatives taken by Trygve Lie. They wanted to get back to the tradition established by Sir Eric Drummond at the League of Nations: high-level administration, behind-the-scenes conciliation, no speaking out in public on behalf of an international point of view. While the UN Charter, unlike the League's, specifically conferred on the Secretary-General the right to take his own initiative in matters threatening peace and security, Britain and France would have preferred more restraint on Lie's part in asserting a political role.

"I wasn't happy with the British on several occasions," Lie later commented. "They were very much disappointed with me. Palestine, Persian oil, to mention just two examples, and I could mention more." The French had "made some difficulties" because of the impact of his blunt-spoken anti-colonialism on French Africa, and also "they didn't like me because I didn't speak French."

Hammarskjold's name was put forward by the French and seconded by the British. There is some suggestion that the proposal originated with the British, and that Sir Anthony Eden, who was then Foreign Secretary, had a hand in it. But the British asked the French to take the lead because they were committed to Lester ("Mike") Pearson of Canada. He was already out of humor with his British colleagues because he felt that by rushing a vote on his candidacy they had precipitated a Soviet veto.

The British and French had come to know Hammarskjold after the war in the European negotiations establishing the Organization for European Economic Cooperation. As the head of the Swedish delegation in very complicated transactions he had acquired a reputation among professional diplomatists for fairness, resourcefulness in devising compromises, a "razor-sharp mind," (the comment of Hugh Gaitskell), unflagging intellectual energy and a physical constitution to match.)

Soviet calculations in accepting Hammarskjold were more obscure. They knew a good deal about him. The previous year the Russians had shot down two Swedish planes over the Baltic. The Swedish Foreign Minister, Osten Unden, was on holiday in Italy and Hammarskjold, the number two man in the Foreign Office, directed the angry exchange of notes that followed the incidents—"so I was very much in their books," he commented later. The Russians, after Trygve Lie, also favored a weak Secretary-General. In 1946, Soviet delegate Andrei Gromyko had been the chief advocate of liberally construing the Charter provisions regarding the Secretary-General's functions and powers. But this was a short-lived liberalism. Dr. Aleksander Rudzinski, who was legal adviser to the Polish delegation in 1946 and who subsequently accepted asylum in the U.S., wrote that after the Korean invasion and Lie's part in organizing UN resistance to the Communist attack, "the Soviet Union, misled by Mr. Lie's intervention in the Iranian affair, favored granting him broad political powers and regrets now its mistake." They organized an all-out attack against Lie, culminating in a veto in 1950 of his re-election when his term of office expired. Vishinsky denied Korea was the reason. Instead, he argued that Lie was a "lackey" of the State Department, that he had agreed to the establishment of "illegal organs," that he was hanging on to the job because "it is quite nice to receive $25,000 a year forever, with another $25,000 thrown in"—actually it is $20,000 and $20,000, tax-free—and when the Assembly extended Lie's term to 1953, Vishinsky announced: "He is unobjective, two-faced; we will have no truck with him."

But by the spring of 1953, new winds were blowing from Moscow. Stalin had died. "Foreign Minister" Vishinsky, after paying tearful tribute to "the great Stalin" in the Political Committee, had journeyed to Moscow and returned "delegate" Vishinsky, a mellower Bolshevik, charged with advancing the peace offensive launched by the new men in Moscow.

A stalemated UN did not fit Moscow's effort to defuse the international situation while Stalin's heirs struggled with the issue of the succession. The day Vishinsky accepted Hammarskjold, Red China's Foreign Minister Chou En-lai removed the final roadblock to an armistice in Korea by announcing acceptance of the principle that no force should be used to bring about repatriation of Korean prisoners of war.

The change in Moscow's policy may explain why Trygve Lie took Hammarskjold's selection with such ill grace, emerging, in fact, as the bitterest behind-the-scenes opponent of the decision. Candidates, official and unofficial, ranging from Pearson to Krishna Menon of India, had not been able to muster the necessary vote. It was understandable that Lie, looking for vindication, would hope that in the end the Council would return to him—hopes that were given added impetus with the change in Moscow's leadership and policies. He turned white when Lodge came in on March 31, on his way down to the Security Council meeting, to say it was all fixed for Hammarskjold and that the meeting would be over in short order. His disappointment vented itself in uncharitable references to Hammarskjold, most of them designed to suggest that the big powers had been able to agree on the Swedish diplomat because nothing in his record indicated he would take any risks in defense of the Charter. His feelings were reflected in his book a year later, *In the Cause of Peace*. Recalling that he had warned Hammarskjold: "The task of the Secretary-General is the most impossible job on earth," he observed: "Any Secretary-General will find it so if he tries to be the kind of officer that I think the San Francisco Charter envisaged. Should his conception be the same as mine, he will find it impossible to avoid the displeasure of one or more of the greater or smaller states during the years to come. He will be the target of criticism from right, left, and center. . . . Just as the Secretary-General is the servant of the UN and not of any single nation, so he is obligated to risk himself in the interest of a just solution."

If the projection of Hammarskjold's name by France and Britain took the U.S. by surprise and plunged Lie into gloom, his nomination by the Security Council came like "a smash on the head" to the man chosen. He had been in New York with the Swedish delegation the previous autumn when Lie had resigned. The Norwegian statesman had finally been harassed beyond endurance by the Soviet boycott and abuse of him as a U.S. "stooge" on one side and U.S. press and congressional sniping on the other for softness toward Communism because of having American Communists in the Secretariat.

It never occurred to Hammarskjold that he might be Lie's successor. A Swedish name that did come up immediately was that of their Ambassador to Washington, Erik Boheman. Sven Backlund, at that time the lean and sharp-spoken Embassy press officer, recalls spending hours with Boheman on how one declines a job which has not quite been offered and which was not likely to be offered. Backlund came up to spend a day with Hammarskjold and talk about Boheman's problem. They went from one restaurant to another, ending up in a movie—all the time discussing Boheman's difficulties without its ever occurring to either of them Hammarskjold might be the man.

In March 1953, in Stockholm, the vivacious Bo Beskow, commissioned by the Bank of Sweden to paint the portrait of their former board chairman, noted the newspaper reports of the Security Council's difficulty in finding anybody it could agree upon. "It strikes me you would make a very good Secretary-General," he told Hammarskjold.

"Nobody would be so crazy as to propose me," Hammarskjold replied, "and I wouldn't be so crazy as to accept so impossible a job."

Two days later, the morning of March 31, among the cables from the Swedish delegation in New York was a message that some woman in New York, "a fussy busybody," was promoting Hammarskjold's candidacy. Hammarskjold promptly cabled back: "Amused but not interested."

Late that night the wire services began ringing his flat, telling him he had been chosen by the Security Council in New York and wanting his reaction. He indignantly dismissed the reports as newspaper speculation. A newspaper editor, a friend, called him with the same story. He had not heard a word about it, Hammarskjold told him. Apart from the wire service stories there had not been a word from the UN—and then he added, rather sourly, "I might have understood it if it had been to-morrow. Even then I would have considered it as a cruel joke." The next day Hammarskjold found on the front page of his friend's paper a box: "Mr. Hammarskjold would have found it perfectly in order if on April 1 . . ." By then it was official. A cable had arrived from the president of the Security Council, Dr. Bokhari of Pakistan, informing him of the Council's nomination. Dr. Bokhari added: "In view of the immense importance of this post, more especially at the present time, members of the Security Council express the earnest hope that you will agree to accept the appointment if, as they hope and believe, it is shortly made by the General Assembly."

Later, after he had settled down in New York, he was to ask his friend, Sir Gladwyn, how the Council could take a chance like that and present him with a *fait accompli?* How could they put someone in such a position? "How could we ask you before?" Jebb replied. "We knew for certain you would have said no."

Hammarskjold talked with his father, Hjalmar, ninety-one years old but still a man of forceful opinions. The surprised Swedish Cabinet, of which Hammarskjold was the only non-Socialist member, met and consented to his release. He was due for a sitting at Bo Beskow's. He arrived punctually "but we did not do much painting," said Beskow. "Instead we talked about the job. His attitude was that he had no alternative but to accept as a matter of duty. When he went down to inform the press that he was accepting, he was in good spirits."

He cabled the Security Council: "With a strong feeling of personal insufficiency, I hesitate to accept candidature, but I do not feel that I could refuse the task imposed upon me should the Assembly follow the recommendation of the Security Council by which I feel deeply honoured."

He was neither "optimistic nor pessimistic" about his chances of success, he told a crowded news conference. "It is the kind of job where one can only do one's best. You can read about its difficulties in the newspapers."

He apologized to the press for his unresponsiveness the night before. The first he had heard of his nomination was when his "phone began buzzing in the middle of the night." He had returned from New York "two weeks ago and neither there nor in Washington had there been any inkling that I was being considered for Secretary-General."

On April 9, he, Ambassador Boheman and a young Swedish Foreign Office official, Per Lind, arrived at Idlewild. "I want you to come with me to New York," he had told Lind who had been in the Washington Embassy from 1947 to 1951. "That is an order. And if it can be arranged, I would like you to join the Secretariat."

Lie introduced Hammarskjold to the press. It was all right to call him "hammer shield," as Assembly President Pearson had suggested, since that was what the name meant, but the correct pronounciation was "Hammarshuld." He declined to answer questions about his private life. "The private man should disappear and the international public servant take his place." With Lie listening intently, he answered a question about his conception of his job. The Secretary-General should "listen, analyze, and learn" to understand "the forces at work" and the "interests at stake" so that he can give the right advice when "the situation calls for it." He was not advocating a "passive" role for the Secretary-General but "active as an instrument, a catalyst, an inspirer." That could mean little; it could mean much, Lie's aides agreed.

Advance press reports had made a great point out of Hammarskjold's fondness for mountaineering. A touch of the poet showed up when he commented that in Scandinavia the mountains are harmonious rather than dramatic, "matter-of-fact rather than eloquent." The qualities required in mountain-climbing "are just those which I feel we all need today: perseverance and patience, a firm grip on realities, careful but imaginative planning, a clear awareness of the dangers, but also of the fact that fate is what we make it, and that the safest climber is he who never questions his ability to overcome all difficulties."

The next day in the high-domed Assembly Hall before the diplomats of sixty nations and thousands of staff members, President Lester Pearson administered the oath of office:

"I, Dag Hammarskjold, solemnly swear to exercise in all loyalty, discretion and conscience the functions entrusted to me as Secretary-General of the United Nations, to discharge these functions and regulate my conduct with the interests of the UN only in view and not to seek or accept instructions in regard to the performance of my duties from any government or other authority external to the Organization."

Lie then introduced Hammarskjold to the officers of the Assembly. They included Vishinsky. The Soviet delegate shook Hammarskjold's hand, and then there was a burst of applause as he and Lie shook hands for the first time in almost three years.

Lie escorted his successor up to the high officers' dais and showed him his chair behind the green marble desk, next to that of the president. As Lie walked off the floor to the guest section to sit next to Mrs. Lie, Hammarskjold took his seat.

He then moved down to the speakers' rostrum for his inaugural speech.

"Ours is a work of reconciliation and realistic construction," he said, ending his brief words with a line of Swedish poetry: "The greatest prayer of man is not for victory but for peace."

3

The Swedish Heritage
"... the private man should disappear."

In Stockholm's Old City, where the cobbled streets are carriage width and houses and taverns date back to the time when the history of Sweden was also the history of Europe, the Swedish Academy has its lodgings in an eighteenth-century palace. Here the *Eighteen* gather for their weekly discussions, retiring afterwards to Den Gyldene Freden for supper. The hostelry's name commemorates "the golden peace" that settled on the land after Sweden's career as a great power came to an end following the defeats suffered by Charles XII.

In the Academy's palace takes place also the annual meeting where, with the royal family and government in attendance and the *Eighteen* seated in the blue and golden armchairs which date back to the Academy's founding, the Nobel prize for literature is awarded.

It is December 20, 1954. Dag Hammarskjold is in Stockholm to confer with the Chinese Ambassador about his coming trip to Peking. But he is also there to be installed as a member of the Swedish Academy. In the office of the secretary, an atlas-sized blue volume is taken out of its box. Engraved on its parchment pages are the statutes promulgated by Gustavus III when he established the Academy in 1786. A companion case houses a red volume in which the newly elected member signifies his acceptance of the statutes. Hammarskjold signs in the greenish-blue ink that is his scriptorial trade-mark. He signs directly beneath the signature of Hjalmar Hammarskjold, his father, who had died the previous year at the age of ninety-one, and to whose seat the son had been elected.

The newly inducted member goes to his chair. It is numbered XVII and had been occupied previously by his father. His installation address, devoted by tradition to the member whom he has succeeded, is an exercise in filial piety.

Explaining the father, the son notes that "between the nation in history and the individual, the family is the primary tie." Seeking to understand the individual, Dag Hammarskjold, the outlook and qualities he brought to his assignment as Secretary-General, there is no better place to start than with his family. To be faithful to one's heritage in all its individuality, he has said, is also the path to the genuine understanding of the heritage of others. "Faced with the worlds of others, one learns," he remarked years later after UN journeys had taken him to all the continents, "that he who has fully absorbed what his own world has to offer is best equipped to profit by what exists beyond its frontiers."

The Hammarskjold family is part of the Swedish aristocracy, not the great nobles and landed gentry who for centuries feuded with the kings over which would rule Sweden, but the civil service aristocracy which developed after the King had won the battle and the aristocracy was transformed into a civil and military bureaucracy with its task "the service of the Kingdom."

The first Hammarskjold, a cavalry captain, was knighted in 1610 at the time this transformation was taking place and from that time on there were always Hammarskjolds in the service of the King, either as soldiers or civil servants. In the family album which is now in the custody of Landhovding Bo Hammarskjold, the oldest of the clan, there is only one deviant from the portraits in breastplate: a poet, Lorenzo, an open-shirted Byronic-looking figure. Since he lived in Byron's day (1787–1827) this may not have been only a coincidence.

The duty that one owes to family and country is one of the most deeply rooted traits of the civil service aristocracy. Another is hard work. Tirelessness had been established as part of the government tradition from the time of Sten Sture the Elder, the victor of the Battle of Brunkeberg in 1471. Today, with the growing democratization of the civil service, to be a nobleman means to work harder than anyone else.

Legal training is also part of the Swedish aristocratic tradition. The national ethos, from mid-fourteenth century on, has proclaimed that "this land shall be built upon law," and the Swedish aristocracy has been described as "soaked in law."

It was not at all certain that the older Hammarskjold would enter the civil service. His early interests were literary and philological. He took to the law, somewhat to his mother's distress, as a way of supplementing the family's income. Unsuccessful timber speculations and an unhappy involvement in a local railway venture in the early 1880s caused the loss of the family's estate at Vaderum. The resulting impoverishment of the family was such that the sons speak of their father as a poor boy from the country, beginning with nothing at all and achieving position and financial security only after bitter struggle. Having shifted to the law, Hjalmar quickly achieved such eminence that by the turn of the century he was serving as Minister of Justice.

The older Hammarskjold was a stern, commanding, patriarchal figure—a man of firm convictions which his political opponents denounced as reactionary and his defenders described as a conservative's faithfulness to the past.

When Dag was born—July 29, 1905—Sweden was in the midst of the "Union" crisis, arising from Norway's demands for dissolution of the union between the two countries. There were pressures for war, and Hjalmar was one of four Swedish leaders sent to Karlstad to try to work out a peaceful solution.

To the relief of most of Sweden, this was accomplished, but the negotiations delayed the christening of the newborn baby until late autumn. Among the christening presents was a silver chalice from Hjalmar's fellow negotiators at Karlstad with the inscription: "For the one too long without a name."

Although close to the Conservative party in his views, Hjalmar Hammarskjold was never a member of any party. He did not consider service to king and country, which were primary with him, as always compatible with allegiance to a party. When Gustavus V, on the eve of World War I, produced a constitutional crisis by appealing over the head of his Cabinet to the people, Hammarskjold assumed the task of forming a new Cabinet. He did this, explained his son, not to uphold personal royal power but because he considered administrative officials as custodians of the national interest with duties and responsibilities that went beyond party conflicts.

But the son concedes that accepting the assignment "brought him into conflict with the movement toward a fully developed parliamentarianism."

Commenting on Dag Hammarskjold's Academy tribute to his father, a friend said: "It was a new Hjalmar Hammarskjold. Not many would have looked at old Hjalmar in that light."

His reputation, Hammarskjold agrees, was that of representing extreme conservatism, "but I did not regard him as such."

Many of Dag Hammarskjold's friends believe that a more important influence in shaping his political values was his mother, Agnes Almquist, who had married Hjalmar in 1890. Of his mother he said in his Academy speech: "Her characteristics, which appear to me to reflect her family origin, had once emerged with particular clarity and with the somewhat frightening overtones of genius in the poet Carl Jonas Love Almquist, a step-brother of her father: a radically democratic view of fellow humans, 'evangelic' if you like, a child-like openness toward life, an anti-rationalism with warm under-currents of feeling." His mother's influence bred in Dag that understanding and sympathy with people that enabled him to support loyally

and with conviction the democratic equalization policies of
the Socialist governments he later served.

There were four sons in the Hammarskjold household: Bo,
the oldest, dark and short-headed, resembled his mother; Dag,
the youngest—there was a span of fourteen years between the
two—resembled his father, medium height, long-headed, blond.
In between there was the gifted Ake, ten years older than
Dag, a judge at the International Court who died of rheumatic
fever in 1937, and Sten, five years older than Dag, a sickly boy
in his youth, the only one of the four sons not to achieve public
eminence.

As the youngest, Dag was also the closest to his mother. He
was bound to her in a very special way. He postponed his own
interests to be useful to her, and most of his friends cite
this attachment as the explanation of why he never married.

A schoolmate from Uppsala days, when the father was
Governor of Uppland and the family lived in the imposing
fifteenth-century palace that dominates Uppsala, and who often
walked up the hill with Dag to the palace, recalls: "There was
a nice feeling in the family. But the whole family was hard
working. His mother was a wonderful woman, perhaps a little
soft. We only thought she had some difficulties getting along
with five hard-working men who were only interested in their
important work. She was an intellectual woman, but in many
ways she represented the emotional side of the family."

Another friend reports that "she was exactly what the father
was not. He was a forbidding figure, authoritative to the point
of being rude. She was exuberantly forthcoming . . . with good
will and friendliness towards everybody around her . . . great
human warmth. She was a sweet woman and Hammarskjold
was very attached to her."

Old Hjalmar used to say: "If I were as gifted as Dag and
had his talent for dealing with people, I would have gone
far." That talent came from his mother.

A friend who knew both father and son cautioned against
being deceived by the son's apparent gentleness: "Old Hammarskjold had great authority and the appearance of great
authority. He was a very strong personality. Dag also has

authority but he exercises it in a different way. He is much more delicate about it."

At Uppsala, both in gymnasium and university, Dag was by far the most brilliant pupil. "I believe he had the best examination certificate in 100 years," a classmate reports, and whether true or not this was his reputation among his classmates. He was outstanding in all subjects, but above all in languages and literature and in mathematics.

There is a penalty to being the best pupil in the class. There is always some distance between the brightest boy and the rest; real intimacy becomes difficult. His classmates were proud of him, admired and respected him, but did not love him. He himself contributed, being already a little withdrawn, and willing to extend intimacy to no one outside of his family, perhaps no one outside of his mother. "He was a good fellow, but not one with whom to get intimate."

At Uppsala University, where he studied literature, jurisprudence and economics, it was even more hard work. He did not take part in the entertainments that were characteristic of a university town; he was not interested in girls or dancing. On Wednesday and Saturday evenings, when all the others were out dancing, "he only worked.

"He had a very strong father. He wanted his sons to work, to accept the necessity of work. The sons accepted his challenge."

Other students lived in student rooms; Hammarskjold lived with his family in the castle of the governor. But Dag was never considered a sissy. It was never possible to push him around, a classmate reports. "He was a rather strong boy, outstanding in gymnastics, and while he didn't take part in our escapades we liked him." Of these school days, Sten said: "He was very good at straightening out problems and finding solutions in differences of opinion. However, he was not a 'softie'! We could never impose our will on him."

Students at Uppsala were grouped by "nations," that is, according to the province from which they came. Each nation had a house with rooms for reading, writing and meetings. The "nations" approximated the fraternity of the American university and the *Burschenschaft* of the German. Uppland

"nation" was the oldest at the university and during Hammarskjold's student days it celebrated its three hundredth an-
niversary with a great festival and other entertainments. The
respect and admiration in which Hammarskjold was held was
indicated in his election as First Curator of the Uppland
Nation during these important months.

"He was already marvelous at languages and it was wonderful to have so outstanding a student at our head," a classmate
recalls.

Hammarskjold's curriculum vitae at the university began with
a humanities degree after two years' study of literature and
philosophy, a *filialia* in economics after another three years,
and a Bachelor of Laws after two more years.

It was not only the faculty and library that stirred him.
His father's wide-ranging interests were reflected in the table
conversations at home. Since Hjalmar Hammarskjold was delegate to the Disarmament Conference, there was much talk about
that as well as of international law whose codification at
Geneva was proceeding under his chairmanship. The father's
literary interests ranged into the fields of Spanish, Portuguese
and South American poetry, carrying the household with him,
as with Hammarskjoldian productivity he proceeded to translate folk songs from those areas.

There was the spur of conversation with his fellow students
as they walked beside the quiet river that divides the town or
carried their argument into the Gästis restaurant. Freudianism,
the skeptical philosophy of their professor of jurisprudence, Axel
Hagerstrom, Spengler's *Decline of the West* became the subjects
of passionate debates. "Sometimes we went to fetch Hammarskjold at the castle to get his point of view, and in the
marvelous spring evenings—as everyone knows spring evenings used to be marvelous in those days—we walked back
and forth in the Odinslun Park solving the problems."

The town of Uppsala itself kindled the historical imagination.
One of the oldest university towns in Europe, it was also a
former seat of Swedish royalty. The red castle in which the
Hammarskjolds resided, on a hill overlooking the town's spires
and gables, had been built by Gustavus Vasa, who mastered

the clergy and the provinces and fused Sweden into a centralized kingdom. It was an even more ancient center of religion. Rune stones are scattered over the Uppsala campus. As late as the twelfth century, the temple at Uppsala was a major center of Viking worship and human sacrifice. Thor and Odin whisper more closely than the Catholic bishops whose tenure was a brief matter of three centuries when the Protestant Reformation swept Sweden, and Uppsala became the archiepiscopal see of Swedish Lutheranism. In the twenties, Uppsala was alive with new intellectual currents emanating from the church.

"Sometime somebody will perhaps describe the Uppsala of the twenties with the same loving care as has been devoted to the age of Geijer," Hammarskjold observes in his memoir of his father. Erik Gustav Geijer, a Gothicist poet and conservative politician, lived in the early nineteenth century, a brilliant period in Swedish literature and intellectual activity. "The strange, brief idyll," Hammarskjold goes on, "which burgeoned all over Europe between two crises and two wars, had a reflection all its own in Uppsala. The church policy of Soderblom in this period made the city an international center. Soderblom and Hjalmar Hammarskjold joyfully shared the burden of the ceremonial tasks which accompanied this development. Both had a strong sense of academic pomp and circumstance."

Archbishop Nathan Soderblom, founder of the "Stockholm Movement," strove to unite the churches and to bring the spirit of the Gospel to bear upon social, economic and industrial relationships.

The families Hammarskjold and Soderblom were much intermixed. Jon Olof, Archbishop Nathan's son, was Dag Hammarskjold's playmate and schoolmate. Mrs. Hammarskjold was born on the same day as the Archbishop and they were often called "the twins." Both were ardent and outgoing. The Governor and the Archbishop's wife would frequently be seen sitting on the logbox in the castle hall while their spouses dallied in a final chat.

Religion in the Hammarskjold household was a matter of tradition and conventional observance for the father but of passionate commitment for the mother. Agnes Hammarskjold was Low Church in her outlook, and evangelistic religion played a very great part in her life. Her husband's Bible and Psalm Book were well worn from use but he did not speak about religious matters. More often than not it was Dag Hammarskjold who accompanied her to Sunday services.

Dag Hammarskjold's effort to come to terms with the religion of his forefathers was to be set forth in 1954 in a gemlike statement on Edward R. Murrow's radio program, "This I Believe." He spoke of "a never-abandoned effort frankly and squarely to build up a personal belief in the light of experience and honest thinking" which had led him "in a circle."

I now recognize and endorse, unreservedly, those very beliefs which once were handed down to me. . . . The language of religion is a set of formulas which register a basic spiritual experience. It must not be regarded as describing in terms to be defined in philosophy, the reality which is accessible to our senses and which we can analyze with the tools of logic. I was late in understanding what this meant. When I finally reached that point, the beliefs in which I was once brought up and which, in fact, had given my life direction even while my intellect still challenged their validity, were recognized by me as mine in their own right and by my free choice. I feel that I can endorse those convictions without any compromise with the demands of that intellectual honesty which is the very key to maturity of mind.

In the twenties, when his mind rebelled at church doctrine, nature and the Swedish countryside drew him with an almost mystical intensity. In his presidential address to the Swedish Academy on Carl Linnaeus, Hammarskjold said: "A great naturalist guided the author, but a great poet permitted the scholar to peer into the secret Council Chamber of God." The Swedish countryside, to the young Dag, as to Linnaeus, not only was a world of color, sound and movement tempting the sojourner to imagery and song but "deep down, it was a world of meaning."

Those who were Dag Hammarskjold's companions on the hikes through the countryside and up into the mountains speak of him as the best of comrades who "saw so many things" they would otherwise have missed. In the summer there was hiking and bicycling; in the winter, skiing. There was also mountain-climbing, to which he had been introduced by his brother Bo when together in 1922 they had climbed in the mountains of Silesia.

As a skier, Hammarskjold's resources were power and endurance. He was better at going up the trail than down. His technique, while good enough to get him down the mountainside, was not superior, but, added a companion of those days: "In the evenings he could discourse on the art and technique of skiing much more beautifully than the rest of us."

His sense of orientation in the mountains or countryside was uncanny. "We had a Sunday hiking club and he would map out the route so that through any wilderness we got back to the right place at the right time to get the railroad back to town," one companion of those days has said. "When you were with Dag you did not need a guide," added another.

Except for his membership in the Academy, the only Swedish post he has retained while serving as Secretary-General has been that of board member of the Swedish Tourist Association. He was the main mover in the association's publication of the little volume, *Swedish Nature,* an anthology of nature descriptions from Swedish poetry and prose. Some thought it was too difficult to do. The next morning a thick envelope arrived from Hammarskjold outlining the project and itemizing suitable poems and prose—"a book in which the cycle of seasons and the varieties of scenery from Sandhammaren in the far south to the Lapland Mountains in the north wove together fragments of our literature into a picture of this country as it has been experienced by Swedes, separated in time, separated also by origin, philosophy and ambition, but joined in their ties to the soil out of which they have grown."

"I thought I knew most things about Swedish nature poetry," commented a Swedish poet at the time, "but Dag Hammarskjold knows more."

Years later he was to take time out from his duties as Secretary-General to fly back to Stockholm to address the Swedish Tourist Association. The statement was a deeply personal one but characteristically objectified in the form of a comment on poems of Verner von Heidenstam on love of homeland and openness to the world.

"His feeling of deep roots in Sweden, which might have degenerated into complacent provincialism, was balanced by his alert awareness of all that the world had to offer, in a way which, in turn, without its counterpoise in his lively feeling for the homeland, might have transformed him into a rootless cosmopolitan."

The association's injunction "Know your country" was not narrow isolationism but the road that led outwards.

"Faced with the worlds of others, one learns that he who has fully absorbed what his own world has to offer is best equipped to profit by what exists beyond its frontiers. . . . We go to other countries and other continents. We may experience the overpowering greatness of the mountain ridges of Asia, the other-worldly calm of the deserts of Africa, the rain forests of South America or the wide waste expanses of Polynesia. We meet people of other races and other creeds. But the more we see and the more we widen our contacts with our fellow beings in other parts of the world, the more it is also revealed to us that the essential beauties and the ultimate human values are equally present among 'the stones where as children we played' as in these other, far larger, worlds. The road inwards can become a road outwards."

The "road outwards" from Uppsala for Dag Hammarskjold first led to Stockholm. In 1930, Hjalmar Hammarskjold, in his seventies, left his post as Governor of Uppland and moved his household to the capital. Dag Hammarskjold, then twenty-five, went along. The impression he made on his contemporaries at that time is conveyed by this extract from the diary of Sven Stolpe who was then at work on his first novel, chapters of which he gave Dag to read when both found themselves together for a few weeks in the little town of Sigtuna. "Dag has such purity of character and an intelligence of such a high order that I do not for a moment hesitate to write that he will be Swedish prime minister at a young age."

In 1930, Sweden, like the rest of Europe, was descending

into a deep economic crisis, from which it was to emerge "a Fabian paradise."

The best university minds were gravitating toward economics. Stockholm, on Dag's arrival, was the headquarters of a remarkable group of younger economists whose discussions and writings in the early thirties were to give them an intellectual identity as the "Stockholm School."

The school's outlook was broadly speaking Keynesian, but the inspiration and guiding spirit were Swedish. "We all read Keynes' *The Theory of Money* and especially the little pamphlet *The End of Laissez-Faire*," recalls Alf Johansson, inspirer and chief administrator of Sweden's housing program, "but the Stockholm School was really a parallel development emanating from the theoretical thinking of Knut Wicksell."

A brilliant economist and political radical, Wicksell had died before Hammarskjold arrived in Stockholm, but his thinking continued to have an almost personal impact on the younger generation of economists.

Because of Wicksell's work, the books of Keynes, wrote Gunnar Myrdal, another member of the school, "appeared to us as brilliant and important writing on familiar lines and caused none of the shock and the sense of intellectual revolution which they did in his own country and elsewhere." The common ground between Wicksell and Keynes was advocacy of an expansionist policy, acceptance of the need for state intervention into economic life, an active fiscal policy. Because of Wicksell, "We were conditioned from the outset [of the Great Depression] to turn to a realistic and practical discussion of anti-depression policy," commented Myrdal.

Karl Marx had little impact on the group. Erik Lundberg, who with Alf Johansson became Dag's closest friends in the group, says: "There were no real Marxists among our economists. There were radicals and socialists—but without Marx. We had no dogmas of that kind at all." Myrdal, a radical and unorthodox thinker, also testified that "in our milieu, Marxism was never the pressing problem which Liberalism had been. We did not have to 'work it off.'" Myrdal credits Hagerstrom, Hammarskjold's old professor, with having helped "to save the whole post-war generation of Swedish intellectuals from becoming Marxists" by his thoroughgoing skepticism and insistence on rigid analysis of concepts used in social theory.

Another distinguishing characteristic of the Stockholm School was the close involvement of its members with the formation and administration of government economic policy. The older generation of economists rarely had ventured outside of the academic milieu. Hammarskjold's generation, although professional economists, was in the thick of the battle. "I can think of no other country where technical economists had as great an impact on government policy," Johansson observed. Lundberg concurred: "At no other time in Sweden has the debate between academic economists been so intense or has left such a legacy of treatises and articles. The main reason for this was no doubt the intimate concern of economic research with current problems of economic policy."

Almost on arrival, Dag was appointed secretary of the Royal Commission on Unemployment. Soon he was serving as a major catalyst in bringing about this marriage between ideas and action. The postwar generation of economists went to work writing learned theses for the commission. Hammarskjold persuaded the commission to have these appendices made part of the report, and they were to have a considerable influence on Swedish economic policy in the thirties.

Myrdal dealt with the fiscal aspects of anti-depression policy; Bertil Ohlin, now leader of the Liberal party, with monetary policy, public works and tariffs in combating unemployment; Johansson with wages and unemployment; Hammarskjold with the diffusion of economic fluctuations.

As secretary, Hammarskjold also had to write a substantial part of the commission's report. He made it a habit to write exactly four pages a day, considerable for a scientific thesis. He established the regime and stuck to it. There were conflicting views about Hammarskjold's draftsmanship. Already there were complaints that the introduction of subtleties and side issues resulted in a complicated structure.

Hammarskjold's appendix, *Konjunkturspridningen,* like Johansson's, was to do double duty. It also served as his doctoral dissertation. It dealt with the dispersion of prices during the business cycle and the influence of prices abroad on prices internally. The main part was abstract and theoretical; the other, a study of actual price developments before the 1931 crisis.

Hammarskjold defended his doctoral thesis in public in 1933. There were two opponents: one appointed by the faculty, Gunnar Myrdal; the second chosen by the candidate. Hammarskjold selected Karin Kock, not because she was a member of the Stockholm School but because she was working in the same field.

Such discussions generally started at ten and ended at four. "But at four," recalls Professor Kock, "Hammarskjold and Myrdal had only finished *their* discussion. So I had only one hour for my little opposition. Myrdal and I had made a division of work, but not of time."

Stolpe, who was present at Hammarskjold's defense of his thesis, entered in his diary: ". . . it was the most subtle debate I ever heard . . . a brilliant performance."

At the customary dinner that the candidate gives afterwards for his opponents and teachers, Myrdal asked him: "Do you speak at home, too, in these long, eloquent, carefully constructed cycles?"

From the Unemployment Commission Hammarskjold had gone to work for the Riksbank under Ivar Rooth. Until the midthirties, the Riksbank was the main playing ground of Swedish economists, but although his advance was rapid Hammarskjold was discontented because he had too many trivial administrative chores.

He would discuss with friends like Johansson and Lundberg whether to go in for an academic career or continue with administration. But others who knew Hammarskjold at the time doubt that he was ever seriously tempted by an academic career. "I think he was rather clear in his mind from the beginning to get into administration, but I don't think he wanted to be an administrator," Professor Kock commented. "His aim was to get into the layer of civil servants where things are decided."

This also was the impression of Ernst Wigforss, Social Democratic Minister of Finance, the man for whom he now was to go to work and with whom he would be intimately associated for a dozen years. In the first talk Wigforss had with Hammarskjold, while he was secretary of the Unemployment Commission, Wigforss asked him whether he did not wish to become an academic economist. If he should write, Hammarskjold replied, it would be more along the lines of flesh-and-blood economics than the algebraic equations and models he had carefully elaborated in his thesis. He seemed to sense the sterility of this approach and the thesis, in fact, has had little influence. Hammarskjold's special aptitude already was for co-operating with people, defining a formula that would permit a step forward and getting the conflicting parties to go along.

In 1932 the Social Democrats, emerging as the dominant party, took over the government, a position from which they were not subsequently to be dislodged except for a brief interlude. Wigforss was one of the giants of Swedish socialism, representing the academic and intellectual side of the movement. A professor of philology at Lund University, he immersed himself in economics in the late twenties, and, though not a professional economist, mastered the literature and became an "adopted member" of the economists' circle.

He and Hammarskjold became acquainted during their work together on the Unemployment Commission, where Wigforss represented the Social Democrats. Hammarskjold found Wigforss an absolutely fascinating human being, a Fabian in the tradition of the Webbs, completely undoctrinaire, selfless, a first-rate economist and linguist. His socialism, while stemming from Marxism, Hammarskjold considered a not unsympathetic form of extreme humanitarian liberalism. "If that is left socialist intellectuality, it seduced me."

As the Depression deepened, the younger economists as a group found the socialists more skillful and interesting, especially Wigforss who had become Minister of Finance, in their approach to the country's problems. With the Finance Ministry supplanting the Riksbank as the main factor in shaping the country's economic policy, Hammarskjold did not need much urging to shift his talents to the Ministry. For a brief time Wigforss and Rooth shared Hammarskjold. Then, when Dag was scarcely thirty, Wigforss asked him to become Under-Secretary, the top civil service position in the department.

It was highly unusual to give so young a man such large administrative responsibilities. Pressed in Parliament to divide the job, Wigforss consulted Dag. The issue was settled by old Hjalmar, whose advice to Dag "seems to have been firm and short," Wigforss wrote later. "It was all or nothing."

There was a brief moment in the mid-thirties, when the Social Democrats were out of office and the new government tried to pressure Hammarskjold into resigning by spreading the word he was too young. But he stood pat. Wigforss returned and concern about his youth soon ended. In an "amazingly short time," Wigforss reports, the new Under-Secretary acquired a position in the administrative co-ordination of policy comparable to that of an old hand. "To a much greater degree than his father, he (Dag H.) had a talent for winning people personally, straightening out differences and filling a leading role in a big organization," Wigforss wrote in his memoirs.

As top civil servant at the Ministry, Hammarskjold established a working pattern that was to re-create itself in whatever post he held. He built up a close circle of talented collaborators, many of them young economists whom he drew into the Ministry because of his close friendship with Wigforss. They would often, if necessary, work the night through . . . at night, also, one was free of the telephone.

Officials dropping in late at night to finish some work would ask: "Is anybody here?" Invariably the answer would come: "Well, Mr. Hammarskjold, of course."

Wigforss and Hammarskjold worked in a rare kind of harmony. Coming from a long line of civil servants, the correct relationship of a deputy to his Minister was almost a matter of blood and breeding with young Dag. To Wigforss belonged the final determination of policy, its defense in Parliament and with the public. It was indispensable that the Under-Secretary have every thread in his hands since Wigforss, in carrying the whole responsibility in Parliament and before the public, had nothing to go on but Hammarskjold.

Hammarskjold was in full agreement with Wigforss' expansionist, full-employment policies. "The policies we followed were as much his as mine," Wigforss said later, "although I did not like to put any responsibility on him for the policies for which I was criticized." The attacks came from conservative business interests which, in the name of economic liberalism and *laissez faire,* resisted Sweden's movement toward a welfare state.

With Bo Hammarskjold at that time Under-Secretary in the Ministry of Social Welfare, the two brothers between them were writing the laws which transformed Sweden into a welfare state. Their father, said Bo, would complain that his sons were keeping bad company and were too far to the left.

But it did not really "shock my dear father," Dag Hammarskjold believes. "He regarded it as perfectly in order. This was government service. You put all the ability you had at the service of the government and Parliament. If you did not, you would be negating the system under which the country was run. To refuse to do so would have been taking sides politically."

At times when the opponents of Wigforss were out gunning for him and looking for scapegoats, Hammarskjold would also be shot at. "Since I came from a notoriously conservative family, I was a tempting target." He would be accused of being a "fellow traveler" of the Socialists, a "stooge" of Wigforss, and the like.

But Hammarskjold was not a party man. His father, although he never joined the Conservative party or took instructions from it, was ideologically a Conservative and elected by its votes.

His son was even more independent politically. There is, he believes, a need for the kind of man who has a great sense of public responsibility, is politically deeply engaged but serves the state rather than a party. There are families in Sweden, even more so in Britain, where this philosophy of state service brings one generation into co-operation with one party, and another with its rival.

That is the Hammarskjold family tradition. It is not a

conservative tradition, Hammarskjold emphasizes: "The strong civil service accent places it rather in an *etatist* line, that is, country first." With that background, in a period such as the thirties, when the Conservatives, under the influence of big business, turned sharply against state intervention, it was, in fact, easier for Hjalmar Hammarskjold's sons to co-operate with the Social Democrats.

"I am a conservative man," said Bo Hammarskjold, "but the best thing a conservative man can do is to put forward social welfare measures. When people feel they have a part in the welfare of their nation, that the nation is something of their own, they will defend and stick by it."

His brother Dag later was to write: "From generations of soldiers and government officials on my father's side, I inherited a belief that no life was more satisfactory than one of selfless service to your country—or humanity. This service requires a sacrifice of all personal interests, but likewise the courage to stand up unflinchingly for your convictions."

There were other reasons, apart from his freedom from Liberalism's ritualistic suspicion of the State, that made co-operation with the Social Democrats congenial to the young patrician civil servant. Planned state intervention in economic life harked back to an older conservative tradition which regarded the State as the guardian of common values. Such an approach moreover, fitted with Dag Hammarskjold's propensity to manage things. A strong hand on the economy fitted him temperamentally as well as by tradition. And also by conviction. The concepts of Wicksell and Keynes were more logical and persuasive than alternative approaches. This was controlling with a mind as superbly gifted at analysis as Hammarskjold's. He had been drawn to economics as a kind of intellectual sport. The greater complexity a financial problem presented, the more pleasure in finding a solution.

Yet, basic to everything else perhaps was a sense of human solidarity, a strong feeling for his fellow human beings and dislike for class distinctions that he had acquired from his mother. "From scholars and clergymen on my mother's side I inherited a belief that, in the very radical sense of the

Gospels, all men were equals as children of God, and should be met and treated by us as our masters in God. . .

"The two ideals which dominated my childhood world met me as fully harmonized and adjusted to the demands of our world of today in the ethics of Albert Schweitzer, where the ideal of service is supported by and supports the basic attitude of man set forth in the Gospels. In his work I also found a key for modern man to the world of the Gospels." This was his answer to Sven Stolpe, who, a convert to Catholicism, asked how Dag with good conscience, although not a Socialist, could put his talents at the service of a government carrying out a socialist program.

Hammarskjold's work at the Ministry included preparation of the government's budget. "Cut" is the watchword of budget bureaus all over the world, and the enjoinder to cut means disputes with other departments. But these disputes never became personal. Hammarskjold had a rare capacity for staying uninvolved personally. He fought hard for his point of view, but he managed to remain on good terms with his colleagues from other departments.

Lundberg testifies to Hammarskjold's skill in putting ideas into action. "When Hammarskjold said something would be done, it would generally come out pretty much the way he had planned." He developed a sixth sense for what was politically possible, knew what strings had to be pulled and was in a position to pull them. Myrdal, a more original thinker than Hammarskjold in economics, had a disastrous spell as Minister because he did not know how things worked administratively and politically.

Hammarskjold's strength was that he knew what ideas could be put through. Some of his economic colleagues, especially those who came into conflict with him after the war, said this also occasionally became a weakness. "I wrote a book about economic policy in which I was critical of Hammarskjold," recalled Lundberg. "His comment was that Lundberg did not know what was politically possible. But I'm an economist, concerned with ideas that should be made politically possible."

Despite the enormous burden of work that he shouldered

at the Ministry, Hammarskjold managed to carry along with him all his other interests: skiing in Jämtland in the winter; Sunday hikes; summer forays on bicycle into the countryside. Then there were expeditions with his friend Gosta Lundquist to Lapland with its mountains and marshy wilderness and the Lapps with "their faithful adherence to a form of society and tradition with roots stretching far beyond historical time."

There were, in addition, reading and music. No group of economists was ever better instructed in contemporary literature than Hammarskjold's friends. Lundberg reports how on hikes Hammarskjold would always bring along a book, read it and then lie down for an hour to memorize and organize its contents into his mind. A tremendous memory is one of his sources of strength. But also, perhaps, a source of weakness, according to Lundberg. "He is always speaking out of memory. As a result, there are no surprises." Alf Johansson recalls how they read the books of the Bloomsbury group, played Beethoven's last quartets, and followed the young proletarian authors who were then putting in an appearance in Swedish literature. Stolpe, who, in the mid-thirties, was introducing several Catholic writers to the Swedish public, found Dag Hammarskjold already familiar with them.

The harder he worked at the Ministry, late at night, the more he read literature to refresh himself. "The need for personal contact with literature of quality reflects an acquired taste," he was to write later.

During these years he lived with his parents. On his way home for lunch he would buy a bunch of flowers for his mother. She was solicitous for his interests, adjuring him as he left on a hike to dress warmly, or urging his colleagues at the Ministry to keep him from working so hard.

His father had become, as Stockholm saw him, a silent old man, sitting in his own study, reading books sent over to him by the Swedish Academy written by Nobel prize nominees. Friends of Hammarskjold would meet his mother, but rarely his father. He explained to them gently that he was old and found it difficult to establish new relationships.

Between his tender solicitude for his parents and absorption in work—"he was always overburdened with work, with projects that had to be finished"—there was no time for romance or courtship. When friends got married, the relationship changed. He was very sweet with their wives, but found it disturbing that they would no longer work at night or take walks at the drop of a hat.

In the summer of 1939, Hammarskjold and the principal assistant secretary at the Ministry—tall, brown-haired Erik Swartling—instead of biking south as they had the previous summer, pedaled northwards toward Norway, to Röros, which was so far north it was devoid of trees. They found lodgings one night in the little village of Elvirum. It was symptomatic of that summer's mood that the two men canvassed Elvirum's possibilities as an escape route in the event Sweden was invaded and evacuation became necessary.

War did come. Sweden proclaimed its neutrality, as it had done in 1914 under Hjalmar Hammarskjold's leadership, but most Swedes fatalistically assumed, after the invasion of Denmark and Norway (King Haakon did flee to safety via Elvirum), that Sweden's turn would be next. This catastrophe was averted, but Sweden, cut off from Western Europe, was faced with severe supply difficulties and inflationary pressures. One of Hammarskjold's jobs was to draft legislation establishing a price control board, write the by-laws, see to it that people worked efficiently.

Although neutral in policy, Swedes were not neutral in feeling and short of provoking the Nazis did what they could to help neighboring Norway. Hammarskjold was deeply involved in this work and for his services was later to be awarded the Grand Cross of the Order of St. Olav, the only official Norwegian order and bestowed very sparingly.

One of his assignments was to fly to London secretly in a military plane to discuss with the Norwegian government-in-exile wartime credits and postwar economic arrangements. "He was very helpful," said Knut Getz Wold, director of the Bank of Norway, and a participant in those negotiations.

A Norwegian diplomat who flew with Hammarskjold to London later reported that at one point their plane was spotted by the Luftwaffe and had to undertake violent evasive actions. The Norwegian said that in the heat of the action he practically forgot his own name, but Hammarskjold went on reading unconcernedly—he thought a book of sixteenth-century French poetry.

In 1941, Hammarskjold had become chairman of the Riksbank, and with the end of the war it was up to him and Wigforss to establish a policy for the transition to a peacetime economy. Faced abroad with the need for reconstruction credits by neighbors like Norway, Denmark and Holland, and wishing internally to promote economic expansion, they decreed a low-interest, "easy money" policy. If it involved certain sacrifices for Sweden this was the price Sweden had to pay for solidarity with Europe.

A storm broke over the Finance Ministry's head because of this policy. The big banks and insurance companies would have none of it. It was also disputed by economists like Hammarskjold's old friend Lundberg. There had been debates in the Stockholm group before the war but the differences on how to achieve recovery were slight; it proved to be otherwise after the war.

Lundberg wrote a report contending that as demand pressure increased, cost control through low interest rates would not be effective in keeping prices down, especially when accompanied by a policy of increasing the value of the Swedish crown. Inflationary pressures could only be curbed by a more restrictive monetary policy, he insisted.

In the ensuing debate Hammarskjold told his critics among the economists that they oversimplified the internal political pressures that had to be compensated. He quoted to them a line from *The Three Penny Opera* to the effect that "the conditions, they are not such . . ."

Lundberg, a tall Viking who emerged as his chief opponent in the postwar debate, describes the difficulties of joining issue with Hammarskjold. "He has a tremendous power of expressing himself orally in a way that people can't quite follow . . . he never tries to express himself in the easiest sort of way . . . he is not a man of simple statements.

"When he came home from the U.S. negotiations on dollar

arrangements, he presented the results to business men so beautifully and complicatedly that no discussion was possible; it was all so interrelated in so complex a fashion that no grip was possible on any part of it."

Wigforss ascribed the involved nature of Hammarskjold's oral expositions to his desire to show the complicated nature of economic phenomena. This led to shadings and qualifications and reservations which marred simplicity. But Wigforss added that Hammarskjold's ability to give the essentials of a question clearly and in a concentrated way made it a pleasure to follow his reports in Cabinet—provided one took the trouble to brief oneself on the issue under discussion.

The most serious consequence of the "easy money" policy was a balance of payments crisis. "What we did not foresee in '46 was what no one foresaw at that time," Hammarskjold said later, "neither in London nor Washington, the development of the general payments crisis in Europe which called forth the Marshall Plan.

"As a result, a policy which, while fairly radical and involving certain sacrifices for Sweden was perfectly acceptable and right, dovetailed with a general crisis in liquidity and so Sweden was the first to develop an acute dollar problem."

But even with Sweden's "easy money" policy, adds Hammarskjold, its balance of payments position was re-established more quickly than that of any other country in Europe—"so much so that Sweden's participation in the Marshall Plan was a little bit on the marginal side of what could be defended."

Hammarskjold's critics also fired away at what they considered an "unholy alliance"—namely, that he should be both Under-Secretary of Finance and chairman of the Riksbank. The latter should be a check on the Finance Ministry's policy, they argued. Hammarskjold was attacked as a "tool" of Wigforss by some and by others as the man primarily responsible for postwar policy formulation.

There is no evidence to suggest that Wigforss and Hammarskjold did not see eye to eye. And the bank's Board of Directors, an all-party group appointed by Parliament, voted confidence in their chairman. "There was not a step in the process when I had not carried them with me," says Hammarskjold, "so it was natural for the Board to back me up, saying we shared responsibility."

Wigforss generously has said it was his deputy's way of handling issues and his ability to give reasons for a policy which Ivar Rooth, the manager of the Riksbank, could accept that long postponed the conflict between the bank and the Ministry. When, in the end, Rooth resigned because of his differences with Wigforss, the latter said: "He might have resigned earlier if it had not been for Hammarskjold's talent for conciliation."

Of the Wigforss-Hammarskjold postwar line, Hammarskjold says: "It was a policy based on certain assumptions that did not work out," but he goes on to note the eulogies of Wigforss, even in the opposition press, when the white-haired Socialist finally left office because of age. "Just as I followed Wigforss down the drain, so I followed him back up," Hammarskjold adds.

Before the war the major problem whetting the interest of the economists was how to bring about economic recovery at home; after the war the primary challenge was how to rebuild the international economy. Increasingly busy with all types of international economic negotiations, Hammarskjold left the Finance Ministry in 1945 and the Riksbank in 1948.

Having renegotiated the U.S.–Swedish trade agreement in 1946 in order to ease Sweden's exchange and payments problems, it was logical that he should be designated as Sweden's top representative in the 1947 meetings that prepared the way for the Marshall Plan and its European adjunct, the Organization for European Economic Cooperation. He was, moreover, a gifted linguist, capable of, as one of his Paris colleagues remarked, "building up those remarkable sentences in French, English and German as well as Swedish."

In launching the Marshall Plan the U.S. demanded that recipient European countries accept two responsibilities—maximum self-help and maximum mutual aid. Each country was required to submit a list of projects for which it wanted help, and it was the job of OEEC to eliminate duplication and ensure that the recipient nations were doing as much as possible for each other.

Paul Hoffman, who was U. S. ECA Administrator, bracketed Hammarskjold and Robert Marjolin of France, a key figure in the European Economic Community, as the "two bright young men" in the operation. In drafting the Charter of the OEEC there was a division along familiar lines. The British supported by the Scandinavians were concerned with expansion and full employment; the Continental nations, with internal financial stability and the dangers of inflation.

Hammarskjold was, of course, in the former camp. But he was not a man who got involved in controversies. His knack was the resolution of difficulties, the finding of formulas of agreement.

Hammarskjold was on the executive committee which was running OEEC. He was head of the Swedish delegation and Sweden was in a special position because it was not a receiving country, had no colonies and, therefore, had few axes to grind.

The first division of aid exercise, recalls Arne Skaug, who was heading the Norwegian delegation to Paris, was very difficult. The countries had submitted requests which in sum exceeded the amount the U.S. was providing. "What the European countries thought they needed added up to more than was available. Hammarskjold was one of a handful of people put to work to negotiate readjustments."

The process of decision-making was a process of drafting and Hammarskjold was extremely adept at that. "European governments welcomed recommendations from OEEC in regard to their internal policies," states Skaug, "because it was easier for governments to re-shape their policies if they could point to an agreement in Paris."

Hammarskjold was active in all the efforts to find compromises. "I never heard of anybody who worked with Dag in those years who was not impressed with his capacity to see things in a realistic way, his ability to hold to a neutral position in seeking a solution that would be just in terms of all the interests involved," says Skaug. "What you are saying is not reasonable," became almost a Hammarskjoldian trademark.

The OEEC was the first experience for Europe in successful international co-operation. Through his participation in it, Hammarskjold became known to large circles of officials in Western Europe and the U.S.

In the view of Wigforss, the respect which Hammarskjold acquired at OEEC "for his acute intelligence, good judgment and ability to find ways out of bothersome situations was principally what made it possible to launch him as a candidate for Secretary-General."

During the early years of OEEC, Hammarskjold spent weekdays in Paris, traveling home every Friday, often with Skaug—the two separating at Copenhagen: one to Oslo, the other to Stockholm—and then back to Paris on Sunday.

The Council would very often have long night meetings. "Dag would read French poetry while I read *Alice in Wonderland*," recalls Skaug. "We would have dinner," says Professor Kock, who was also on the Swedish delegation; "then Hammarskjold wanted us to go to some highbrow play. Then afterwards we were supposed to resume our discussions and have as clear a mind as his."

Another member of the delegation, Lief Belfrage, recalls how they would often search out a small restaurant together and talk through half the night. When they had a few days' grace, they would travel through France, with Hammarskjold instructing his companions in French history and culture. "He knew all about the old churches and cathedrals."

In the course of his work for the OEEC, Hammarskjold had become a special adviser to the Ministry of Foreign Affairs. When the work slackened off in Paris, he was made Secretary-General of the Foreign Ministry and in 1951 became Vice Minister of Foreign Affairs under Osten Unden and a member of the Cabinet, a non-party Minister without Portfolio. In the Foreign Office he was in charge of economic affairs and his particular interest the growing movement toward European economic co-operation.

Hammarskjold's mother had died in 1940. Until 1945 he

lived with his father in Sturegatan in an apartment in a house owned by the Nobel Foundation overlooking the tree-shaded park that encompasses the Royal Library. In 1945 he moved into a seven-room flat on the top floor of an ivy-covered house surrounded by lilac bushes and lofty trees whose branches reached up to his windows.

A very lonely man, his friends encouraged him to marry. They thought they had all the pre-conditions of success when they brought him together with the daughter of a Swedish financier. "She was pretty, charming, intellectual, a Doctor of Philosophy." But when they asked Dag how he had liked her, he put them off with the comment: "She didn't appreciate T. S. Eliot." To a friend he once remarked that it might have been better if he had married, but how could he invite a woman to share his kind of life, when he was always at the Ministry, at work until early hours of the morning. He had seen how much his mother had suffered from his father's absences on public business.

Hammarskjold carried into the Foreign Ministry methods of work he had developed in the finance department. He quickly brought together a small personal secretariat of outstanding young men. It was "not a brain trust," one of its members observed, because "he was his own brain trust," but it was a group in which they talked out loud and through which "he kept his fingers on every lever."

There were some raised eyebrows at this unorthodox outcropping, but "because of Hammarskjold's authority and fantastic ability, the little organization never caused any ill will as it might have done with anyone else." The group disappeared when Hammarskjold left the Foreign Office but the episode left some feeling in the department that he tended to keep the reins too tightly in his hands.

It was summer, 1952. Unden, Hammarskjold's taciturn chief, was in Italy on holiday and Hammarskjold himself was up in his beloved Lapland. A half-year before Stalin's death, Soviet foreign policy was in its most paranoid phase. On a Friday and Sunday Swedish planes were shot down by the Russians over the Baltic.

A military plane was sent up to Lapland to fetch Hammarskjold. He was rushed to the Foreign Office in mountaineering garb to take charge of the running exchange with Moscow. For a small country like Sweden, the episode constituted a major crisis. There was deep anger with Soviet policy, but Hammarskjold and his aides, Sverker Aström and Sven Backlund, were also fascinated by the intellectual sport of outmaneuvering the Russians. The latter would present their notes late in the evening, in time to catch the morning headlines in Sweden but too late, they thought, for the Swedes to react officially.

Hammarskjold and his group established a midnight watch. The game was played night after night. After their reply was out, or no Soviet note had appeared, the trio would walk home talking animatedly in the spectral light of Stockholm's summer night.

The episode, although unsettling, did not cause Sweden to reconsider its policy of staying out of NATO. Sweden was in the anomalous position of being linked to Western Europe economically through OEEC and politically through the Council of Europe. But it was determined not to permit these ties to pull it into NATO. In the 1948–49 debates over Scandinavia's relationship to the germinating Atlantic Pact, Sweden had proposed instead a Scandinavian defense bloc that would remain neutral between East and West.

Hammarskjold sympathized with this line, but he was also Sweden's ministerial representative to Paris and Strasbourg. Sweden did not want to appear to be dragging its feet in the movement toward unity. Hammarskjold wrote an article, "To Choose Europe," in which he underscored Sweden's ties— ideological, political and economic—with Europe but denied that to be a good European either excluded or necessitated membership in NATO. That depended on specific national conditions and the Swedish position "was fully justified by our situation."

In other ways, too, the Hammarskjold who came to the UN

in 1953 was very much a product of Sweden's distinctive approach to foreign affairs. It is worth outlining the relevant elements. Basic to the Swedish outlook is the fact that it has not been involved in a war in 150 years. Until Charles XII's defeat by Peter the Great in the early eighteenth century, Sweden was one of the great powers. Its greatness in this sense finally came to an end in 1809 when it lost Finland to Russia. This was a hard blow to national pride. Complexes of revenge and bitterness lasted well into the nineteenth century, but greatness henceforth was sought elsewhere. With Charles XII's death, said Hammarskjold, "a conquest of the homeland had started, in art and science . . . the conquest in the world of intellectual culture, of a position which genius, courage and effort cannot alone create in the political world."

Another concomitant of Sweden's 150-year reign of peace is that it tends to regard the status quo as a natural state of affairs. Since the loss of Finland it has had no dispute with a foreign power where it has had to claim a right, nor has any power had any claim against Sweden, that meant upsetting the status quo.

Although it has had no dispute with Russia since the early nineteenth century, the Swedish problem, standing as it has for centuries between East and West, is to maintain its ties with the West while keeping itself secure to the East. For Swedes it is important that both the Soviet Union and the U.S. be in the UN.

Sweden has not had to claim a right that meant going against international law. Its vital interests have been best served by the development of international law, and with the oldest written constitution in Europe it was temperamentally disposed toward such a development. When international disputes do arise it is part of the Swedish tradition to look first for a solution by isolating the legal factors. If these can be isolated and submitted to arbitration, tempers will calm down and even the political elements may become more susceptible of solution.

The Swedish background is indispensable to understanding Hammarskjold. Yet it would be unwise to try to draw a one-to-one correspondence between his actions and policies at the UN and the Swedish viewpoint.

He had his views on the great international issues, he said, on taking over the UN job, but "those views are mine as a private man.

"In my new official capacity, the private man should disappear and the international public servant take his place."

4

An International Priesthood

Administration had first claim on Hammarskjold as he settled in on the thirty-eighth floor. It was to be his major concern that whole initial year lending weight to those who thought he intended to model himself on the civil servant-diplomat, Sir Eric Drummond, rather than on the politician-statesman, Trygve Lie.

And yet the way he took over what he called the "overwhelming job as chief administrator of the UN Secretariat" quickly indicated that here was a man who would establish more precedents than he would follow, and a man who was certainly no "clerk."

The administrative problem, when Hammarskjold assumed office, was explosively political. That secular priesthood known as the UN Secretariat, whose holy writ is the Charter and whose church is the UN organization, had become a badly demoralized body as a consequence of the U.S. loyalty investigations.

The concept of an international civil service, impartial, independent and objective, whose members during the time of their appointment served not the states of which they were nationals but only the UN, was a relatively new one.

It originated with Sir Eric Drummond at the League of Nations. It was enshrined in Articles 100 and 101 of the UN Charter.

Article 100 stipulates:

1. In the performance of their duties the Secretary-General and the staff shall not seek or receive instructions from any government or from any other authority external to the Organization. They shall refrain from any action which might reflect on their position as international officials responsible only to the Organization.

2. Each Member of the United Nations undertakes to respect the exclusively international character of the responsibilities of the Secretary-General and the staff and not to seek to influence them in the discharge of their responsibilities.

Article 101 provides that:

"The Staff shall be appointed by the Secretary-General" and that "the paramount consideration in the employment of staff . . . shall be the necessity of securing the highest standards of efficiency, competence and integrity." It adds that "Due regard shall be paid to the importance of recruiting the staff on as wide a geographical basis as possible."

The UN Preparatory Commission, in a gloss of these articles that was endorsed by the First General Assembly, observed that "loyalty to the Organization is in no way incompatible with an official's attachment to his own country, whose higher interests he is serving in serving the UN. It clearly involves, however, a broad international outlook and a detachment from national prejudices and narrow national interests."

The heyday of the McCarthy era was 1953. U.S. pressures were posing a major challenge to this concept of a truly international civil service.

Congressional investigating committees, a federal grand jury, a raging press had forced the harassed Trygve Lie into a position where he appeared to be dismissing Americans who had invoked the Fifth Amendment. Henry Cabot Lodge, on arriving at the UN in January 1953, felt obliged, as part of his effort to restore American confidence in the Organization, to make his first official action a well-publicized request to the FBI to initiate a full check of the 1680 Americans on the UN payroll. Americans lined up to be fingerprinted and fill out questionnaires and FBI agents were allowed to come onto UN premises to question non-Americans as well as Americans.

Lie called the loyalty investigations a "purgatory." By his American critics he was under fire for permitting "an overwhelmingly large group of disloyal U.S. citizens" to infiltrate the UN. He also came under sharp criticism from delegations and staff for yielding to American pressures. This criticism did not dispute the presence of some Communists among the Americans in the Secretariat.

Nor did Lie's critics necessarily defend the behavior of those who invoked their constitutional privileges against self-incrimination. While UN staff members were not expected to give up their "political or religious convictions," the same staff regulation stipulated that "they shall at all times bear in mind the reserve and tact incumbent upon them by reason of their international status."

But many member states held that automatic dismissal of staff members who pleaded the Fifth Amendment amounted to acceptance of a purely national standard of employability rather than the universally applicable criteria laid down in the Charter of "efficiency, competence and integrity." No individual should be dismissed at the mere request of a government, they argued. The UN must itself determine whether or not just cause existed for dismissal. In particular, diplomats from West European countries with long-established traditions of due process felt that findings made in extrajudicial, inquisitional procedures, such as characterized congressional loyalty inquiries, could not be binding upon the UN.

It was not an easy situation for Hammarskjold when he arrived. He was later to call it "a short nightmare." Rightly or wrongly, the interpretation given abroad to Lie's personnel policies was that he had caved in to McCarthyite pressures. Delegations feared that the Secretariat's independence from Washington had been seriously compromised.

It was a crucial moment. He had to put his foot down right away. One of his first moves was to order FBI agents off the premises. "You can't be here; whatever permission may have been given in the past is withdrawn," he notified them. Their presence was "intolerable, absolutely intolerable," he commented to friends.

A more serious problem was to find a platform on which to stand up to U.S. dismissal demands without antagonizing the U.S. Lodge would come in with a dossier forwarded from the State Department and seek discharge of some Americans. U.S. support for the UN was indispensable; U.S. support for the Secretary-General equally so. But yielding to the U.S.—or appearing to yield—would jeopardize his standing with the rest of the UN. He and Lodge had their difficult moments, but they avoided a public quarrel. "Cabot was very good about this," Hammarskjold said. What Hammarskjold did was to build up, by decisions in individual cases, a body of rules, "creating a kind of common law." This judicial procedure then served as a buffer against yielding to pressures. The U.S. delegation and the State Department were quite satisfied because they themselves being unhappy about trespassing on the Secretariat's independence could now simply reply to the Senate Internal Security Subcommittee that matters had to take their judicial course.

When allegations against a staff member were brought to Hammarskjold, his reply would be: "We'll put it in the mill. We have a judicial process—no anonymous testimony, no evidence that doesn't stand up in a court of law." There was not a single case of a staff member being discharged for political cause, although a few were dismissed for other reasons.

"The system provided Cabot with a highly dignified reply to those who were trying to discredit the Organization," said Hammarskjold. By the end of 1953, when the Assembly approved Hammarskjold's proposals for amending the staff regulations, this particular challenge to the independence of the Secretariat was over. The revised staff regulations made more explicit the prohibitions on activities that might reflect adversely on a staff member's "integrity, independence and impartiality," stiffened the curbs on political activity and enlarged the Secretary-General's power, under certain safeguards, to terminate permanent appointments.

The line that was followed was one of "stricter criteria for the conduct of the staff member combined with increased checks and controls on the way in which the Secretary-General exerts his powers."

To the Staff Committee, which was worried by his proposals, he explained that he could not successfully defend "the truly international and independent position of Secretariat against attacks from any quarter . . . unless every staff member fully lives up to the standard of strict impartiality laid down in Article 100 (1) of the Charter and to 'the highest standards of efficiency, competence and integrity,' of Article 101 (3)."

The highest standards and absolute independence of the Secretariat were important because they were its only weapons. "Countries are arming in order to be able to negotiate from a position of strength," he said in a message to the Geneva UN staff. "The Secretariat, too, has to negotiate, not only in its own interest, but for the cause of peace and a peaceful development of our world. The weight we carry is not determined by physical force or the number of people who form the constituency. It is based solely on trust in our impartiality, our experience and knowledge, our maturity of judgment."

By the end of 1953, Hammarskjold could feel that the "previous controversial chapter" was closed and that in regard to the independence of the Secretariat they were off to "a new start."

The concept of a truly international civil service, wrote Hammarskjold in 1953, is "not yet fully understood and accepted." No member state was to challenge it frontally again until the Soviet Union in 1960 was to issue its demand for a three-bloc secretariat, but the nations which wholly refrained from pressures of any sort were the exception rather than the rule.

In 1954, India indicated discontent with the presence of Americans on the UN teams observing the cease-fire between India and Pakistan in the Kashmir region. Hammarskjold defended the Americans. Their actions "are actions as agents and nothing else." Whatever their national uniform or passport, when they took action or passed judgment on behalf of the UN "they may be considered 'denationalized.'"

But is an international civil service possible in a divided world? Hammarskjold was to return to this problem time and again in his thinking as well as his practical arrangements. The UN staff is a secular priesthood but it must not uproot itself from the world of which it is part. The staff may in ideal foreshadow the international community that is slowly coming to birth, but to work effectively it must be in touch with and mirror the split world of today in which the most strident notes were ideology and division.

The Charter discreetly recognizes the need for roots. In addition to prescribing the "paramount" standards of integrity, efficiency and competence, it states that due regard shall be paid to recruiting on "as wide a geographical basis as possible." To meet the geographic criterion, the General Assembly said the Secretary-General should, in allocating posts to nationalities, use the scale of contributions to the UN budget as a rough index of the desirable range of posts: 33 per cent to the U.S.; 14 per cent to the Soviet Union, and so on.

Almost from the outset of the UN there has been clamor for a wider dispersion of posts. It is a regular feature of Assembly debates, and Hammarskjold's annual tabulation of number of people employed by country is one of the most closely scanned Assembly documents.

The problem was inherited by Hammarskjold. Trygve Lie had to assemble a staff of three thousand in less than nine months. Not only was Lie in the position of a fire chief trying to recruit his firemen while rushing to put out several fires, but in the early years the Soviet bloc was not eager to second its people for international duty and most of the countries of Asia and Africa were not yet in existence as independent states. As a consequence, there were recognized imbalances. National grievances focused particularly on twelve hundred-odd "professional" posts, where the U.S. in accordance with its share of the budget was entitled to 350 to 450 posts and actually had slightly over 350, while the Soviet Union had less than 50, although having a claim to 140 to 190 posts.

Hammarskjold considered it axiomatic that "national accent" and "national experience" can be a "great asset in international cooperation." No one could free himself entirely from his background and why should he, he asked. But the Secretary-General's problem was "to find ways to make the national elements an asset, to overcome the divisive influences and try to create a unity in which the diversity of national backgrounds of the members are fully respected and preserved, but in such a way as to be an asset rather than a liability in the work."

But to have a Secretariat that was geographically representative did not mean members of the staff were selected to represent their piece of geography. Hammarskjold underscored the exclusively international responsibilities of staff members in the Assembly's discussion of his proposal to reorganize the top level of the Secretariat. The Soviet bloc representatives challenged his proposal to merge the Assistant Secretaries-General and Principal Directors into a single echelon of Under-Secretaries, whose responsibilities would be essentially administrative. They argued that suppression of the post of Assistant Secretary-General would violate a "gentlemen's agreement" made in 1946 for the distribution of the top-level posts. The Soviet Union was concerned about holding onto the position of directing the Political Department that was accorded to it by the gentlemen's agreement. The Assistant Secretaries-General had a semblance of political status under Lie. They would be sworn in at a special meeting of the General Assembly's General Committee. They substituted for Lie when he was away. Lie thought the Assistant Secretary-General could and should give him the thinking of the country from which he came.

Hammarskjold considered this incompatible with the Charter provision that the international civil servant should be free of such ties. He could get the thinking of the countries from their permanent delegations, he argued. The Eighth General Assembly approved his reorganization plan by a vote of 53–5.

Essentially, what he sought through the reorganization was to streamline and temper the Secretariat so that it could meet any and every crisis with unbureaucratic dispatch and excellence.

"The very nature of its [the Secretariat's] task necessarily involves a capacity to adjust easily and quickly to new demands and unforeseen developments," he wrote in his 1954 Report. This could only be assured if the Secretary-General had "a large measure of administrative discretion in such measures of internal management as the scheduling of work and the utilization of Secretariat staffing and resources."

Hammarskjold thus brought into the UN the pragmatic and highly personalized approach to administration he had developed in Sweden. He had always been concerned with getting things done rather than worshiping tables of organization. And the best guarantee of accomplishment was to keep the reins in his own hands. The UN Secretariat was now reorganized around his own formidable capacity for work and insistence on perfection. Since the Charter's provisions regarding administration had been deliberately framed to ensure the Secretary-General's administrative pre-eminence, it was a case of job and man fitting neatly together.

According to the chart, the top-level group at the UN consisted of a dozen to twenty Under-Secretaries or officials with Under-Secretary rank. But titles were not necessarily indicative of responsibilities nor of who happened to have Hammarskjold's confidence. The Under-Secretaries met with Hammarskjold on Friday mornings. All presumably were of equal rank, and precedence was determined alphabetically beginning with the official whose country happened to be first in General

Assembly seating arrangements. Very little of moment happened at these meetings.

There were a few aides who were in on everything—or almost everything. They varied from time to time. In the early years they included the late Ahmed Bokhari, a witty and scholarly Pakistani; Andy Cordier, a chunky, blue-eyed former Hoosier political scientist associated with the UN from its earliest days; Nobel Peace Prize winner Ralph Bunche, a superb negotiator with an intimate knowledge of Africa and the Middle East; and Per Lind, his Swedish aide.

Philippe de Seynes, a former Mendès-France protégé, a man of style and an analytical bent of mind, was part of the top team of intimates, working as Under-Secretary for Economic and Social Affairs. When African affairs came to the forefront, the politically astute Wieschhoff, a Frankfurt University anthropologist who made his first trip to Africa and the Congo in 1928 and who quit Hitlerite Germany in the thirties, entered the inner circle. More recently C. V. Narasimhan of India, a quiet, studious civil servant and author of the Mekong River Project, whom Hammarskjold drafted from the UN Economic Commission for Asia and the Far East, became Hammarskjold's *chef de cabinet*.

With members of this group Hammarskjold was on easy, intimate terms, frequently darting into their offices to exchange a tidbit of information or to try out an idea. Often as not they lunched together and in the evening reviewed the day's developments over a whisky and soda.

A special position was occupied by Cordier. Invariably cheerful and relaxed, full of good common sense, with a retentive memory, a capacity for work second only to his chief's and a detailed knowledge of the Secretariat, Cordier served as Hammarskjold's executive assistant. Anything of concern to Hammarskjold was in Cordier's domain too. He kept the machinery moving when the SG was away from headquarters and was, in effect, if not in title, Deputy Secretary-General.

This method of work produced grievances. The Russians complained that Anatoly Dobrynin, a highly intelligent official who for several years was the top-ranking Soviet member of the Secretariat, was given nothing to do, although nominally in charge of the Political Department.

The Indians registered the same complaint for a time about Narasimhan. Sir Humphrey Trevelyan, a first-rate British diplomat, left partly because there was not enough for him to do, as did Geoffrey Murray, an outstanding younger official in the Canadian Foreign Ministry whom Hammarskjold begged the Canadian Government to let him have.

Who can say what chemistry of thought, feeling, and personality, what constellation of political circumstances and administrative requirements caused Hammarskjold to favor one man rather than another? Despite all complaints about Hammarskjold's highly personal methods of dealing with the higher levels of the Secretariat, the salient fact was that it worked, that with a relatively small staff, the most difficult and complex tasks were to be carried out successfully.

This was largely a result of Hammarskjold's intensive intellectual direction of the entire enterprise. Memos flowed into him from all departments. Often they would come back with *vidi* written on them. Ideas suggested would turn up months later in some speech or proposal enriched and transformed. He read fast with tremendous comprehension and a sixth sense for detecting if something was wrong or hidden. His *élan* infused the whole enterprise.

"If an Under-Secretary brings a paper to his office Monday night, it will be dealt with Tuesday morning," said Cordier when the Assembly's Administrative Committee began worrying about the Secretary-General's far-flung activities. "Does the Committee want him to have the paper back by midnight?"

5

Mission
to Peking

"My first job is to run this House," Hammarskjold said on taking up his post.

His next was to move the UN back into the center of serious diplomacy. Ever since the collapse of the UN cease-fire effort after the Chinese "volunteers" swarmed into the Korean War, the world organization had been elbowed to the sidelines, a forum for invective and propaganda, manager of a modest technical assistance program, but exercising only peripheral influence on the major issues affecting peace and security.

When Hammarskjold assumed office the UN had atrophied alarmingly. It was serving neither as an instrument for collective security nor as a center for negotiation and conciliation. Great national weeklies were carrying articles with titles like "The UN Is Dying." On a disquietingly large number of world issues the great powers were by-passing the world organization.

An opportunity to begin restoring the political prerogatives of the UN came with Hammarskjold's first important political assignment—an Assembly resolution in December 1954, asking him to do what he could to bring about the release of American airmen held prisoners by Red China.

In late fall of 1954 the Peking regime suddenly tried and sentenced as "spies" eleven American airmen who had been shot down in January 1953, while flying a Korean War mission. The Chinese claimed the plane had violated Chinese air space; the U.S. said it had been shot down over North Korea. At the same time it was disclosed Red China was still holding in custody four American jet pilots also shot down during Korean War missions.

Since the Korean Armistice Agreement obligated both sides to repatriate all prisoners of war, a wave of anger swept the U.S. Senator Knowland wanted the U. S. Navy to impose a "tight" blockade on the mainland of China. Faced with demands in Congress and the press and from the China Lobby for retaliatory measures, which President Eisenhower warned were "acts of war" and might split a Western alliance already divided over China policy, the U.S. brought the issue to the General Assembly on December 4.

A resolution presented by the sixteen nations which had provided troops to the Unified Command in Korea, called the detention of the airmen a "violation" of the Armistice Agreement, condemned the trial and conviction of prisoners detained illegally, and then, not knowing what else to do, requested the Secretary-General to make "continuing and unremitting efforts" to bring about the release of the airmen "by the means most appropriate in his judgment."

A friend, Hans Engen, recalled how Hammarskjold made up his mind on what these "means" might be. Engen, a buoyant, blond-haired old UN hand, was Norway's permanent delegate. Extremely helpful to Hammarskjold at a time when the UN was *terra incognita* to the Swedish diplomat, his advice and judgment were highly valued.

Hammarskjold was very dubious about the sixteen-power resolution, which was then only in the drafting stage. In particular he questioned the usefulness of asking the Secretary-

General and the UN to do this kind of job when denying one party in the dispute access to the organization. Sending a note to China would fail and further damage UN prestige. But as Hammarskjold talked with Engen, the creative possibilities of the assignment matured in his mind. He ended the conversation by saying: "If they do, I'll go to Peking."

Hammarskjold's decision shocked some members of the U.S. delegation. The Administration was already under attack by Senator McCarthy for "weakness" in taking the issue to the UN. When the news got out that Hammarskjold would go to Peking, the China Lobby group denounced it as a kind of "blood barter."

"Hat in hand, suppliant, and ready to pay a ransom to the blackmailers," was one national news magazine's comment on Hammarskjold's decision. But there was little the U.S. could do, even if it had wished (which it did not) to stop Hammarskjold. The resolution made him the sole judge as to the ways and means of accomplishing his difficult mission.

Hammarskjold's first objective was to "crash the gate" in Peking. This was not at all a foregone conclusion since his mandate originated with a resolution of condemnation. "You either condemn or negotiate; you can't do both," was Hammarskjold's view. He concluded that it would be impossible to work with the resolution and be received at Peking as agent for the Assembly's decision. He never even sent it on to Peking. He calculated that his main card with Chinese Communists was their realization that an affront to the Secretary-General would not help them gain entry to the UN, something they very much wanted at that time. A rebuff to Hammarskjold would only slam the UN door more tightly shut and strengthen demands in the U.S. for extremist measures.

Hammarskjold cabled Premier Chou En-lai that he would like to take up with him personally in Peking the matter of the imprisoned personnel. Chou cabled back: "In the interest of peace and relaxation of international tension, I am prepared to receive you in our capital, Peking, to discuss with you pertinent questions." But in a second cable that was received at the same time, Chou declared there was no justifica-

tion for the UN to try to interfere in such an internal affair
as the conviction of spies by a Chinese court. Chou obviously
considered it politically advantageous to have the Secretary-
General of the UN come to Peking, but it was still unclear
whether he would be willing to discuss the prisoner issue with
him and even less clear that there could be any meeting of minds
on the issue.

But first the practical arrangements had to be made. Hammarskjold cabled his friend Uno Willers, Librarian of the Realm,
to invite him and the Chinese Ambassador to Willers' home for
lunch in Stockholm. He held three meetings with General
Keng Piao, discussing possible routes to Peking, the duration of
the visit, the set-up of the discussions, the staff that would
be needed. One meeting had to be held at the home of
Willers' mother in order to avoid the press which by then
dogged his every step. The less he was willing to say, the more
the world's interest mounted in the movements of this un-
pretentious man.

It was not only the pathos and human interest of the imprisoned airmen which engaged the imagination of the world,
there was the larger drama of American-Chinese relations. In
September 1954, the Chinese Communists had begun to bom-
bard the offshore islands, announcing their intention of "liberat-
ing" Formosa. Faced with what appeared to be preparations
to invade the offshore islands, the U.S. concluded a mutual
defense treaty with Nationalist China and President Eisenhower
sought authorization from Congress to use American forces in
the defense of Formosa and related areas. On both sides there
were extremists who wanted a showdown. It was a delicate
assignment. Peking's interest was to break out of its isolation. U.S. public opinion still was bitterly opposed to recognition
of Red China.

The larger issues were reflected in the farewells to Hammarskjold and his little group of aides. Ambassador Lodge, who
had led the fight in September to prevent Assembly discussion
of the issue of Chinese representation, and in October rebuked
Hammarskjold for distributing a message from Chou, was at
the airfield to wish Hammarskjold Godspeed on a journey

ending Peking's post-Korean ostracism and the first leg of which would be flown in a U.S. military Constellation piloted by a major who had seen service in Korea.

The delegate of the Soviet Union which had voted against the resolution threw a party for all the permanent delegates the night before Hammarskjold left, at which the UN chief was the honored guest. Leading the contingent of Secretariat aides who saw Hammarskjold off at Idlewild was Ilya Tchernyshev, a Soviet Under-Secretary, whom Hammarskjold left in charge rather than Dr. Ralph Bunche.

En route to Peking, Hammarskjold obtained appraisals of Chou from Eden in London and French Premier Mendès-France in Paris, both of whom had negotiated with the Chinese Premier in Geneva. Both advised him there were very few negotiators in the world as good as Chou. He would find a man on whom it would be hard to get a grip. Mendès-France added that in the Chinese Prime Minister he would find a *grand seigneur,* a statesman not only conscious of his own power, but a man who spoke with the self-confidence of a family which had been part of China's ruling class for a thousand years.

It was bitterly cold in Peking when Hammarskjold and his party arrived. The winds from the Mongolian plains blew down icily. But within the Heavenly City, Hammarskjold and Chou talked for four days amid a growing thaw. The two men were remarkably alike. Both were patricians, one a Marxist mandarin and the other a welfare state aristocrat, and a rapport was quickly established. Their formal conversations in the Hall of the Western Flowers lasted more than 13½ hours over four afternoons. "The whole atmosphere was of great earnestness," said Dr. Bokhari, the scholarly Pakistani who served as Hammarskjold's political adviser on the trip. "There was not a sound, not a noise of any kind in the whole room," he added, except for attendants unobtrusively serving Chinese tea in tall lidded Chinese cups.

There were also dinners and receptions in the Hall of the Purple Light with menus that included consommé of swallows' nests, Peking duck, lotus seed soup, mandarin fish. There were excursions to the summer palace and the Ming Dynasty tombs, with Hammarskjold walking "at a terrific pace, without a hat," according to Bokhari, a partisan of less strenuous pleasures.

The formal talks were very involved and subtle. "If I express myself in circumscribed terms, it is nothing compared to Chou," Hammarskjold commented later. Chou used exceedingly indirect language and expected the Secretary-General to do the same. The subtlety of Chinese diplomacy made him feel like a vulgar barbarian, "and you know I am not a complete amateur at this business."

Their first problem was to find a formula to get around the difficulty of Chou's discussing a matter which China maintained was its own internal affair with an international organization from which it was banned.

The prescription invented by Hammarskjold subsequently came to be known as the "Peking formula." The discussion was held not on the basis of the General Assembly resolution, which Peking rejected, but on the basis of the authority of the Secretary-General under the Charter. Agreement by Chou to discuss the issue of the airmen did not require prior recognition by Peking of the UN's authority or advance agreement to accept the Secretary-General's conclusions.

In cutting himself loose from the resolution, and dealing with Peking on the basis of his general authority under the Charter, Hammarskjold was able to discuss with Chou not only the issue of the airmen but "other pertinent" issues as well. This involved the whole gamut of Far Eastern problems. Hammarskjold took the view that if the Secretary-General finds that a situation may become a threat to peace and security, he is entitled to raise the matter with the government involved to ascertain whether it might be possible to take preventive action.

In the case of the airmen, Hammarskjold was familiar with the strength of U.S. feelings aroused by their sentencing as well as post-Korean pressures in the U.S. regarding China policy. The conviction of the airmen under Chinese law might be a domestic affair, but it could have the most serious international repercussions, he told Chou. While the Secretary-General did not have a right to mix into the internal affairs of

China, he was entitled to discuss the matter in view of its international repercussions.

Chou replied that the People's Republic of China recognized the UN Charter, the Secretary-General and his concern in the matter. It was legitimate for him to bring the issue up.

That having been established, Hammarskjold went on to place before Chou the full and complete case for the release of the convicted men.

By the time he left Peking, Hammarskjold's conclusion was that the airmen would be freed, but it would jeopardize the outcome to say so. Peking needed time to dissociate the freeing of the airmen from any appearance of yielding to pressure. Hammarskjold figured six months.

Secondly, Hammarskjold felt Peking would need a peg. That was the idea of permitting the families of the fliers to visit them. The family visits were never posed as a condition, but would enable Peking to save face, being in accordance with a traditional amnesty pattern in China.

The communiqué at the end of the talks was much less communicative. It said only the talks had been "useful," would "continue," and that reference "was made at the same time to questions pertinent to the relaxation of world tensions."

No deals of any kind had been made, he told a mammoth press conference back at UN headquarters. "The door has been opened and can be kept open, given restraint on all sides," which meant, he explained, no reacting "prematurely" or "blasting" away.

One hitch developed very quickly when Secretary Dulles flatly turned down the idea of family visits. A State Department announcement said that the U. S. Government could not "in good conscience encourage those who may wish to go into an area where the normal protections of an American passport cannot be offered." This was not the real issue. The UN declared publicly that "Secretary-General Dag Hammarskjold has no doubt about the safety of those members of the families wishing to visit China to see their men." The real issue was not safety of the families, but fear on the part of the U.S. that Peking would exploit the family visits to push the U.S. further in the direction of negotiations than it was prepared to go. Dulles was persuaded it was first necessary to convince Red China that the U.S. was no "paper tiger."

"One of the most curious and most upsetting features about the present world situation is that everybody is afraid of everybody," Hammarskjold commented at the time.

It was his duty, he thought, to explain to Peking and Washington the other side's viewpoint, "as well as one can and as deeply as you can understand them. . . ."

Many of America's allies were urging it to make some military adjustments, such as withdrawal from the offshore islands, but Hammarskjold did not have any particular measure in mind. He sought instead to create an atmosphere which would give those in China and the U.S. who wanted a *rapprochement,* something with which to work. But he also was very anxious not to be in a position where he appeared to be prodding the Americans.

Despite the rebuff on the family visits, Hammarskjold continued discreetly to press both sides—the U.S. to keep the door open, Peking to go ahead with the release of the airmen.

As the weeks passed and nothing happened, clamor began to mount again in the U.S. on the subject of the airmen. On April 19 he told the press at UN headquarters that he was going to Stockholm to attend a working session of the Swedish Academy. In fact, he went to meet with the Chinese Ambassador. He had considered the matter as settled, he told General Piao, at the time he had been in Peking, except for China's need for time and a peg. The General agreed with his assessment of the situation. Time was running out, Hammarskjold noted. What remains was the need for a peg. Was there anything that could be done?

The Chinese found their peg. A representative of the Chinese Embassy met Uno Willers at a Soviet party at about this time. He learned on inquiry that Hammarskjold would be in Sweden during the summer and that it would be his birthday. That was "very interesting," he commented. What would Hammarskjold like for his birthday? "Books, Chinese paintings, but, most of all," replied Willers, "release of the airmen." Twice, subsequently, the Embassy called to check the date of Hammarskjold's birthday.

On August 1, two days after Hammarskjold's birthday, he was at his cottage in Löderup, a small village in the south of Sweden. There he received a message from the Chinese Government that they would in a few days release the airmen, not because of the Assembly decision but in order to maintain and strengthen friendship with the Secretary-General, ending with congratulations to Hammarskjold on his birthday. Personal courtesy was what they finally used as the peg.

To get his friend away from the press, Bo Beskow rented a cod-fishing boat and together with Bo's shy young wife, Greta, they spent the day on the water. But when they put in, the hills around were aswarm with people, very young and very old, waving little flags. The Chinese cable had arrived.

He deprecated efforts to assign credit. All sorts of factors influenced the outcome and all sorts of personalities entered the picture and it would be presumptuous to try to interpret the arguing and reasoning of Peking, he said. But "no event or anything which I have been permitted to do ranks higher on that list of causes for gratitude than my trip to Peking."

It still is difficult to assess the impact of Hammarskjold's intercession—how much of a part it played in the relaxation of tension that preceded agreement on direct talks between the U.S. and China. In a recent interview with Edgar Snow, Chou said that the eleven airmen were released following the mediation efforts of India as well as Hammarskjold. The purpose, added Chou, was to create "a favorable atmosphere" for the ambassadorial talks between China and the U.S. that began August 1, 1955, in Geneva.

The contact between Chou and Hammarskjold continued. At that time Hammarskjold felt that Peking certainly counted on the UN as a very important factor in international politics. That appears to have changed, perhaps because of U.S. ability to keep the UN door tightly shut. In any event, Chinese diplomats now give the impression the UN no longer figures in their policy. They brush it aside. The Chou-Hammarskjold correspondence ceased.

In 1959 Willers was invited to visit Red China where he met Chou. "I gave him a little book from Hammarskjold with his regards. There was no reaction from Chou."

The mission to Peking did not open the UN doors to the People's Republic of China but a major consequence was the sudden realization by member states—both East and West— that in Hammarskjold they had a diplomat of balance, discretion and extraordinary resourcefulness in finding solutions, and that in the office of the Secretary-General they had an organ that could fill the vacuum created by the impotence of the Security Council as an agency for negotiation, mediation, initiation.

6

Holding the Line
in the Middle East

The mission to Peking became the forerunner of a long series of assignments in the Middle East aimed at checking the fatal slide toward a renewed Arab-Israeli war.

The area was beset by that whole cluster of turbulences that the postwar world has come to associate with the retreat of empire—a convulsive nationalism intent on driving out the remnants of imperial rule, internal instabilities stemming from governmental inexperience and an acute social problem, intra-Arab feuding and rivalries and the East-West competition for client states.

All of these collisions of interest fed on the most perilous of all—the festering dispute between Israel and the Arab states. In 1948–49 the UN had done only half a job after voting for partition of Palestine and establishing the state of Israel. It stopped the war waged by the Arabs to overthrow that decision. It encouraged the conclusion of formal armistice agreements. And then it halted, finding it easier not to face up to the problem of the hundreds of thousands of Arab refugees nor to press the two sides to move on from armistice to settlement.

About the time of Hammarskjold's accession to office, events in the area took an ominous turn. The rise of Nasserism and the ebbing of British power were accompanied by Soviet Russia's active entry into the Middle East, following the death of Stalin. From a policy of abstention in the Security Council Moscow moved to vigorous and automatic advocacy of the Arab cause. "A sinister event," Sir Gladwyn Jebb cabled the Foreign Office after Andrei Vishinsky's first veto of a Palestinian resolution—one that would have permitted Israel to go ahead with a life-giving water project in a demilitarized zone along the Syrian-Israel frontier.

Israel turned from the UN to a policy of reprisal and retaliation. "Two blows for one," decreed David Ben-Gurion. Armistice demarcation lines were transformed into zones of guerrilla warfare. The agenda of the Security Council between 1953 and 1956—Qibya, Patish, Nahhalin, Scorpion Pass, Gaza, Nahal-Oz, Khan Yunis, Galilee—were grim markers on a road that appeared to be leading inevitably to war when the Council, in March 1956, turned to Hammarskjold.

The British were unhappy over reliance on Hammarskjold in the Middle East, not because of any lack of confidence in him, but they favored direct intervention by the Western Big Three—a policy that Sir Anthony Eden, then Prime Minister, called "putting teeth" into the Tripartite Declaration of 1950. This pledged the U.S., Britain and France to take action, inside or out of the UN, against any move to alter the Palestine status quo by force or threat of force.

Eden favored preparatory military measures by the Tripartite powers that would indicate to Arabs and Israelis alike that if war broke out they would intervene. But the U.S. was hesitant. The Tripartite Declaration was regarded by the Arabs as an instrument of Western imperialism. It was a red flag to the Soviet government which declared formally that "military measures undertaken outside of the UN and without the participation of the countries of the U.S.S.R. and Middle East cannot fail to constitute a threat to the U.S.S.R. and Middle East." President Eisenhower informed Eden during the White House talks in February 1956 that constitutional difficulties stood in the way of such precautionary moves.

The upshot was the decision to turn to the UN. And the further decision to make use of the Secretary-General was dictated by the problem of the Soviet Union. A resolution "giving it to Dag" might get by the Soviet Union where a more specific directive might not; moreover, giving the mission to a Council subcommittee would immediately raise questions about its composition. And if the mission failed, the blame would be on Hammarskjold rather than on them.

Hammarskjold was not unready; he had, in fact, already moved into the situation. Special responsibilities for maintaining and strengthening the armistice regimes had been conferred upon the UN by the Security Council in 1949 when it requested the Secretary-General to maintain a Truce Supervisory Organization. Two dozen countries supplied UNTSO's staff of 120, of whom 35 were military observers. Hammarskjold had taken a firm hold of UNTSO, whose chief he appointed. The chief of staff was a Canadian general, E. L. M. Burns, scholarly, steady of nerves, fair-minded.

In late 1955 Hammarskjold in New York and Burns in the Middle East had acted energetically to halt certain military moves and dispositions by Israel and Egypt which to all war offices signaled an explosion was imminent. These took place in the sensitive El Auja–El Quesima–Abou Aoueigila triangle, road junctions in the Negev-Sinai area that were the doorway to invasion of either Israel or Egypt. The Israel-Egypt Armistice Agreement had stipulated that El Auja on the Israeli side should be a "demilitarized" zone and severely limited the number and kind of troops and armor Egypt could maintain on its side of the line.

Both countries were in flagrant violation of these armistice provisions when in January 1956 Hammarskjold made an "introductory" visit to the Middle East. Although not a Security Council assignment but simply a leg on a longer journey that took him to South Asia and Australia, his talks with Colonel

Nasser and Ben-Gurion centered around the dangerous situation in El Auja. Nasser not only had strengthened Egyptian dispositions on his side of the Armistice demarcation line but had sent Egyptian forces into El Auja, because, he said, an Israeli *kibbutz* and police in that area were only disguised military forces.

Hammarskjold's advice to Ben-Gurion was that instead of attacking Egyptian forces in El Auja, he should rely on the UN to get them out. The UN had been unable to do so, Ben-Gurion replied, and therefore he had acted as the head of any other state would have done in similar circumstances. "How would you like to be sitting where I am?" Ben-Gurion flung out at him, carrying as he did the responsibility for the security of a people surrounded by an Arab world intent on its destruction.

Nasser told Hammarskjold he had sent his forces into El Auja only after Israel had begun to fortify the area and outlined the long list of Arab grievances against Israel, beginning with the situation of the Arab refugees.

A "map of the problem" took shape in Hammarskjold's mind as a result of these initial talks. On his return to headquarters he had advised the Western Powers against action in the Security Council or the General Assembly. He thought "quiet diplomacy" in which Secretariat efforts to re-establish compliance with the Armistice Agreements, backed by the discreet pressure of the great powers in Middle Eastern capitals, would be more productive than a public debate which might further entangle the issues in the coils of the cold war.

But if the West insisted on formal action in the Security Council, he cautioned against moves that in any way carried a "tripartite" flavor. This would only tempt a Soviet veto, he warned. The Secretary-General had power to act on his own in a situation threatening peace and security, especially in the Middle East. However, if a resolution requesting the Secretary-General to move into the situation were vetoed, his authority to do so on his own would be considerably impaired.

With armed forces building up on both sides, with the propaganda war in full swing, and Fedayeen terror and forays a daily occurrence, some striking within five miles of Tel Aviv, the Security Council met on March 20, 1956, at the request of the U.S. alone—the first time Britain and France stayed aside—to consider the status of compliance with the Armistice Agreements. A U.S. draft resolution asking Hammarskjold to survey the compliance situation was adopted unanimously. Israeli Ambassador Eban welcomed this decision to utilize the office and person of the Secretary-General to restore operation of the Armistice Agreements to their full integrity. But he emphasized that the Agreements were defined in their own first articles as indispensable steps towards the restoration of peace.

The Arab spokesmen also welcomed the assignment to Hammarskjold, but insisted that its scope should be limited to the Armistice Agreements and not deal with the basic problems standing in the way of peace settlement. Soviet Ambassador Sobolev, in voting for the resolution, emphasized that no decision affecting peace and security in the area should be taken outside of the UN and that all measures should have the agreement of the parties concerned.

In effect, what the Council was asking Hammarskjold to do was to pull the contending parties back from the brink of war— an unenviable assignment considering that the Western Powers on their own had been unable to accomplish it.

He welcomed the mandate, Hammarskjold told the Council, but noted that the specific responsibility placed upon him by the request neither detracted from nor added to the authority of the Secretary-General under the Charter. He considered himself to be acting in two capacities. He was agent of the Council with a clearly defined mandate. But the Secretary-General always remained Secretary-General, and, as such, had the unlimited right under the Charter to bring up with the parties any matter affecting peace or security as, for example, the arms race.

His immediate aim was concrete, limited and urgent. As he flew out to Beirut, which was to serve as his headquarters for almost a month, he construed the Council's mandate as a directive not only to "survey and report" on the state of compliance but also to "re-establish compliance" to the greatest extent possible.

Hammarskjold's problem was that of a field commander whose forces are in disorderly retreat, establishing a line where he can take a stand, regroup and rally to recover the lost ground.

His report of May 9 on his Middle East trip was not only a superb piece of craftsmanship; it reflected brilliant political generalship and the agreements it registered showed diplomatic skill of a high order.

A "chain of actions and reactions" had been engendered in the Near East, he reported to the Council, which, unless broken, would lead to war. The way he had decided to break out of the chain was to lift the cease-fire provision out of the Armistice Agreements and give it a special sanctity. The cease-fire obligation was to become an obligation independent of the Armistice Agreements to which no exception would be permitted. Infringement of other articles in the Armistice Agreements would not serve as justification for infringement of the cease-fire.

Hammarskjold had, therefore, asked the governments concerned for assurances—which he had received and attached to his report—that they would observe the cease-fire clause unconditionally provided the other party complied with the same clause, reserving only the right to self-defense under Article 51 of the Charter.

If the retreat could be halted on the line of the cease-fire, that would then pave the way for a balanced return to the full implementation of the other clauses of the Armistice Agreements.

"There are quite a few situations," Hammarskjold told an impatient newsman, "where we must live and learn to live with provisional arrangements, because there is no solution to the long-range problems which we can find overnight. We must simply grow into the solution. . . . I think that for the time being if we can get compliance with the Armistice Agreements in their integrity, we should be quite happy and not too impatient."

Extracting the unconditional cease-fire pledges had involved a delicate campaign of synchronization as well as persuasion. Just as the package appeared to be glued together in Jerusalem, it would come unstuck in Cairo or Damascus. Each ruler had his own reason for opposing an independent and absolute cease-fire commitment. Ben-Gurion was skeptical of "palliatives" so long as Nasser asserted the right to maintain "a state of war" with Israel in violation of Article I of the Armistice. Nasser wanted to make the cease-fire conditional on Israel's withdrawal from the strategic El Auja demilitarized zone. The Syrians, and to a lesser extent, the Lebanese, wanted to condition the cease-fire on Israel's agreement not to tap the waters of the Jordan.

Hammarskjold took with him to the Middle East George Ivan Smith, a soft-spoken Australian who shared his tastes in painting, literature and music and who served as his spokesman. Before he would go into a session with Ben-Gurion, Nasser or one of the other luminaries of the region, he would assemble Burns, Smith and a few of Burns's aides and do some thinking out loud with them on the line he proposed to take. After his meetings he would reassemble the same group and review the conversations he had held. These were essentially monologues.

Perhaps the most remarkable aspect of Hammarskjold's entry into the Middle East picture was the way he established his personal ascendancy over the situation and his authority with the strong, vivid personalities in the area. His most difficult problem was with Ben-Gurion, who was hostile to Hammarskjold because he considered Hammarskjold hostile to Israel. Hammarskjold on his first visit to Israel in January had asked the Israelis to cancel a Jerusalem reception because he felt that he not only had to be impartial but appear impartial; his aides without his knowledge had objected to Israeli customs officers stamping his passport, presumably out of deference to Arab sensitivities on the point. But most upsetting of all to Ben-Gurion was a significant question that Hammarskjold had put to Dr. Nahum Goldmann, the leader of the World Jewish Congress. Hammarskjold had told Goldmann he knew his position on the partition of Palestine having seen the memo on the subject initialed by Goldmann and Dean Acheson. He wanted to ask Dr. Goldmann a question and would understand if he did not feel he wanted to answer it: "Would you still today be in favor of partition?" The question suggested that Hammarskjold was against the idea of a Jewish state and it upset Ben-Gurion greatly.

Yet the two men also fascinated each other and the more dealings they had, the greater their mutual respect and admiration. Ben-Gurion appreciated Hammarskjold's quickness of mind and refinement of instinct. The UN chief was attracted by Ben-Gurion's combination of earthy vitality and sage-like learning. Over "oceans of tea" they would talk for hours, with Ben-Gurion's blunt-spoken wife, Paula, coming in and out with sharp comments. "Why don't you get married?" she asked Hammarskjold. "Then you would have to worry about your wife and would leave us alone."

In Cairo he hit it off very well with Dr. Mahmoud Fawzi, the Egyptian Foreign Minister. He admired Fawzi's diplomatic skill, his knowledge, his soft subtleties. He liked him as a human being. He respected President Nasser but gained the impression after several talks that the Egyptian leader was insecure and not well understood in the West. He would go out of his way to explain Nasser's views to Western leaders. As with Ben-Gurion, he had problems with Nasser, although of a different sort. At one of his first meetings he thought he had reached an understanding with the Egyptian leader on one of the crucial points regarding El Auja, but when he arrived at the Cairo airport he was handed an agency report that meant Nasser would not hold to the understanding. He drove right back to Cairo, demanded an immediate meeting with Nasser, entered the room and told him he was completely mistaken if he thought the Secretary-General would be satisfied with the appearance of an understanding.

As a result of Hammarskjold's cease-fire achievement, a milder tone was heard in the opposing capitals, specific measures were under active consideration for preventing clashes along the demarcation lines, incidents were less frequent and serious. When the Council met in June, its members spoke in high praise of the Secretary-General. In the two months since the

Council had adopted its resolution, "war has not broken out in Palestine," Ambassador Alphand of France noted. If not peace, the cease-fire has been re-established and strengthened, he went on. "Mr. Hammarskjold's stature has been increased by the test to which we subjected him, and the same applies to the prestige—which I know to be dearer to him than his own prestige—of his office."

The Council session was called "operation momentum." The hold-the-line arrangement was so successful, officials in Western chancelleries concluded the momentum should not be lost and consideration should be given not only to bolstering the Secretary-General's compliance efforts but to edging the parties toward a settlement. London especially was anxious to test the meaningfulness of Soviet statements to that effect. Khrushchev and Bulganin in an April visit to the British capital had agreed in the final communiqué to the need to create conditions in which a peaceful settlement "on a mutually acceptable basis" could be achieved.

In line with this communiqué, the British representative on the Security Council, Sir Pierson Dixon, offered a resolution with a preambular clause on mutually acceptable agreements. Violent Arab protests caused its deletion. Retention of the clause, they warned, would jeopardize the Secretary-General's task. The Soviet delegate backed them up. Perhaps he would not have if the U.S. had been willing to sanction a four-power approach. But the U.S. opposed dealing the Russians in. Hammarskjold thought this was a mistake. The British lamely explained to the Russians that they would have had a cause for complaint only if they had been left out of a *tripartite* resolution, not otherwise. In the end, Sir Pierson regretfully withdrew the offending words. It was neither the first nor would it be the last occasion on which great power ambitions in the area prevented the UN from exercising its influence to achieve a settlement. As finally adopted, the resolution was limited essentially to supporting Hammarskjold's efforts to secure full performance of the undertakings already given him.

In anxiety-shrouded words, after this vote, Israeli Ambassador Eban warned the Council that his people would be wise and prudent to conclude from the debate, especially from the tone and content of the Arab speeches, that their national security was gravely threatened.

An even more ominous development, known at the time only to a handful, was President Eisenhower's lack of success in persuading President Nasser to turn his efforts towards a peace settlement. Eisenhower sent a secret, top-level emissary to Cairo for this purpose in the spring of 1956. He was Robert Anderson, later to become Eisenhower's Secretary of the Treasury. The failure of this mission was a crucial turning point in Israel's attitude. More than ever it felt events were moving toward a fatal clash.

His position obliged Hammarskjold to take a more hopeful view. Asked after the Council meeting whether the belligerence of the Arab spokesmen on the "peace issue" did not cast doubt upon the "will to peace," which he insisted was basically operative in the region, he replied: "A will to peace is one thing; a will to peace-making on certain conditions, at a certain time, is necessarily another." When it came to peace-making, the basic fact, he emphasized, was the existence of over 900,000 Arab refugees. That is "very much on everybody's mind in the region." His goal at the moment was to see "the legal cease-fire converted into a state of mind." From that he would move toward getting both sides to undertake "unilateral, though related" steps to improve conditions, such as disarming of the demilitarized zones and "defense areas," re-establishment of freedom of navigation for Israel ships in the Suez Canal, repatriation and resettlement of refugees, utilization of the Jordan waters—all areas "where decisions by the UN have for long been neglected or even challenged."

Hammarskjold was sufficiently sure that the cease-fire would hold and lead to new and fruitful developments that he embarked on a tour of East European capitals. But on July 19 he was back in Jerusalem for talks with Ben-Gurion because of Israel limitations on the movement of UN observers in the El Auja demilitarized zone. This violated the Armistice Agreement, but Ben-Gurion argued the "indivisibility" of the Armistice Agreements. Except for the cease-fire clause, he contended that Egypt's refusal to accept Article I with its stipulation that both sides would refrain from undertaking, planning or threatening aggressive action against the other and would move toward peace, freed Israel from complying with the Articles which would prejudice its security in the face of Arab threats.

Hammarskjold was in the middle of trying to break out of this dangerous deadlock when the event occurred which British Prime Minister Sir Anthony Eden said transformed everything in the Middle East. On July 26, Nasser, in reprisal for Secretary Dulles' abrupt withdrawal of an American offer to help build the Aswan High Dam, nationalized the Suez Canal.

This is neither the place, nor are the materials available, to describe the way events now began to move toward their tragic climax—the maturing of the Anglo-French decision to use force to regain their rights in the Canal and settle with Nasser and Ben-Gurion's parallel resolve to strike the dagger from the upraised Arab hand, as Eban was later to put it.

So far as Hammarskjold knew, he still had the backing of all the members of the Security Council in his "round-the-clock" efforts to obtain compliance with the Armistice Agreements. There were ugly incidents during the summer, heavy casualties and sullen, seething tension between Israel and its Arab neighbors. Hammarskjold warned the Council the cease-fire was in danger of becoming "a dead letter."

But in the early autumn the flaming borders of Israel became flickers in the distance compared to the thunder and lightning of the Suez crisis and Anglo-French determination to compel Nasser to let go of the Canal.

When Nasser rejected the international management proposals of the eighteen "users" who accounted for more than 95 per cent of the tonnage passing through the Canal, Britain and France decided to bring the issue to the Security Council. They viewed it as a final effort to get justice by peaceful means, but few knew that.

The Council began its discussions on October 5. Seven foreign ministers were in attendance, including Dulles, Lloyd, Pineau, Dmitri Shepilov for the U.S.S.R., and Fawzi. The Western maritime powers were insisting that the nationalized

Canal be placed under international management as the only way by which freedom of navigation could be assured. The Canal should be insulated from the politics of any one country was the slogan coined by Dulles. Egypt, on the other hand, considered an international management board, on which it would be only one voice among many, "collective colonialism."

Under a plan proposed by Hammarskjold, the Council, after an initial round of statements, turned itself into a Committee of the Whole for the purpose of private discussions. He was out to prove the Security Council, if used imaginatively and flexibly, could foster businesslike negotiations. Preliminary Council sessions gave way to direct talks (also at Hammarskjold's suggestion) between Lloyd, Pineau and Fawzi. These were held in Hammarskjold's office on the thirty-eighth floor around a low coffee table with Hammarskjold acting as "chaperon," as he jokingly put it to Dulles. But the role of the chaperon, as Dulles pointed out to Hammarskjold, was to keep the parties apart, and on the thirty-eighth floor Hammarskjold was more catalyst than chaperon, helping by his formulations to crystallize agreements. He did not so much propose solutions, said Pineau, as note the points on which he visualized the possibility of agreement.

The result of the discussions on the thirty-eighth floor was agreement on what became known as the "six requirements" which should govern a Suez settlement. They included the vital principle that "the operation of the Canal should be insulated from the politics of any country," and Fawzi's acceptance of this narrowed the issue down to a dispute over the mechanism that would ensure fulfillment. It was agreement on the six principles that caused President Eisenhower to announce on television that progress in the Security Council was "most gratifying" and that it looked as though "a very great crisis is behind us."

The six principles were now incorporated as Part I of an Anglo-French resolution. Part II stated that the eighteen-power proposals, including international management, corresponded to the six requirements. It invited Britain, France and Egypt to go on negotiating and requested Egypt "to make known" alternative proposals that would meet the requirements in view of its rejection of the users' proposals.

Everyone knew there was risk of a veto by Shepilov when this two-part resolution was brought into the Council, but the assumption was that he would veto the whole thing. To the consternation of almost everyone, Shepilov moved that the two parts be voted on separately; the six requirements were approved unanimously, the second part endorsing the users' proposals was vetoed.

Dulles quickly declared in the Council that Hammarskjold should continue to encourage "interchanges between the governments of Egypt, France and the United Kingdom," to which Hammarskjold replied that the resolution provided "a valuable starting point" and that his own efforts to help would be along the lines indicated by Dulles.

It was not only Dulles and Hammarskjold who thought they were on the road to a negotiated settlement despite the Soviet veto. French Foreign Minister Pineau, the president of the Security Council, declared ". . . we have been able to achieve results which, while incomplete, are nevertheless positive. . . ." In a final private session of Western diplomats, Dulles was very emphatic in stating they had now reached a basis for negotiations. Pineau and Lloyd reportedly agreed and Lloyd went back to London quite satisfied with the six principles and fully expecting to meet Fawzi in Geneva at the end of October for further discussions under Hammarskjold's chaperonage.

Hammarskjold held further talks with Fawzi in New York which persuaded him it would be possible to get a satisfactory solution of the Suez dispute—that is, an *international* agreement regarding freedom of navigation rather than a unilateral declaration by Egypt.

For Hammarskjold, the Suez exercise was enormously gratifying, not only because it meant another dangerous world crisis surmounted but equally because it testified to the indispensability of the UN. He had constantly sought to give greater emphasis to the UN as an "instrument for negotiation of settlements, as distinct from the mere debate of issues." He had long been trying to persuade the great powers that "with only slight adjustments, discussions on major issues of a kind that have occurred outside the UN could often be fitted into its framework, thus at the same time adding to the strength of the world organization and drawing strength from it."

And he had been calling the attention of foreign ministries to the "so far unused" Charter provision for special periodic meetings of the Council attended by foreign ministers, or even heads of states, as a procedure for continuous and intensified treatment of certain questions of world concern.

Now, the Council's seeming success on Suez corroborated and reinforced his views on the valuable role the UN could play.

But in London, Eden had drawn opposite conclusions from the Council's proceedings. The vetoed part of the resolution was what counted. There was no point in going to Geneva to get an agreement "dressed up to look fairly reasonable." He could not understand how the UN, set up to build an international order, could have failed to censure or regret the seizure of a great international waterway by force.

On October 16, he and Lloyd flew to Paris for meetings with Premier Mollet and Pineau, at which the decision was taken for what Eden called "the crunch with Nasser."

7

*Back from
the Brink*

On Monday, October 29, the Israeli Government announced to the world it had invaded Sinai in order to destroy
the bases from which the Fedayeen groups operated. With the
end of the Security Council debates on the Suez Canal, Colonel
Nasser, Israel said, "felt himself immediately free to authorize
the Fedayeen units to resume their incursions into Israeli territory."

In Washington, after hurried conferences at the State Department and White House, Dulles' deputy, Herbert Hoover,
Jr., frantically sought to reach Lodge to instruct him on behalf of the President to ask for an emergency meeting of
the Security Council the next morning. Unable to reach Lodge,
who, along with other UN diplomats including Sir Pierson
Dixon, was at the opening of the opera, Hoover located James
W. Barco, brainy number three man on the U.S. delegation
and asked him to find Lodge. Barco immediately called the

Secretary-General and requested him to convene the meeting; then he went to the opera and fetched Lodge, who, in white tie and tails, went with him to talk with Hammarskjold.

He told them that if the U.S. had not asked for the meeting he would have done so himself. They were all deeply angered and aroused over the Israeli attack, and flabbergasted at hints of Anglo-French support for the Israelis. They discussed the line the Council might take the next morning to compel Israel to cease and desist. The drafting of resolutions is up to Council members, but that was a time when Lodge, as a matter of course, consulted Hammarskjold to be sure the U.S. was not out of line with his thinking on the Middle East.

More blows were to fall as became clear when the Council convened. After a debate that went on all day, Britain and France vetoed the U.S. cease-fire resolution. They informed the Council their countries had addressed an ultimatum to Israel and Egypt to end hostilities, withdraw ten miles from the Canal and permit Anglo-French forces temporarily to occupy the Canal Zone.

The Council adjourned at 11:05 P.M. Hammarskjold was deeply shaken by the day's events and distressed by the behavior of the attacking powers, especially by the British with whom he felt special ties. He had never had an easy time with Nasser, but now he saw Nasser as the victim. He was up all that night trying to decide on his course of action. By dawn he had worked out a statement in longhand. When the Council met that afternoon he read it as the first order of business. In a high-pitched voice that betrayed tension but without dramatics he told the Council that he would himself have acted along the lines of the vetoed Lodge resolution had not the Anglo-French ultimatum and attack rendered his mandate and "such an initiative pointless."

The Secretary-General was the servant of the principles of the Charter, he went on. "A Secretary-General cannot serve on any other assumption than that—within the necessary limits of human frailty and honest differences of opinion—all member nations honor their pledges to observe all Articles of the Charter."

That was the basis on which he was serving. It would be the basis on which he would act in the future. "Were the members to consider that another view of the duties of the Secretary-General than the one here stated would better serve the interests of the Organization, it is their obvious right to act accordingly."

There was a quick and unanimous expression of confidence from the delegates around the horseshoe-shaped table. "We regard him as being both able and fair," said Lodge. "We share the opinions that he has just expressed and his concept of his duties." The Soviet Union "has confidence in the Secretary-General . . . and lends him its support," said Sobolev. Despite Hammarskjold's hint that he would press them hard, the delegates of Britain and France concurred. "We have the highest regard for the integrity and impartiality of Mr. Hammarskjold," said Sir Pierson Dixon.

With the Council barred from acting by the Anglo-French veto, Yugoslavia, at the instigation of the U.S., now proposed convoking an emergency special session of the General Assembly, under the Uniting for Peace resolution, in order "to deal with the deepening crisis." There was some question about the legality of the move. Barco and "Chuck" Cook went up to the thirty-eighth floor to discuss with Hammarskjold and his aides how to get around a possible challenge as well as how to word the item on the Assembly's agenda. Most of the next day the U.S. delegation, in close touch with the Secretary-General's office, spent persuading other delegations to write letters to the Secretary-General, saying they noted the decision of the Security Council to convene an emergency session and concurred in it. They obtained more than the necessary number of concurrences, but the issue of legality was never raised.

As dusk fell over New York, the seventy-six-nation body convened. The Israeli Army had sealed off the Gaza Strip and was mopping up the last pockets of resistance in the Sinai Peninsula. Anglo-French bombings of Egyptian airfields in the Suez Canal Zone were preparing the way for an airborne assault.

Dulles was ordered by the President to fly to New York and take over personal leadership of Assembly efforts to stop the fighting. His plane was delayed by rain and he entered the somber Assembly Hall as Sir Pierson was explaining Britain's willingness to have the UN take over in Egypt if it would undertake to police the area pending a lasting settlement of the Palestine and Suez issues.

Dulles ignored this offer. The first thing that must be done, he declared, was to stop the fighting as rapidly as possible lest it become a conflagration endangering all. He presented a U.S. draft resolution. Adopted in the early hours of the morning, it was to become known as the November 2 cease-fire resolution. It called for an immediate cease-fire and a halt to the movement of military forces and arms into the area. It urged the parties to withdraw behind the armistice lines, desist from raids across those lines and to observe scrupulously the Armistice Agreements. It recommended to all member states that they refrain from introducing military goods into the area. It urged also that with the cease-fire, steps be taken to reopen the Suez Canal "and restore secure freedom of navigation."

Finally, it gave the Secretary-General the task of observing and reporting on compliance to the Council and Assembly "for such further action as they may deem appropriate."

Dulles rejected Sir Pierson's argument that events were developing in such a way as to give the UN "a unique opportunity to bring peace in the Middle East." Unless the principle of renunciation of the use of force was first vindicated, he said, "we would have, I fear, torn the Charter into shreds and the world would again be a world of anarchy."

The resolution was approved 64–5 with six abstentions. One of the abstentions came from Canada, and Lester Pearson, in explanation of Canada's vote, spoke of "one great omission" in this resolution. It did not provide for any steps to be taken by the UN for a peace settlement without which a cease-fire would be only of temporary value at best. There was another shortcoming. Allowing the armed forces of Egypt and Israel to resume their old positions confronting each other in fear and hatred would lead again to incidents, bloodshed, and "ultimately another explosion." He would have liked to see a provision authorizing the Secretary-General to establish a UN force large enough to keep the borders at peace while a political settlement was being worked out. Canada would be happy to participate in such a "truly international peace and police force."

Pearson had urged Dulles to delay his cease-fire resolution so that it might incorporate some of these ideas. "We have to get them off the hook," he remarked to his colleague Hans Engen, meaning that France and Britain already gave indications of wanting a graceful way out. Dulles was not unsympathetic, especially to the idea of a UN force. But he did not dare delay the call for a cease-fire. He was afraid the Russians might jump in and pre-empt the leadership of the aroused Afro-Asian group. The U. S. Government was, moreover, furious at the invaders. They were aggressors and aggressors should not be rewarded.

Nevertheless, just before the weary Assembly adjourned at 4:20 A.M., Dulles arose to say that he agreed with Pearson, as did President Eisenhower with whom he had talked a few hours previously. The U.S. would be happy if Pearson formulated and introduced "a concrete suggestion" along the lines he had outlined.

Pearson had informed Hammarskjold of what sort of suggestion he had in mind. With a British and French invasion force approaching the coast of Egypt, the Secretary-General seriously doubted that the moment was propitious for talking about a lasting peace settlement.

In a before-dawn statement hailing the Assembly's approval of the cease-fire resolution, Hammarskjold noted the calls for "a fresh, positive approach to the problems of the Middle East." One should have a clear view of the conditions under which concrete proposals might prove useful. He did not believe that confidence, co-operation and peace in the Middle East could be achieved through force, violence, illegality and disregard for the spirit and decisions of the UN.

This was the protector of the UN Charter speaking. There were also doubts on the score of practicality. The British and French, in urging the UN to take over from them, were suggesting the UN commission them as its agents. Prime Minister

Nehru was urging that the U. S. Sixth Fleet be deputized as the UN Force.

Later that morning Lodge and Barco went to see Pearson to inform him the U.S. would support a UN force if he would formally propose it. Pearson was willing but first wanted to consult Ottawa. When the three met again Lodge had a draft resolution requesting the Secretary-General to submit a plan for an emergency force. What did Hammarskjold think of it, Pearson asked. Lodge said he had talked with the Secretary-General and he had approved—but talk to him yourself, Lodge added. At lunch Pearson outlined his plan to Hammarskjold and Cordier. Hammarskjold, who had been depressed, was persuaded of its workability and discussion turned to how it should be gotten under way. By the time the Assembly reconvened Saturday evening, November 3, the preparatory work had been done. Engen had been drawn in for the Scandinavians, Arthur Lall of India for the Afro-Asians, and Francisco Urrutia of Colombia for the Latin Americans. Lodge and his aides worked discreetly. Egypt had been consulted and Pearson was in touch with the Commonwealth countries.

Speed was essential. Egypt had signified a willingness to comply with the cease-fire, but Britain and France had conditioned compliance on the establishment of a UN force. Meanwhile, their air offensive had destroyed the Egyptian air force, and an invasion armada was converging on Port Said.

Four resolutions were before the Assembly. An Afro-Asian draft renewed the call for a cease-fire and with an eye to the invasion force set a twelve-hour deadline for compliance. There were two U.S. resolutions to establish UN commissions to work out new approaches to the Palestine and Suez problems. These were submitted in response to widespread demands from allies and the American press that the U.S. do more than press for a cease-fire and withdrawal. They were promptly attacked by leaders of the Soviet and Afro-Asian blocs. "Appeasement," cried Hashim Jawad of Iraq. A maneuver to divert the Assembly from "the real issue which is halting aggression," said Arkady Sobolev. The only purpose of Assembly action, said Arthur Lall of India, should be "to restore the *status quo ante.*"

As a consequence, the fourth resolution on creating a UN Force was presented by Pearson as establishing the machinery by which compliance could be secured with the Afro-Asian cease-fire proposal. The Pearson resolution simply requested the Secretary-General to submit "within 48 hours, a plan for the setting up, with the consent of the nations concerned, of an emergency international UN Force to secure and supervise the cessation of hostilities in accordance with all the terms of the aforementioned (November 2) resolution."

Given the enormous Assembly majority for "vacating the aggression" and Soviet-American agreement on that point, Hammarskjold would have had little leeway for another approach, even if he were so minded. "How could the Secretary-General of the UN oppose a position shared by the U.S., U.S.S.R., dragging in their wake the majority of other nations?" Pineau asked. But Hammarskjold's own view also was there was an aggression and that to appear to reward an aggressor in the context of the UN would undermine the Charter.

Another view was possible, as Pearson indicated. Aggression could not be rewarded, but it was not only Britain, France and Israel which had a stake in Palestine and Suez settlements. It was in the whole world's interest to press for such solutions. But Hammarskjold did not want to do it. Neither did the U.S. And Britain and France did not have the standing to do it. As Sir Pierson Dixon noted later, "No one was talking to us."

The November 2 cease-fire resolution did have some reference to longer-range considerations. It called on the parties to the Armistice Agreements, following a cease-fire and withdrawal, to observe those Agreements scrupulously. It also urged the restoration of secure freedom of navigation through the Suez Canal.

These were precisely the lines along which Hammarskjold had been working before the attack. Full compliance with the Armistice Agreements was, he had concluded in the spring of 1956, a necessary stage on the way to Arab-Israeli peace and he still held to this view. And on a Suez settlement he expected to pick up where he and Fawzi had left off in October.

Not the least of Hammarskjold's qualities is what a fellow Swedish economist noted as "a strong feeling for consistency and continuity."

The upshot was an Assembly decision—59–5, with 12 abstentions—approving the Afro-Asian cease-fire demand coupled with a vote at 2:17 A.M. on Sunday—57–0, with 19 abstentions—directing Hammarskjold to submit a plan for a UN force in forty-eight hours.

As they left the General Assembly Hall, Hammarskjold turned to Bunche and said, "Now, go get a force together." A message went to General Burns in Jerusalem telling him he would have to take over at least temporary command of this first emergency international force. He was also asked to send in his views on what would be required and to begin to assemble a staff from his UNTSO officers.

That was also the night the Red Army began its final tank and artillery assault on Budapest. At three in the morning, the exhausted diplomats, including the Secretary-General, trooped down the carpeted hall to the blue and marble Victorian precincts of the Security Council. A Soviet veto of an American desist-and-withdraw resolution brought from Hammarskjold the same terse statement on how he envisaged his duties that he made after the British and French vetoes. There was, however, no chivalrous Soviet response.

It was dawn when the Council rose, having voted to convene an Emergency Assembly on Hungary later that day. Hammarskjold went directly to the thirty-eighth floor to continue work on the plans for a UN force. A senior Israeli diplomat had commented skeptically after the Pearson resolution was adopted that the UN had been laboring on the police force idea for forty-eight months without result, let alone forty-eight hours. The first blueprint was to be ready in seven hours.

His initial pessimism and doubts overcome, he embraced Pearson's idea with his customary energy, enthusiasm, and imagination. Even before the Assembly vote he had sounded out several delegations, especially the Scandinavian on supplying contingents in a hurry. Pearson had offered a Canadian levy, a self-contained battalion of the Queen's Own Rifles, ready to ship for Port Said. Saturday night Hammarskjold received word from President Nasser he could not accept contingents from NATO powers. He put in a call to Urrutia, who had flown to Washington. Would he come right back to New York? Urrutia was in Hammarskjold's office at 8 A.M. agreeing to get in touch with Bogotá about Colombian troops.

By 9 A.M. Pearson and Engen had come in and soon after that, Lall. Hammarskjold had a working paper ready for them to discuss. When the Assembly resumed late that afternoon Hammarskjold was ready with a first installment on a plan for UNEF. As an immediate step the Assembly should establish a UN Command, headed by General Burns, the UNTSO Chief of Staff. Burns should be empowered to recruit a small staff of officers as a beginning. Neither officers, nor the troops that would come later, should be drawn from the great powers, the report stipulated.

The Assembly's approval of this report by a vote of 57–0, with 19 abstentions, had profound implications. It established the first genuinely international peace force. It rebuffed British and French pressure that their forces be given a UN flag; and it was a step forward from the Unified Command concept in Korea, where a group of nations under a UN flag acted for UN purposes but were not under the authority of the General Assembly or the Security Council.

Hammarskjold, Pearson and the U.S. hoped that approval of a UN Command would be sufficient evidence of the UN's intentions to persuade the British and French to postpone the invasion that was imminent. But they replied that no UN force was yet in being and went ahead with their plans.

Now Hammarskjold's job was to assemble the troops at the same time that he drafted a second report on what they were going to do. Bunche, whom he jocularly designated as his "Minister of Defense," assembled the Washington military attachés of the countries which had been sounded out on supplying contingents. They met almost continuously in Bunche's conference room on the thirty-eighth floor. The U.S., which was to provide the airlift, assigned a couple of officers to work with this group, and General Coulter, head of the UN Command in Korea, happening to be in New York, was pulled in to help.

At Hammarskjold's end conferences went on without interruption on the principles that should govern the new force—its functions, duration of duty, where it would be deployed and the hundred other matters on which governments wanted answers before they committed their troops to him. He would first talk these principles over with his aides, and then consult Pearson, Engen, Lall and others. He worked phenomenally long hours, dictating reports between 2 and 3 A.M., relaxing afterwards with a book of poetry. A British diplomat presented him with Isaiah Berlin's *The Hedgehog and the Fox*. Almost the next day he had a message that the Secretary-General had read and enjoyed it.

Lief Belfrage recalls being at his desk at the Foreign Office in Stockholm when a call came through from Hammarskjold about a possible Swedish contingent. After discussing the offer, Belfrage asked, "Aren't you very tired?" "Oh, no, no," replied Hammarskjold, "I don't think I've slept more than two or three hours this past week, but I'm doing fine."

In Oslo, the Cabinet, meeting on Sunday to consider Hammarskjold's request, discovered it had no legal right to send troops out of the country. An order went out, convening Parliament the first thing on Monday. An emergency bill was submitted, processed through committee, and by 3 P.M. Oslo time, unanimously approved. The Secretary-General on Monday morning, New York time, had a cable saying the first company was ready for dispatch to the Middle East that night.

Monday, November 5, was a critical day. The airborne invasion of Egypt had begun. And the Soviet Union, which up to that day had been preoccupied with Hungary and East Europe, now thrust itself into the Middle Eastern picture with savage threats and ultimatums. On the night of November 5, Eden, Mollet and Ben-Gurion received letters from Premier Bulganin stating that the Soviet Union was ready to use force "to crush the aggressors and restore peace in the Middle East" and warning that West Europe's capitals were within reach of its rockets.

The Bulganin letter caused Mollet to convene an emergency meeting of his Cabinet at one in the morning, with several of the members tumbling out in pajamas and dressing gowns. In a parallel letter to President Eisenhower, Bulganin proposed that the U.S. and U.S.S.R. join forces to put an end to the Middle East fighting. And in New York the Security Council convened at the request of Sobolev to consider a Soviet draft resolution calling on the U.S. and U.S.S.R. to aid Egypt with air, naval power and volunteers.

The Council rejected the Soviet proposal, which President Eisenhower had already branded as "unthinkable." It was easier for the Council to do so because of the progress Hammarskjold was able to indicate on setting up the UN force which the British and French were insisting was the prerequisite to a cease-fire. Eisenhower pressed Eden to accept the UN force plan immediately to forestall Soviet intervention.

November 6 was another frenzied day at the UN. President Nasser, responding to the Soviet offer of help, had issued an international appeal for volunteers. Israeli military operations had ceased and Eban had transmitted to Hammarskjold an unconditional acceptance of a cease-fire, but the Anglo-French invasion force was pushing down the Canal.

Racing to prevent enlargement of the conflict—the Soviet threat was taken very seriously—Hammarskjold early that day completed his second and final report on the establishment of UNEF and transmitted copies to Britain and France.

The essential elements of this report were that the Force would be an "emergency"—that is, not permanent—body; would be recruited from the small, not great, powers; would function under the control of the Secretary-General aided by an Advisory Committee; would be a buffer, not a fighting body, with aims limited to those set forth in the November 2 cease-fire resolution; would not be used to affect the political balance; and, in accordance with international law, would require the consent of Egypt for it to be stationed and operate on Egyptian territory. Appended to the report were six annexes, letters from Canada, Colombia, Denmark, Norway, Pakistan and Finland, stating the readiness of those countries to contribute contingents.

On the basis of this report, Britain and France informed Hammarskjold that they had ordered a cease-fire pending confirmation that Israel and Egypt had accepted an unconditional cease-fire and that the international force to be set up would be competent to secure and supervise the objectives set forth in the November 2 resolution.

Hammarskjold immediately summoned the press and while his hands trembled his voice was firm as he told reporters that he had "an important communication to make." He read the British and French letters, said he could confirm the Egyptian and Israeli cease-fire acceptance, and added that it was his "personal conviction that if the General Assembly, as I certainly hope it will, accepts the proposals I have made in my second and final report on the international force, the force will be competent to secure and supervise the objectives set out in the General Assembly resolution."

When the Assembly reconvened the next day, November 7, it was in an atmosphere of general relief. Pearson summed up the body's feelings when he said: "We may have been saved from the very edge of catastrophe" by the action of the UN.

How much of a part did the Assembly, and its agent, the Secretary-General, play in halting the fighting? Creation of the UN force was advanced by the two countries as their reason for doing so. It was certainly the peg for their action, and the speed and resourcefulness with which Hammarskjold implemented the Assembly's decision on a force was a significant element in their decision as was their discomfort at being in defiance of the UN.

But there were other, perhaps more decisive, pressures at work. Eden later said the main reason for his decision to yield to the UN was "a run on the pound which threatened disaster to our whole economic position." There was also the threat of dissolution of the Commonwealth, a split country, the unremitting pressure of the U.S. and the dangers of Soviet intervention. It is difficult to gauge how much these were activated by the Assembly's almost unanimous refusal to countenance the resort to force. Vindication of this key Charter provision was certainly a crucial factor in U.S. policy.

It was the absence of comparable pressures that accounted for Hammarskjold's lack of success with the series of mandates that the Assembly handed him at the same time in regard to Soviet Russia's military suppression of Hungarian independence.

That same Sunday that he was asked to put together a UN force for the Middle East, he was requested to "investigate and report" on the situation in Hungary, dispatch "observers" to Budapest, suggest methods for ending foreign intervention, provide humanitarian relief, and, at a later stage, do what he could to obtain compliance with the Assembly's repeated calls for withdrawal of the Soviet Army from Hungary.

The Soviet and Hungarian authorities rebuffed the Assembly and its agent at almost every point. His observers were barred and his own offer to go to Budapest personally to discuss humanitarian aid was rejected. The Hungarians suggested they meet in Rome. "I turned thumbs down on that," Hammarskjold said.

With the exception of one or two smaller powers, no one was prepared either inside the UN or outside to urge measures going further than moral pressure.

In the crucial week when it was unclear whether the Red Army was moving out or back into Hungary, no suggestion was ever made to him that he fly to Budapest, Hammarskjold noted later. "And if you will read the records of the Security Council and the General Assembly for the week which started the twenty-eighth and in fact went up to, let us say, the fourth and fifth of November, you can very well see why there was not any such proposal.

"There was certainly not a single member of the Security Council who at that stage felt that the situation was clear enough to make such a proposal or felt that it was a good idea to send the Secretary-General away. There was never any choice from that point of view."

Neither had the precedent yet been established that the Secretary-General on his own initiative could move into a situation without some enabling directive by the Council or Assembly.

The Suez crisis did not have a higher priority with Hammarskjold over the tragic events in Budapest because one appeared a more iniquitous form of aggression or a greater threat to peace. The two problems never presented themselves in a way that would have provided for choice.

"It was only on the night between the 3rd and 4th of November that the General Assembly reached the first decision on UNEF. That first decision, as you know, was a very meager one. It was really only asking the Secretary-General to make a proposal within 48 hours. It was on the morning of the 4th—that is to say, in the late night of that Saturday, the 3rd—three o'clock in the morning—that the Security Council met in the final and decisive meeting on Hungary which later on led, as you know, to the question being transferred to the General Assembly.

"If you disregard all other aspects and look at the time sequence, I think it is perfectly clear to you that Suez had a time priority on the thinking and on the policy-making of the main body in the UN. That was not their choice. It was history itself, so to say, which arranged it that way.

"On the 4th I had in my hand a request for a report on UNEF within 48 hours. I do not think that the General Assembly or any member of the General Assembly would have asked me to do that and at the same time to check what was going on in Budapest. They could not have done it."

8

The Steep Hill of Suez

The cease-fire established, the tasks handed Hammar-skjold and his aides were only beginning. He now became the Assembly's agent in negotiating the withdrawal of the Anglo-French-Israeli forces. At the same time he had to translate UNEF from blueprint to reality. And a few weeks after the cease-fire he took on the job, monumental in itself, of clearing the Suez Canal of the forty-eight ships, tugs, barges and two bridges which the Egyptians had sunk and scuttled into the 105-mile waterway.

The political tug of war over the UN's purposes in inter-vening in Suez was in the next few months to dominate the attention of the Assembly—whether its responsibility was simply to "vacate the aggression" or to ensure a more durable peace.

While the Assembly's debate focused around this central issue, the Secretariat under Hammarskjold's leadership dis-charged administrative and organizational responsibilities in a

manner that provoked universal praise—even from those most
critical of the Assembly's—and Hammarskjold's—approach to
the political issues involved.

The Assembly approved Hammarskjold's second and final
report on UNEF on November 7, and by November 10, 100
Danors (Danish and Norwegian troops) had arrived at Cap-
odichino Airport in Naples on their way to Egypt.

Hammarskjold hurried to get token UNEF elements into
Egypt before one side or the other had a change of heart.
There were indications that Nasser, prodded by the Soviet
Union, might turn against the scheme. Moscow already was
suggesting the Force was an American scheme to gain control
of the Suez Canal. In Cairo an Egyptian spokesman announced
that Egypt had only "agreed provisionally" to the Force. On
November 14, however, Egypt agreed to permit the entry of
UNEF troops, and the next day a first blue-helmeted contingent numbering forty-five officers and enlisted men flew to
Abu Suweir Airfield, ten miles west of Ismailia. They wore
battle dress and were equipped with Sten guns and bazookas and
personal identification cards signed Dag Hammarskjold saying
in Arabic and Hebrew, "We testify that bearer is a member
of the UN Emergency Force." Within four weeks the Force
numbered 3700 men from eight nations and by February it
reached its final target of 6000 men from ten countries. Mine
detection and clearance, patrol guard, and buffer duties were
the Force's main tasks in those early weeks, supplemented by
such housekeeping functions as signals, engineering, communication, transport, medical, postal and pay.

First, the Force took over from the British and French;
subsequently from the Israelis as they withdrew eastwards. General Burns headed the operation in the field; Ralph Bunche
and General Martola of Finland at UN headquarters. A pio-
neering force symbolizing more a moral than a military com-
pulsion, it was something new in world history which had
to prove itself to skeptical general staffs and doubting diplomats.

A comparable feat was performed in regard to Suez Canal
clearance. The British and French assembled a salvage fleet

in Port Said, hoping that the clearance job would of necessity be entrusted to them, thus giving them some leverage in future negotiations about the status of the Canal. When Nasser told Hammarskjold he would like the UN to do the job and the Assembly so voted, British Foreign Secretary Selwyn Lloyd summoned Cordier, who was handling the clearance job at headquarters, to his Waldorf suite. This was a Sunday night. He told Cordier the Queen's Salvage Fleet was the best in the world—the only salvage fleet that could clear the Canal.

"The only one in being," Cordier corrected him. To think that another one could be assembled was "amateurish," countered Lloyd. "Yes, but by Thursday we'll be professional," persisted Cordier. The discussion was repeated to Hammarskjold Monday morning and he told Cordier to move into high gear, to assemble a UN salvage fleet.

On November 8 the Secretary-General had already made approaches to Dutch and Danish salvage firms. Now he called in John J. McCloy, chairman of the Board of Directors of the Chase Manhattan Bank, to serve as consultant on financial matters. McCloy was asked to recommend a first-rate army engineer. Without hesitation, he replied: "Jack Wheeler." They should not take his word for it, McCloy went on, but call General (Lucius) Clay and ask him simply: "Who is the best army salvage engineer?" Clay recommended Wheeler immediately.

Lt. Gen. Raymond A. Wheeler, ret., former Chief of the U. S. Army Corps of Engineers, was then working for the International Bank. Cordier called (Eugene) Black and asked whether the UN could have General Wheeler. Black wanted to know for how long.

"Four months."

"When?"

"The first plane."

"Then we called Rotterdam and said we don't have a penny but McCloy is our financial adviser and we can't wait. Will you send salvage ships to the Canal at once? They started on that same day. Then we contacted the Germans who had the largest salvage ships in the world. The Germans said O.K., but were under contract to the British. So we called the British to ask them to release the Germans from the contract. Soon we had our salvage fleet."

It consisted of thirty-two vessels mobilized from Belgium, Denmark, the Federal Republic of Germany, Italy, the Netherlands, Sweden and Yugoslavia. The British kept on making comments about how much better they could do the job. Viscount Hailsham, First Lord of the Admiralty, remarked that it was typical of the UN to send an "old middle western grocer" to do this most difficult technical job. Hammarskjold and his aides kept silent.

Nasser would not permit salvage operations to begin until the British and French had completed their withdrawal at the end of December. It became a point of honor with the UN team to finish the job in a shorter time than the British might have taken. Each time a ship was raised, there was a celebration. By the end of April 1957 the assignment was completed. "We have been able to establish unprecedented records in salvage," commented General Wheeler.

Underlying the technical achievement was the more fundamental question of the UN's purpose in clearing the Canal and establishing UNEF. On November 16 Hammarskjold flew to Cairo for intensive talks with Nasser and Fawzi on the functions of the Force, its composition, how long it would stay, where it would be deployed. There had been complete agreement in principle, but between a principle and its fulfillment a hundred controversies could arise. Token elements of UNEF reached Egypt November 15, but the door still had not been fully opened.

The Advisory Committee, which consisted of representatives of nations contributing troops to UNEF, was exercised over Nasser's pressure to exclude all Western Pact countries and weight the force in favor of the Bandung powers. Its members were even more apprehensive that after two weeks, Nasser would say: "Thank you. You can go home now."

In the Cairo talks, Hammarskjold prevailed upon Nasser to leave the composition of the Force in the hands of the Secretary-General and the Advisory Committee, and to include the

General Assembly in any ultimate decision on when the Force should be withdrawn, its functions fulfilled.

These agreements were embodied in a declaration of the Egyptian Government that "when exercising its sovereign rights on any matter concerning the presence and functioning of UNEF, it will be guided, in good faith, by its acceptance of the General Assembly Resolution 394 of 5 November, 1956 (establishing the UN Command)." This formula was the key that finally unlocked the Egyptian door to permit the rescue squad to enter.

Britain and France with some U.S. backing wanted UNEF to be stationed along the Suez Canal after the withdrawal of the British and French, pending a Suez settlement. Egypt violently resisted this as a violation of assurances that UNEF would not be used in any way that would affect the political balance. Soviet Russia equally firmly opposed the stationing of UN troops in this area.

Hammarskjold's assurance to Nasser that UNEF, except for a token force during clearance, would not remain in the Canal Zone, his agreement that clearance would not begin until after the British-French withdrawal, his refusal to use clearance as a lever with which to get a Suez settlement, produced charges he was giving way to Nasser. Even some State Department officials began to say, "Wait a minute, he's going too far with Nasser." The French and Israeli press were bitterly hostile. Paris *Match* accused him of a greater concern with holding onto his $40,000-a-year post than with justice. It was bitter for Hammarskjold, European to the core, to read accusations that he was the destroyer of Europe.

Hammarskjold's position was complex—his opponents said "excessively legalistic." There was an international stake in the creation of peaceful conditions in the Middle East and in a Suez settlement. But the international community had an equal stake in establishing respect for the basic principles of the Charter, especially the overriding principle that aggression should not be rewarded. ". . . to have peace with justice, adherence to principle and law must be given priority and cannot be conditioned," he said.

The Secretary-General was an upright man and certainly not an antagonist of France, said Pineau, "but his stand on the Suez affair was vitiated from the start when he failed to view the nationalization of the Canal by Nasser as a warlike act which ran counter to the UN Charter."

The British and French hoped to use the withdrawal as a lever with which to compel Nasser to negotiate a Suez settlement. Their withdrawals would be paced to Nasser's willingness to settle the arrangements under which the Canal would operate once it was reopened. They were prepared, Eden said after the cease-fire, to admit UNEF to Port Said, but would go no further than token withdrawals until the General Assembly debate showed that the UN would, in fact, carry out the responsibilities it had assumed—that is, internationally acceptable arrangements on Suez.

The crucial test of strength between the Afro-Asian and Soviet blocs on one side and the West Europeans on the other came in the vote on the "Spaak amendment." Belgian Foreign Minister Henri Spaak, with the backing of West Europe, moved on November 23 to strike out the call for "withdrawal forthwith" from a new Arab resolution to that effect. Had his amendment carried, which the British thought possible if it had U.S. support, the Anglo-French bargaining position would have been considerably enhanced. The vote was 23 in favor, 37 against, 18 abstentions. The latter included the U.S. and many Latin American states. Dulles was in the hospital and the U.S. vote was largely Lodge's decision. He argued that a U.S. vote for the Spaak amendment would undermine Hammarskjold's efforts to organize UNEF and clear the Canal.

Hammarskjold kept out of this crucial engagement. He was then almost completely wrapped up in the practical details of UNEF and getting Canal clearance started. But he concurred with the U.S. and Egypt that withdrawal had to be unconditional. He stayed out of the showdown on the Spaak amendment, but the opposition to it reflected his own views. He was in fact a central pivot in the U.S. decision to apply and subsequently lift the oil sanctions against Britain and France. The U.S. looked

to him as the Assembly's instrument in obtaining compliance
with its withdrawal demands to give the signal that would
open up U.S. oil reserves to its allies.

After the rebuff to the Spaak move Britain and France
concluded they had no alternative but to pull out. On December
3, they confirmed to the Secretary-General their previous decision to continue their withdrawal, and on December 22
Fort Fuad was turned over to UNEF and the last Anglo-
French transport sailed from Port Said.

Once the British and French withdrew, Hammarskjold began
to press Egypt to negotiate about Canal arrangement. But these
efforts were unavailing even though they had the support of the
U.S. In February, the U.S., Britain, France and Norway submitted a joint proposal to Hammarskjold to be transmitted
to Egypt for interim operation of the Canal. Under it, Egypt
would have operated the Canal, while the tolls would have
been collected by some international agency such as the World
Bank. The plan was rejected by Nasser.

Various governments took over the job, negotiating directly
with Nasser, including the U.S. and India. The latter urged
him to accept an international advisory board. Nothing came
of it. Hammarskjold never abandoned his October 24 proposals as the basis for his effort to arrange a Suez settlement.
In early April as the clearance operation was coming to an end,
he told a news conference these proposals still were "the direction in which I try to influence the developments to the best
of my ability and with the somewhat meager equipment which
I necessarily have." But later in April, at the same time that
Egypt notified the Secretary-General that the Canal was "open
for normal traffic," Egypt submitted a *unilateral* declaration,
promising compensation, reaffirming its intention to abide by
the Constantinople Convention guaranteeing freedom of navigation, and stating that differences over interpretation of the
Convention should be referred to the International Court of
Justice. This was a far cry from insulating the Canal from the
politics of any one country, as Dulles and the Security Council
had demanded, and Nasser underscored his triumph by keeping
the waterway closed to Israeli shipping.

A Security Council meeting was convened by the U.S. to "take note of the situation." Lodge said that in the absence of any "organized co-operation" between the users of the Canal and Egypt "there is no assurance that the six requirements would in fact be implemented." This was the postscript to Lodge's hopes that after withdrawal and the reopening of the Canal, Nasser would co-operate with the maritime powers in establishing a permanent regime for the Canal.

Could Hammarskjold have been tougher in these negotiations? He was banking a good deal on Dr. Fawzi with whom the negotiations were being carried on. He found Fawzi an attractive, reasonable and reliable statesman and assumed that once the withdrawals were completed it would be possible to negotiate a Suez settlement along the lines he and Fawzi had been discussing in October. But Fawzi's influence with Nasser, as Hammarskjold was to learn later, was much less than he thought.

Suppose Hammarskjold had taken the matter to the General Assembly and asked for its backing in trying to restart the negotiations. There was never any doubt that close to a majority of its members would have supported the Egyptian position. Hammarskjold did persuade Egypt to submit, in July 1957, a new declaration agreeing to accept as compulsory the jurisdiction of the International Court in disputes arising out of Suez Canal operations, and for a time cargoes bound for Israel in non-Israeli vessels were not molested. And compensation was paid to the Suez shareholders.

Inducing the Israelis to withdraw unconditionally proved a much more difficult and protracted undertaking. The Israeli evacuation began December 3, first from the Suez Canal area, then eastward out of the Sinai Desert. By the middle of January, under Hammarskjold's insistent pressure, Israeli armies had completely left the territory overrun except for a strip on the west coast of the Gulf of Aqaba and the Gaza Strip. There the Israelis stonewalled, declining to pull back any further without assurances that the Gulf of Aqaba, which leads to the Israeli port of Elath, and which had been blockaded from 1950 until

the Sinai attack, would remain open, guarded by UNEF, and
that the Gaza Strip, former Fedayeen base, would not revert
to Egyptian control.

There was more sympathy in the Assembly for Israel's position than there had been for Britain and France. But, on the
other side, Dr. Fawzi reminded the Assembly that the entry,
stationing and deployment of UNEF required the consent of
the Egyptian Government.

Hammarskjold has been criticized for establishing UNEF
with a key principle the recognition of Egypt's sovereign rights.
In effect, this placed the Force legally at Nasser's mercy. The
Assembly "could not request the Force to be stationed or
operate on the territory of a given country without the consent
of the Government of that country," Hammarskjold said in
his second report on UNEF.

The only possibility for overriding the sovereign rights of
member states, Hammarskjold pointed out, was through Security Council action under Chapter VII of the Charter. This
provides for enforcement measures but requires the concurring
votes of all the great powers.

UNEF was set up by the Assembly, not the Council,
which is the reason why the Soviet bloc of nine called the
decision illegal and refrained from voting no only because of
Afro-Asian pressures. No nation ever suggested that UNEF
did not require the sovereign consent of Egypt.

In fact, the first country to raise the issue of sovereign rights
was Israel. It did so the night the first UNEF report was
debated. The consent required, said Eban, was not merely of the
states invited to contribute troops "but chiefly the consent
of the state upon the territory of which it is proposed to
station these forces." Such consent was "axiomatic under the
Charter." If the question of sovereign consent was not absolutely
clear, he warned, "then a precedent would be created whereby
a majority of the General Assembly could decide to station
forces on the territory of any state irrespective of its prior
consent." It never gave its consent to stationing UNEF on the
Israeli side of the armistice demarcation lines. Israel did not
want UNEF stationed inside its borders because it feared that

the force acting at the behest of a transient Assembly majority could become an instrument of political pressure.

The "consent" clause was an important lever in Nasser's hands, one that he pressed more boldly as the invading forces withdrew. In January, when Israel was demanding guarantees in Aqaba and Gaza, Fawzi replied that UNEF was in Egypt for the sole purpose of giving expression to the determination of the UN to put an end to the aggression committed against Egypt and for securing the withdrawal of Israel's forces behind the armistice demarcation lines. It was not in Egypt as an occupation force or as a replacement for the invaders, he said, "or to resolve any question or to settle any problem be that in relation to the Suez Canal, to Palestine, or to freedom of passage in territorial waters. . . ." Krishna Menon of India backed up Fawzi.

Lester Pearson, a tireless exponent of a "middle position" between Israel and Egypt, agreed that complete withdrawal of Israeli forces should be "first in order of priority," but the Assembly should also agree on arrangements regarding the use of UNEF in Gaza and Aqaba "which will take effect only after Israel has accepted the decisions of the UN to withdraw." Israel had no right to attach conditions to its withdrawal. "But, as delegations to the General Assembly, we have, I think, the right, and, indeed, even the duty to relate these two matters: withdrawal, and proposals which may make impossible the kind of situation in the future which we have been facing during the last two or three months." The Assembly is an unwieldy body. In November despite top-heavy majorities in favor of a cease-fire, it would have been unable to translate parliamentary recommendations into operational decisions if it had been unable to entrust to the Secretary-General the elaboration and execution of its intentions. In the new impasse created by Israel's refusal to withdraw from Gaza and Aqaba in the absence of guarantees, it again turned to Hammarskjold. It wanted through negotiations and reports on implementation of the November 2 cease-fire resolution to chart a way out of the deadlock which it could endorse.

Hammarskjold was as concerned as any delegate with laying

a basis for peaceful conditions in the area but only by a
route that scrupulously respected international law and the UN
Charter. The four legal signposts that the UN had to obey,
as he outlined them in a report to the Assembly were:

1. The UN could not condone a change of the *status juris*
—that is, a situation which had been in conformity with law—
resulting from military action contrary to the Charter.

2. The use of UNEF required the consent of the state in
which the Force operated.

3. UNEF could not be used as a means to force a settlement
in the interests of one party or of political conflicts and legal
issues recognized as controversial.

4. UN actions must fully respect the rights of Member Governments recognized in the Charter and in international agreements.

Moving from these guiding principles to the specifics of Gaza
and Aqaba, Hammarskjold reasoned that the Egyptian-Israeli
Armistice was such an international agreement. It provided for
Egyptian control of Gaza and could not be altered to permit
either Israeli or UNEF control unless Egypt agreed. Deployment of UNEF in Gaza would have to be along both sides of
the armistice demarcation line. Any broader function for UNEF
in Gaza would require the consent of Egypt. Not even an Assembly vote could override the requirement of Egyptian agreement.

Similarly, in the Sharm el-Sheikh area dominating the approaches to the Gulf of Aqaba, Israeli military action should
not be an element influencing the solution. The international
significance of the Gulf of Aqaba might be considered to justify
the right of innocent passage and cast doubt on Egypt's claim
to invoke the right of belligerency in order to close it. UNEF
would follow Israeli troops on their withdrawal from Sharm
el-Sheikh and would assist in maintaining "quiet in the area."
But Hammarskjold would not say explicitly that UNEF would
assure freedom of passage through Aqaba, or for how long.

Instead, his reports emphasized that full implementation of

the Armistice Agreement would bar the assertion of belligerent rights which Egypt had used to justify the blockade.

Hammarskjold was a persistent man; the blueprint for Middle East peace, focusing on full compliance with the Armistice Agreements that he had set out a year earlier when he had brought about a cease-fire, was the one which he felt still to be valid in terms of legal requirements and political realities. UNEF should move into the El Auja demilitarized zone in the Negev and Israeli military forces should move out. Both Egypt and Israel should, in accordance with the Armistice Agreements, henceforth maintain only "defensive forces" in the militarily strategic El Auja–El Quesima–Abou Aoueigila triangle.

Withdrawal, like the cease-fire, was a preliminary and essential phase in a development through which a stable basis would be laid for tranquillity in the area. The Assembly, in giving high priority to a cease-fire and withdrawal, was in no way disregarding other aims which must be achieved in order to create more satisfactory conditions, Hammarskjold argued with Eban, but, withdrawal was the precondition. The basic function of UNEF, "to help maintain quiet," gave the Force great value as a background for efforts towards resolving other problems, such as refugees, water development, frontiers.

"It is essential that, through prompt conclusion of the first phase of implementation of General Assembly resolutions, Member Governments should now be enabled to turn to the constructive tasks to which establishment and the maintenance of the cease-fire, a full withdrawal of forces behind the armistice lines, a desisting from raids and scrupulous observance of the Armistice Agreements should open the way."

Hammarskjold's views were incorporated in two Assembly resolutions adopted on February 2. One called on Israel to withdraw "without further delay." The other noted "with appreciation" Hammarskjold's report on the measures to be carried out after withdrawal, called for scrupulous compliance with the Armistice Agreements, and stated that this required the placing of UNEF "on" the armistice demarcation lines and the implementation of "other measures" set out in Hammarskjold's report.

Did this mean UNEF would stay in Sharm el-Sheikh until there was an Israeli-Egyptian settlement? Eban wanted to know. Did it mean Gaza would, in fact, be under the control of the UN? Pearson had refused to sponsor the two resolutions because their answers were ambiguous on these points. Pineau had sought to persuade Hammarskjold to favor a more explicit formulation on freedom of navigation in Aqaba. Hammarskjold had insisted the formulation should not be open to the interpretation that Israel was getting a reward. Pineau replied that freedom of navigation was not a reward but a right and that other interests were involved. But Hammarskjold was unyielding. In all of his statements setting up the situation that would follow Israel's withdrawal, he never gave any assurances on subsequent arrangements except that UNEF would be there to "maintain quiet."

Protracted discussions between Eban and Hammarskjold only emphasized the deadlock. Both men were canny, subtle and persistent. There was no rapport with Eban as there was with Fawzi. As the Israelis stubbornly refused to yield, pressures were mounting in the Assembly for sanctions.

At this point, Dulles took a hand. Sometime in January Eban had gained the impression that Dulles was sympathetic to the Israeli case on Gaza and Aqaba. Discussions were broken off in New York and shifted to Washington. Hammarskjold said he welcomed this development; he was doubtful about sanctions, fearing they would introduce "new elements of conflict."

By February 22, Dulles and Eban were approaching agreement. But aspects of it required UN action. In a statement to the Assembly, February 22, Hammarskjold said he had been kept "well informed" about the Dulles-Eban discussions and warmly approved Dulles' efforts to break through the impasse that had developed in the Assembly. "Insofar as UN activities and positions are concerned," he could state with confidence that the take-over in the Gaza Strip "in the first instance would be exclusively by UNEF" and that Egypt was ready to make "special and helpful arrangements with the UN and some of its auxiliary bodies."

Eban thought the U.S. was ready for complete internationalization of the Gaza Strip and flew up to New York to find out whether this was the meaning of Hammarskjold's February 22 statement. But Hammarskjold poured cold water on the concept of internationalization. Gaza was Egyptian by virtue of the Armistice Agreements and whatever was done in the miserable strip required Egypt's consent. Agreement between the U.S. and Israel could not obligate UN action.

Eban returned to Washington less clear than ever about the meaning of Hammarskjold's statement. At this point the French took a hand in Washington. Since there was doubt that a two-thirds vote could be mustered in the Assembly giving Israel the assurances it wanted with regard to Gaza and Aqaba, Hervé Alphand, the French Ambassador, suggested a way out. Israel should make a statement in the Assembly on its "expectations and assumptions" as to what would happen following its withdrawal from Gaza and Aqaba, and the Western maritime powers, led by the U.S., would make answering statements in which they would declare those "expectations and assumptions" reasonable and announce their intention to act accordingly. Such an exchange would have some standing in international law, he and Dulles agreed. Alphand drafted the key paragraph.

Another crucial point on which the Israelis were dissatisfied was vagueness over the length of UNEF's stay in Gaza and Aqaba, whether it would be exclusively up to Egypt. Alphand suggested, and Eban agreed, that Israel pick up Hammarskjold's statements that Egypt would notify the Advisory Committee of its belief that UNEF's mission had been discharged and that it should be withdrawn. The Advisory Committee could be expected to bring the matter to the Assembly's attention.

That was the way it finally worked out. Gaza and Aqaba, said Pineau, was an arrangement "between Dulles, Eban and myself. Only afterwards did I speak to Hammarskjold. He agreed to the arrangement but it was not sealed by any public statement. And the Egyptians never said 'yes' or 'no.'" Pearson thought the Israelis were foolish to settle without a resolution. He upbraided the Israeli Ambassador to Canada, Michael Comay, for willingness to settle for unilateral assurances as the basis for getting out instead of an Assembly resolution. "O.K., you get the votes," replied Comay.

On March 8, Hammarskjold announced to the Assembly that the last Israeli troops had cleared Rafah Camp in the Gaza Strip and that UNEF troops were entering Sharm el-Sheikh with the Israeli withdrawal by sea "proceeding as planned."

The Secretary-General thus was "now in a position to report full compliance" with the Assembly's February 2 resolution on withdrawal. He added that completion of the withdrawal put into effect the operative part of the other February 2 resolution in which it was recognized that "withdrawal by Israel must be followed by action which would assure progress towards the creation of peaceful conditions" in the area.

On March 8, also, the longest and one of the most difficult sessions of the Assembly adjourned. In banging down the gavel, the Assembly's president, Prince Wan Waithayakon of Thailand, said: "The General Assembly rapidly passed resolutions couched in general terms, and the Secretary-General has implemented them by delicate and arduous negotiations, supported therein by the force of world opinion."

One final crisis had to be surmounted. Three days after the Israeli withdrawal from Gaza, Nasser announced the appointment of an Egyptian Governor over the Strip. Egypt's agitators stirred up demonstrations in the Strip demanding the return of Egypt. There were reports from Cairo that this was a prelude to a return of Egyptian troops. Mrs. Meir, who was back in Jerusalem, promptly flew to New York and stormed into the Secretary-General's office to lecture him like a schoolboy. When Cordier tried to interrupt her, she lashed out at him: "Don't try to censor my remarks."

Developments in Gaza, she said wrathfully, were "exactly the opposite" of what should have happened under Israel's understanding with Dulles. Israel had been assured there would be *de facto* UN control of the Strip.

He had not been present in the room when these discussions took place, said Hammarskjold, but had no reason to
believe her account of them was not completely accurate. There
had been no understanding so far as the Secretary-General was
involved. There was only one international instrument guiding
his and the UN's actions in the Gaza Strip, and that was the
Armistice Agreements.

Nevertheless, Hammarskjold was concerned. The legal status
of Gaza was one thing. The return of an Egyptian Governor
to symbolize Egypt's juridical rights could not be prevented, although the news that it had been done so soon produced dismay on the thirty-eighth floor. But if it meant pushing UNEF
into a corner where it could not carry out its function of
tranquillization, that was something else.

On March 19, Hammarskjold was on his way back to Cairo,
stating: "I think we may be able to establish a situation in
Gaza that will give all parties satisfaction, including Israel."
Both he and Dulles were sure that when the dust had settled, it
would be seen that the UN was still the paramount force in
the area. A few days later he was able to confirm to the
Advisory Committee that there were no Egyptian troops back
in Gaza, and none would be coming. The talks with Nasser
ended with a "gentleman's agreement" that he would do nothing
to upset calm and quiet in Gaza and Aqaba.

Throughout this period, Hammarskjold had been criticized
for obscurity and excessive legalism. Lloyd commented in the
House of Commons that "first prize" seems to go "for ambiguity
in these matters," referring to some of Hammarskjold's statements on Gaza and Aqaba. And Ben-Gurion complained of
the "legal pedantry" in Hammarskjold's approach.

Hammarskjold's ambiguity was calculated. The balance of
forces was overwhelmingly in Egypt's favor in the Assembly.
Hammarskjold was in favor of the maximum amount of UN
responsibility in Gaza and Aqaba, but no resolution saying
these things could get through the Assembly. Moreover, he does
not believe that the way to solve thorny international problems
in which many national interests conflict is by frontal attack;

he prefers to circle around them, weaving back and forth, like a broken field runner, so no one can bring him down.

As for his legalism, Pineau tells of a private dinner which Hammarskjold gave for Premier Guy Mollet in February. "The latter, in New York for the first time, was appalled by a juridical formalism which I had had time to get used to. Toward the end of the meal the atmosphere was rather tense."

Actually, what appalled Mollet, the politician, was that Hammarskjold would not go for a purely political compromise. Staking out a legal position is what permitted him to walk firmly without bogging down in a series of expediencies. He saw solutions pragmatically, but tested them against juridical concepts.

This was not legalism. Hammarskjold's view of his position is that in an organization whose stock in trade was conflict, involving two and often more parties, there is need for someone who will say what is right according to the rules by which the game is supposed to be played, someone who constantly reminds the parties of the rules of the game—and especially the supreme obligation to settle conflicts by peaceful means.

Pragmatically, the Gaza and Aqaba agreements have worked reasonably well. Gaza has been pacified and is no longer a base of Fedayeen activity. Aqaba has remained open. And the Western Powers, although not Israel, are content with the way Nasser has operated the Canal.

Could more have been achieved in the way of Middle East stabilization? Perhaps—if India, the U.S. and Hammarskjold had seen Nasser as the provoker as much as the victim of the attack.

In his memoirs, Sir Anthony Eden wrote that he never would have anticipated that the cards that were in the hands of the U.S. and the UN would have been thrown away as he thought they were.

"What were the cards that the UN had?" Hammarskjold commented. "The presence of French and British and Israeli troops in or close to the Canal Zone, regarded as enemies by the country through which the Canal runs—regarded as enemies by the whole Arab world. Is that a card which is a useful one for a negotiation about peace if it is not an imposed peace, or do you believe that any peace imposed on the Middle East would be a lasting one?"

9

Arab "Good Neighbors"

Shortly after the Suez crisis in a period which Hammar-skjold variously described as "convalescence," "the lull after the sound and fury," "germination time," he was asked what his next move might be toward peace in the Middle East.

He was "groping for the best road," he said. His mind was completely open, trying to spot "where there seems to be a road between the trees." But the road suddenly took a sharp turn into another part of the forest as intra-Arab rivalries and disputes in which the great powers were dangerously entangled, moved to the forefront, with Israel a sidelines spectator.

The issue was Nasserism—whether pan-Arab aspirations could only be achieved through unification under President Nasser and Egypt. Cairo's attractive power as the center of Arab nationalism had been enhanced by the Suez events. The union of Syria with Egypt in early 1958 gave another great boost to the concept of one Arab nation radiating from Cairo.

But there were strong counter-tendencies. King Hussein's Jordan violently resisted absorption. Baghdad, under King Faisal and Nuri as-Said, was a rival for Arab leadership. Arab countries complained of Nasserist pressures—inflammatory radio broadcasts, subversion, bribery and the like. Tunisia and the Sudan threatened to go to the UN. All proclaimed their support for Arab nationalism, but all wanted to maintain their national identities.

The East-West split further envenomed these rivalries. Iraq was aligned with the Baghdad Pact. The pro-Western government of President Camille Chamoun in Lebanon had boldly asked for the protection against Communist or Communist-inspired attack offered by the U.S. under the "Eisenhower Doctrine."

The Soviet Union backed President Nasser. "We want solidarity with the Arab people under your leadership," Khrushchev told Nasser in Moscow in May 1958. It "is the guarantee that no colonizers will return to your sacred land."

The intra-Arab issue was dumped into the UN's and Hammarskjold's lap when opposition to the re-election of Chamoun erupted into armed rebellion which the Lebanese Government charged Nasser with instigating. A complaint to the Security Council in May alleged "massive, illegal and unprovoked intervention" by the United Arab Republic with the purpose of "undermining the independence" of Lebanon. Lebanon did not wish to be *"anschlussed"* was the burden of the appeal of Charles Malik, the country's scholarly Foreign Minister, to the Council. There should be room in the Arab world "for a small, independent, free Arab state."

The Western Powers backed Lebanon, but the strongest supporting speech came from Fadhil Jamali, the Foreign Minister of Iraq. Nasserism exploited the ideal of Arab unity, he asserted, to bring about "the domination of Egypt and the rule of President Nasser rather than a union based on freedom, equality and fraternity." All Arab states "have had to a greater or lesser degree a taste of Nasserism." There might be a dissatisfied opposition in Lebanon, but the magnitude of the disorders was internationally produced. "If subversion and interference in Lebanese affairs are permitted to continue and succeed in Lebanon, no country in the Middle East can feel safe and secure."

Omar Loutfi, the mild-mannered and universally liked representative of the UAR, contended that Lebanon was trying to give an international aspect to a purely internal problem. The disturbances were domestic in origin and stemmed from Chamoun's efforts to keep himself in power. It was the opposition to Chamoun that wished to preserve Lebanese independence by freeing it from imperialist subservience.

Loutfi was supported by Soviet Ambassador A. A. Sobolev. The Lebanese disorders reflected a popular, nationalist revolt against a regime that had subordinated itself to the Eisenhower Doctrine and isolated Lebanon in the Arab world. There was no ground for any intervention in Lebanon's internal affairs "from any side, including the Security Council."

Malik insisted the Lebanese case was a test "whether the UN machinery and whole conception is fit to deal with subversion, with indirect aggression." This was very much the view also of Dulles. But the issue was more complex. The UN could not be a twentieth-century form of Holy Alliance intervening in a country at the instigation of a UN majority to support one form of government or political party, or undertaking to prescribe the pattern of relations Arab countries should have with each other and with the rest of the world. Only if there were international elements in the situation did it have a legitimate role.

The result was a resolution introduced by Sweden simply noting the charges of Lebanon and the reply of the UAR and directing the Secretary-General "to despatch urgently an Observation Group" to Lebanon "so as to ensure that there is no illegal infiltration of personnel or supply of arms or other materièl across the Lebanese borders."

Since the observers would be stationed in Lebanon and thus were a concern of Lebanon alone, Loutfi did not oppose the resolution, and, in light of Loutfi's attitude, Sobolev abstained.

The decision was approved June 11. By June 16, the UN Observation Group in Lebanon (UNOGIL) numbered a hundred observers. Its equipment included aircraft, helicopters, white jeeps. Heading the operation was a three-man group: Galo Plaza, a former President of Ecuador; Rajeshwar Dayal, an experienced Indian diplomat; Major General Odd Bull of Norway.

Controversy immediately arose over the function of UNOGIL. They were an "observer team," Hammarskjold stressed, "not a police force in the UNEF sense at all." Their aim was to stop infiltration by spotting and exposing it to world opinion.

This was not what the Lebanese wanted. They emphasized the ensure-against-infiltration language of the resolution. In his private talks with Hammarskjold, Malik asked for an international force that would seal Lebanese borders. The Council had left it up to Hammarskjold to define the meaning of the resolution. He had given it a restrictive interpretation. What the Lebanese wanted was a fighting force that would put a damper on the civil war. Hammarskjold said he could not do it.

In Washington, Dulles backed up Malik. The U.S. was ready to support any move to increase the size of UN border patrols, and if called on by Lebanon, would be prepared to give it military as well as diplomatic support if necessary to preserve its independence.

A quick tour of Middle East capitals in the middle of June left Hammarskjold unpersuaded that massive outside intervention was the cause of Lebanon's troubles. In Beirut, Chamoun had presented him with a big cake inscribed with the words, "UN Save Lebanon." Hammarskjold's rejoinder was: "Only Lebanon can save Lebanon." The most obvious indication of outside intervention was Cairo's inflammatory radio broadcasts. He tried to persuade Nasser to curb these. No assurances had been given in Cairo, he told a news conference, but "I preach my gospel or my law, whatever it is in this case, there as here. Naturally, I hope that it makes some impression."

UNOGIL's first report to the Security Council on July 4 failed to bear out Lebanese charges of massive infiltration and described the situation as essentially "a civil war." Lebanese diplomats disputed the report, said massive intervention continued with "several thousand infiltrators taking part. . . ." Lebanese claims were backed up in Washington where stories were leaked, presumably originating with the CIA, that the U.S. had evidence of large-scale outside interference.

Fundamentally, the divergence between Hammarskjold and UNOGIL on one side and Lebanon and the U.S. on the other reflected different assessments of Arab nationalism.

Except for the Suez interlude, U.S. officials, while publicly welcoming the rise of nationalism, feared it as an instrument, especially in its Nasserist version, not only for pushing Western interests out of the Middle East but for bringing the Russians in. The only safety lay in binding as many Middle East countries as possible to the West through military alliances. National independence was equated with sympathy with the West.

Hammarskjold was more sanguine about Arab nationalism. He did not believe U.S. military power could move in to replace the ebbing might of Britain. The healthiest development would be to take the area out of the cold war, to neutralize it as between the two blocs. So far as Lebanon was concerned, his talks in Cairo and Beirut had led him to expect that the elections in July would produce a new government that would be genuinely neutral.

He considered American military intervention in Lebanon a dangerous and backward step and counseled Dulles against it. He had made an impact on Dulles when on July 14 the world learned that an army revolt in Iraq had overthrown and massacred King Faisal and Nuri as-Said. Chamoun called for help. King Hussein felt imperiled. The little sheikdoms in the Persian Gulf, the main British oil holdings, seemed about to be engulfed in the rising tide of nationalism.

Dulles phoned Hammarskjold. All bets were off. The U.S. in response to an appeal from Lebanon was landing Marines in Beirut. Two days later, Sir Pierson Dixon called Hammarskjold to inform him that British paratroopers were being flown in to Jordan in response to an appeal from King Hussein.

Ironically, the Marines landed in Beirut the day after the

parties in Lebanon had agreed on a solution of the government crisis, which was exactly the solution to which they returned later in the month. The compromise was the election of General Chehab, the Maronite Christian, who commanded the Lebanese Army.

But the Marines really came in to stiffen the Western position throughout the Middle East. Lebanon was the only place they could enter. For a few days, it was thought they might go to the help of survivors of the Nuri as-Said era in Iraq. But there was no one left of the former regime to appeal for outside help.

The Soviet Union, meanwhile, had entered into the picture. Nasser had secretly flown to Moscow. Premier Khrushchev ordered demonstrative "maneuvers" on the frontiers of Iran and Turkey. A major crisis was at hand.

Both the U.S. and Britain in landing their troops in Lebanon and Jordan said they would remain only until the UN would be in a position to safeguard their independence. In making the withdrawal of the Marines contingent on the Council's establishing arrangements to protect Lebanese independence, the U.S. was, in effect, adopting tactics employed unsuccessfully by Britain and France, and successfully by Israel, in the Suez crisis. Not without malice, the Soviet Union, in its resolution condemning U.S. intervention in Lebanon, used the same phrase "withdraw forthwith" which had been employed against Britain, France and Israel.

Aware that he was being criticized in Washington and Beirut for his restrictive interpretation of the Council resolution setting up UNOGIL, Hammarskjold defended his policy line in the Council. Had he "changed the observation operation into some kind of police operation," he said, he would have "overstepped" the Council's mandate. He would also have violated the Charter principle that the use of force had to be explicitly authorized by the Council under the appropriate section of the Charter. He noted, moreover, that at the "initial stage" his interpretation of the resolution met with the "full approval" of all Council members and Lebanon.

A slight chill developed in the relations between Hammarskjold and the U.S. delegation. During the Suez crisis the U.S. had applauded him right down the line. Now it was Lodge's turn to sit in the Council with hands expressively folded. A statement released by Hammarskjold that UNOGIL would avoid contact with the newly landed Marines caused considerable irritation. When Hammarskjold claimed it was only "a coincidence" that the observation group was given full access to Lebanese borders by the rebels the day the Marines landed, Lodge suggested tersely the Marines might have had something to do with it. And a Lodge admonition against the danger of being diverted from the "big picture" by "technical administrative considerations" echoed Anglo-French-Israeli complaints of "legalism" in the Suez crisis.

But the U.S. and Britain were in a dilemma. Their troops could not remain in Lebanon and Jordan. The day had passed when nationalism could be mastered by military force. The Western troops had been rushed in to keep the coup in Iraq, which at that time was mistakenly thought to be Nasserist in origin, from triggering off Nasserist revolts in Jordan, Lebanon and the Persian Gulf. The Western problem now was how to pull them out without starting new landslides.

The Soviet Union vetoed a U.S. resolution to send an international force into Lebanon. Ambassador Matsudaira of Japan, who had criticized the landings, tried another approach. UNOGIL, backed by Hammarskjold, had urged a substantial increase in its personnel and equipment. Matsudaira now proposed that the Council authorize Hammarskjold to augment UNOGIL in order to safeguard Lebanese independence and make possible a U.S. withdrawal.

Sobolev said that unless Matsudaira's resolution also called for immediate withdrawal, it would constitute "moral sanction" of the intervention. He did not oppose enlarging UNOGIL, but since the resolution omitted the withdrawal demand, he vetoed it.

Hammarskjold moved into the breach. By adroit marshaling of provisions from the Charter, phrases from speeches delivered in the Council and paragraphs from the resolution which had been endorsed even though the resolution itself went down, he built up a typically tangled thicket of jurisprudence where few could find their way. It was an exercise in liberal construction of the Secretary-General's powers that left the strict constructionists breathless.

But the purpose was clear and, advance soundings had indicated, *acceptable to all:* he would proceed to do what he would have done had the Japanese resolution been adopted— that is, to strengthen UNOGIL in line with a broadening of its purposes to include the protection of Lebanese independence as well as the prevention of infiltration. The broadened purpose was justified by reference to Charter principles. If Council members disapproved of the way he translated his intentions into practical measures, he would desist.

Now another major prize for the UN seemed to loom within Hammarskjold's grasp. On July 19 Premier Khrushchev suddenly proposed a summit meeting on the Middle East. Although Khrushchev suggested that Hammarskjold should be one of the participants, President Eisenhower replied on July 22 that such a meeting outside of the UN would make the world organization a "rubber stamp" for a few great powers.

He proposed instead that the meeting take place within the framework of the Security Council, noting that the Charter made it possible for heads of governments to represent their countries at the Council. British Prime Minister Macmillan was more eager and cordial. "I would certainly be ready to go to New York for such a meeting if you would also go," he replied.

Khrushchev agreed with alacrity. He was ready to come to New York the following Monday to begin work, he said.

Ever since the correspondence about a summit meeting had begun in late 1957, Hammarskjold had been seeking discreetly to have such a parley take place within the UN framework. A few weeks earlier he had been rebuffed on all sides. The best he could obtain was permission to provide the housekeeping services at the East-West technical talks in Geneva on a nuclear test ban.

He was determined to show that the UN was a flexible instrument which could be used for businesslike multilateral negotiations. Above all, he wanted to avoid a propaganda spectacle.

He recalled the fruitful Suez negotiations on the thirty-eighth floor in October 1956, which had produced the six requirements, and suggested that after a brief opening session the heads of the governments should withdraw and confer in private. Their recommendations could be reported back to the Council.

Hammarskjold had always considered a great power agreement a condition of Middle Eastern stabilization. The presence of the heads of governments would give him a chance on the basis of his unique and intimate knowledge of the area to set forth his views on Middle East needs. A program that had the backing of both East and West could immeasurably enhance the chances of acceptance. Hammarskjold instructed his lieutenants to review the position papers on the Middle East and began to discuss a policy line with them.

But the summit meeting fell through. After a sudden and quick visit to Peking, Khrushchev did a somersault and rejected the proposal for a Security Council summit meeting because the Council was "dominated by the U.S." and because Eisenhower, unlike Macmillan, had left no room for informal gatherings. It never was clear whether Mao Tse-tung had talked Khrushchev out of the UN meeting or whether it was a genuine misunderstanding of Eisenhower's position on informal talks that caused Khrushchev to back out.

With summit hopes scuttled, there still remained the problem of Jordan and Lebanon. Moscow intensified its withdrawal propaganda. In Beirut on July 28, General Fuad Chehab had been elected President. He promptly proclaimed the withdrawal of foreign troops as one of his foremost aims.

The scene now shifted to an emergency special session of the Assembly which both the U.S. and the U.S.S.R. demanded following the collapse of the hopes for a summit. Dulles wanted to make the keynote of U.S. policy at this session the need to establish UN controls over "indirect aggression," which he defined as the technique of foreign-inspired inflammatory propaganda, fifth column activities, incitement to civil war, assassination. On his instructions, Lodge had warned the Council that the Iraq revolt showed "a common purpose, masterminded from one source" to take over everywhere. "If the UN cannot deal with indirect aggression, the UN will break up."

But this approach was considered too negative. Ambassador Ritchie of Canada, in voting for the emergency assembly in the Council, said it should be used for constructive solutions, not sterile recrimination.

Hammarskjold and the group of middle power diplomats with whom he frequently worked hand in hand did not relish an Assembly debate in which Gromyko would bang the drum of intervention and Dulles that of indirect aggression.

Hammarskjold decided that he would try to influence the tone and course of the debate by taking the floor right after President Munro brought down his gavel to set forth his own views of what was required in the Middle East.

A little while back a reporter had asked whether he had some kind of picture in his mind of what a peace with justice in the Middle East might look like.

"I have my dreams," he replied.

Would he care to share them with the press?

"I very rarely share my dreams with anybody."

But he was prepared to use the opportunity presented by the eighty-one-nation Assembly to challenge it to deal with the underlying tensions of the area in specific, practical terms. He set forth a five-point program:

Continuation of UNOGIL until it could be superseded by "some form of UN representation" that would express "the continued concern of the organization for the independence and integrity of Lebanon."

A special status for Jordan with "special measures" that might be "adequate in the specific situation prevailing in Jordan."

Joint reaffirmation by the Arab states of the noninterference and nonaggression pledges embodied in the Charter of the Arab League and "accommodation of policies to these principles" through "joint practical action" with the help of the UN.

An East-West hands-off pledge "assuring the peoples there that they may shape their own destinies in the best interest of each nation within the region and of the region as a whole."

Joint action by the Arab states, with the support and technical help of the UN, in the field of regional economic development. This might include arrangements for co-operation between "oil-producing and oil-transiting countries" and joint utilization of water resources.

The Palestine refugee problem was urgent, but its solution might "have to await the creation of more favorable general conditions which would follow were the other needs to which I have referred to be successfully met."

Hammarskjold's proposals helped sway the debate in Washington on the approach President Eisenhower should take when he addressed the Assembly five days later. The President presented a constructive program which included:

Measures to implement UN concern for Jordan and Lebanon.
Action to monitor subversive propaganda broadcasts.
Creation of a "regional Arab development institution." The U.S. would contribute its share to such an institution if the Arab countries wished it.
Establishment of a UN stand-by force to help curb infiltration and the fomenting of civil strife from without.
Steps to avoid a new arms race spiral in the region.

But a grim-faced Gromyko who followed Eisenhower would have none of this. Regional development programs were "surely something good" and deserved "careful consideration," but first of all the chief question must be solved: "U.S. and British troops must be withdrawn. Talk of economic assistance is designed to divert the Assembly from this paramount issue." The reports of UNOGIL and the Secretary-General had refuted allegations of interference by the United Arab Republic. The Assembly had become necessary because of the armed intervention of the U.S. and United Kingdom, whose real purpose was to repress the Arab national liberation movement. The Soviet Union could not "remain indifferent to the fact that in the immediate neighborhood of its frontiers there is a focal point of military danger." A Soviet resolution called for Anglo-American withdrawal "without delay" and requested the Secretary-General to strengthen UNOGIL and send an observation group to Jordan.

Lloyd proposed that "so far as the particular problem of the Lebanon and Jordan are concerned, the Assembly should request the Secretary-General to take the necessary steps in consultation with the governments concerned to help maintain the independence and integrity of these two countries and so to create the conditions under which the U.S. and United Kingdom forces can be withdrawn."

Lloyd did not go into detail, but privately he recalled that at the time of Suez, Hammarskjold was given a very vague resolution and he produced UNEF, which had "operated frightfully well."

The Assembly now began to operate on three levels—very private talks among the key foreign ministers and the Secretary-General, dickerings over resolutions in the delegates' lounge and the various bloc caucuses, and the public speechmaking in the Assembly chamber. Hammarskjold, since he cannot intervene directly in the resolution-drafting process, very often works through "fire brigades"—groups of middle and smaller powers which seek for an opening for constructive action despite the public collisions.

This particular fire brigade was headed by his good friend Hans Engen. Hammarskjold was also in close touch with Fawzi, whose viewpoint was that "the Middle East countries should have the final say in Middle East affairs." The political problem was to draft a resolution that was acceptable to Dulles, who was quite emotional about guarantees against "indirect aggression," to Gromyko, who insisted on unconditional withdrawal, and to the Arabs who were divided. As usual in such deadlocks, the talk more and more turned to a resolution which would hand the problem over to Hammarskjold and trust to his impartiality, discretion and competence to produce a solution that did justice to all the interests involved.

Nevertheless, the assignment had to be defined in some fashion. Finally, after much behind-the-scenes politicking, Engen presented a draft on behalf of Norway, Canada, Colombia, Denmark, Liberia, Panama and Paraguay. While it omitted any call for withdrawal it did note the explicit withdrawal assurances of the U.S. and the United Kingdom, provided the

Assembly authorized UN arrangements in Jordan and Lebanon.

The nub of the resolution was a request to the Secretary-General to take such action as he deemed adequate to uphold the purposes and principles of the Charter in relation to Jordan and Lebanon, bearing in mind earlier UN resolutions against indirect aggression.

As interesting as the resolution itself was Engen's introductory statement on what Hammarskjold might reasonably be asked to do. The formula not only had to win the approval of an Assembly majority but had to be one which did not give the Secretary-General an impossible task or push him into an untenable position. No Assembly action could be carried out in matters directly concerning member states without the consent of those member states.

The terms of the request to the Secretary-General were admittedly rather general in nature and left a fairly wide field to his discretion, but this was necessary since the practical arrangements Hammarskjold was being requested to make could not be made without the consent of the governments concerned.

Gromyko did not like the seven-power resolution. It was nothing but the British-American draft, he alleged, and was backed up in this by India. He did his best to torpedo the project by pressing the Arabs not to go along.

Fawzi gave the impression of being ready at least to abstain on Engen's draft when India presented a withdraw "at an early date" resolution to the Afro-Asian caucus. While it ran into a chilly reception, it made it impossible for Fawzi to go along with the Norwegian text. The Arabs were opposed to the resolution, said Gromyko. With whom would the Secretary-General negotiate if that were the case? he asked.

Some fast diplomatic footwork saved the day. Fawzi and other Arab delegates set to work on their own text. Within a matter of hours they produced an Arab version of the Norwegian draft, one that reflected even more closely the ideas set forth in Hammarskjold's opening speech.

Because it incorporated Hammarskjold's formula of emphasizing Arab League pledges not to interfere in each other's affairs, it became known as the Arab "good neighbor" resolution. It was adopted unanimously, with all of the leading protagonists —Dulles, Lloyd, Gromyko, Fawzi—contending it was a victory for their viewpoint. Gromyko, however, noted "some inadequacies of formulation" in that it did not speak of "immediate withdrawal" and privately his objections were much more vigorous. Dulles and Lloyd also had private misgivings but felt constrained to go along in the hope that giving this vote of confidence to Arab nationalism would help direct its energies into more constructive channels.

Hammarskjold worked hard behind the scenes to convert Lloyd and Dulles to this experiment. They came to the Assembly determined that Western troops would get out of Jordan and Lebanon on the basis of firm commitments to UN arrangements rather than Arab pledges. But by the end of the Assembly they were emphasizing that no resolution, no matter how clearly worded, nor a UN presence, no matter how formidable, could save countries like Jordan from a Baghdad-Cairo effort to undermine them, if that was the intention of Nasser. The important thing was a change in attitude in Cairo.

Hammarskjold and Fawzi had a great deal to do with persuading Lloyd and Dulles that Nasser now was disposed to deal constructively with the West. Lloyd, exuberantly, and Dulles, dourly, regarded the Arab resolution as an earnest of Nasser's willingness to exert himself along more conventional lines in the region.

The day after the adoption of the Arab "good neighbor" resolution, Hammarskjold met with the press and asked its pardon "for banging the drum a little bit," but yesterday "was one of those days in the life of this Organization when it showed its invaluable contribution to present politics in the international field and to present diplomacy."

He was about to embark on another journey to the Middle East. He declined to spell out what kind or size of UN presence he envisaged in Jordan and Lebanon. It could be "practically anything from one man up to quite a few" and would depend on what the governments themselves thought useful.

But one result of the resolution should be "some kind of radio truce" followed by "radio disarmament."

There were long talks during his tour of Arab capitals with Hussein, Nasser, Chamoun and Chehab and a get-acquainted session with Kassem in Baghdad. The results were summarized in a report to the thirteenth session of the General Assembly. No "practical arrangements" were required in Lebanon beyond the strengthening of UNOGIL; in Jordan he would station a special representative with a staff whose size would depend on the way events developed. There would be liaison offices in Beirut and Damascus. Hussein had expressed a preference for similar UN presences in Cairo and Baghdad, but the governments of the UAR and Iraq would not agree to an arrangement that implied they had to be watched. To assuage Jordanian sensitivities the reason given in Hammarskjold's report for stationing a special representative in Amman was its centrality in the Arab world which made it a good listening post and not that Jordan needed special protection. A UN delegation in Amman would need a line of communications, which justified the establishment of liaison offices in Damascus and Beirut. A senior diplomatic official working out of UN headquarters would visit the capitals of the Middle East from time to time in connection with the resolution and he had persuaded the other Arab countries to resume the supplying of oil to Jordan. The desert kingdom was under economic siege by Nasser, and part of Hammarskjold's problem had been to synchronize the lifting of this blockade with the British withdrawal. Along with his report Hammarskjold submitted annexes from the U.S. and the United Kingdom stating that in view of these practical arrangements, withdrawal decisions would be announced shortly.

There was one dissent from Hammarskjold's report—Gromyko. Although British and American troops were on their way out, he pressed the Arabs to demand a full dress debate on the withdrawal issue. He criticized Hammarskjold for the vagueness of the withdrawal statements in his report. Hammarskjold was as much an author of the Arab resolution as the Arabs themselves; nevertheless, Gromyko took issue with Hammarskjold's interpretation of it.

"Can one, for instance, agree with the assertion contained in the [Hammarskjold] report that the 'political essence' of the resolution adopted at the emergency session consists not in the demand for an early withdrawal of American and British troops but in those elements which concern relations between Arab states? To draw such a conclusion means presenting it all upside down," Gromyko maintained.

Gromyko mustered little support from the Arabs and finally abandoned his effort to raise the withdrawal issue as a separate item. But it went down in his little black book as another count against Hammarskjold.

What did the resolution accomplish? The Arabs have not turned into "good neighbors" to each other, although the drive toward *"anschluss"* abated. The concept of an "Arab fatherland from the Atlantic to the Persian Gulf," of an "Arab nation" heading up in Cairo, lost much of its drawing power, and Arab nationalism turned toward the federation and commonwealth concept.

There were no overnight miracles—no East-West agreement to neutralize the region, no regional bank, no permanent radio truce. But one more crisis was surmounted, one more brink drawn back from with the help of the UN, one more stage passed in the historic withdrawal of Western power from the Middle East with the UN rather than a new imperialism filling the vacuum as the peoples of the region took over responsibility for their own destinies.

10

"Constantly Rebuffed but Never Discouraged"

Hammarskjold has always been dubious that the Palestine problem was soluble unless it could be lifted above intra-Arab politics and rivalries. The "good neighbor" resolution was a chance to moderate those disputes. When the Assembly unanimously approved the Arab draft, Eban arose to say it was his understanding that all member states in the Middle East— Arab and non-Arab—"will fall under the clear applicability of these principles."

This was also Hammarskjold's view, but he did not press it very loudly. Israel was the great unmentionable at the emergency session on Jordan and Lebanon, but the Arab-Israeli dispute was never far from the thoughts of all the major participants— especially Hammarskjold.

The Suez crisis over, he had set about repairing his relationship with Israel. The authority of the Secretary-General derives from his firm independence and objectivity, but if he is to remain useful he must keep open his lines of communication with member governments.

There were several trips to Jerusalem and a walk in the Negev with Ben-Gurion. The first encounter after Suez was a difficult one. Hammarskjold felt Ben-Gurion had violated a commitment to him not to start a war. He suspected the Israelis of inspiring much of the criticism of him for partiality to Egypt. And Ben-Gurion had publicly charged Hammarskjold with "legal pedantry" in favor of Nasser.

When, after Suez, Hammarskjold sent over a signal to Ben-Gurion that he would like to see him, the Israeli leader was in no hurry to respond. He could not come, Ben-Gurion indicated, if his purpose was to try to reinstate the Israel-Egypt Armistice Agreement, which Ben-Gurion had proclaimed a dead letter. But, for Hammarskjold, the Agreement remained a "valid document" which could not be set aside by a unilateral denunciation.

A letter arrived from Hammarskjold regarding the purposes of his visit. Ben-Gurion considered it an evasion on the point of the Armistice Agreement and dictated an angry reply. When the Foreign Office came back with the reply translated into English, Ben-Gurion had it carefully scrutinized by a personal aide to be sure his diplomats had not toned it down in translation.

The two men finally found a formula which enabled them to stand on their positions and yet resume their dialogues. The pattern of their talks was always the same. The first few hours were tempestuous. Ben-Gurion would lash out at the Secretary-General with volcanic, elemental violence. Hammarskjold would reply precisely, firmly, sometimes coldly, sometimes angrily as his own gorge rose.

"He gave me the whole business and then we relaxed," Hammarskjold would report to his aides. With their talks for the record disposed of, they would range over the whole intellectual waterfront. "He's mad, absolutely mad; he's mad like a genius. He is a genius," would be Hammarskjold's comment.

During Hammarskjold's stay at Sdeh Boker, Ben-Gurion presented one of the *kibbutz* members to him with the words, "He's a real terrorist." Was he a member of the Stern Gang? Hammarskjold wanted to know. There was some unfinished business between the Stern Gang and his country, he added. This was a reference to the assassination in 1948 of Count Folke Bernadotte, the Swedish UN mediator in Palestine. Several times Hammarskjold has suggested to Jewish leaders they should do something to set the record straight on Bernadotte, who had been charged by the Israelis with anti-Semitism and hostility to the Jewish state.

There were many visits also to Cairo and meetings with Fawzi, especially when the United Arab Republic stepped up its blockade from Israeli flag vessels to Israeli cargoes transiting the Suez Canal in foreign bottoms.

At times he had the impression Nasser considered the Palestine question a nuisance, a distraction from the really important problems of Egyptian development that pressed in on him, and thus interpreted Nasser to diplomats at the UN.

But the stiffening of the Suez blockade after two years of relative quiet shook him. Initial interventions by Hammarskjold in Cairo after it began to molest Israeli cargoes gave him the impression that Cairo would return to the post-Suez policy. "We shall get round this corner and be able to look at the Canal as we have been looking at it now for a couple of years," he predicted to a news conference.

But always something arose to frustrate hopes and expectations arising from his talks with Nasser and Fawzi. For the first time he was politely cold-shouldered by Cairo. Queries would remain unanswered, and when after long delays replies did come in, they were studded with evasions and ambiguities. The problem was not only an Arab-Israeli one. There were the difficulties caused by intra-Arab rivalries. Concessions by Nasser were jumped on by his foes in the Arab world as "appeasement." Conversely, a sure-fire formula for silencing Nasser's Arab critics and for holding the Syrians in line when they sought to escape from their "union" with Egypt was to get into a scrap with Israel. Around Nasser, his advisers were divided, ranging from the extremism of Ali Sabry and Farid Zeineddine to the polished subtleties of Fawzi.

Hammarskjold worked out a way around the problem—distinguishing between effective and declaratory policy. Nasser might feel obliged publicly to bar Israeli cargoes, but this could be circumvented provided Israel did not hold legal titles to the cargoes when they passed through the Canal. If Israel would agree to send its export cargoes through the Canal in the ownership of the purchaser (that is f.o.b.) and import goods intended to pass through the Canal towards its own ports in the ownership of the seller (that is, c.i.f.), UAR authorities would not obstruct their passage.

"Israel should keep its mouth shut, and we will keep our eyes shut," was Fawzi's summary of the formula.

But it broke down the first time it was tried, when the Greek vessel *Astypalea* with a cargo of 400 tons of cement, sold f.o.b. Haifa, was halted at Port Said. The news reached Hammarskjold just as he was on the point of setting off for Stockholm and a subsequent tour of Africa. He was furious. He asked SAS to hold up its flight as he angrily called Cairo. He fired off one angry message after another to Fawzi and Nasser but without any satisfaction.

Hammarskjold felt betrayed. On January 1, 1960, he and Mrs. Meir were together in Yaoundé, for the independence ceremonies of the French Camerouns. "Happy New Year and a free passage through Suez," he greeted her. A few weeks later Hammarskjold saw Nasser in Cairo but could not budge him. An Israeli campaign against a World Bank loan to improve the Suez Canal was a "provocation" and violation of the agreement, he said. He argued further that the documents of the *Astypalea* were not in proper order.

The Israelis turned to the U. S. Government for relief, reminding it of President Eisenhower's pledge at the time of the Sinai withdrawals to deal firmly with any renewed blockade. President Eisenhower and Secretary Herter passed the buck back to Hammarskjold. It was in his hands, they said, and he might still succeed in working out "a *modus vivendi* which will take care of that problem."

There were similar suggestions from London. Privately, Hammarskjold expressed some exasperation with this buck-passing. He recalled that the British, when they controlled the Canal, had not been able to do anything about the Israeli vessel *Bat Galim* when it was seized by the Egyptians.

Publicly he noted that his means of obtaining compliance were limited. Those who were saying the UN carries a responsibility should follow up their statements "by appropriate re-actions and actions in the UN and in support of the UN." Some things were easier for the Secretary-General, but "there are things which the other organs can do and the Secretary-General cannot do." There was a certain tendency "in some quarters to forget this difference of responsibilities and to ex-pect from the Secretary-General action which rightly belongs to the Security Council." He would continue to do what was possible for him to do "to keep the situation on the rails with the means at my disposal and with the support, or lack of support, which I have to register."

Western diplomats felt there was a certain disposition on the part of Hammarskjold to hand the Middle East back to the Security Council, but they were not quite ready to take it back. None of the Western powers were prepared to challenge Nasser over the issue, especially in the Security Council, where the only outcome would be to give the U.S.S.R. another chance to pose as Nasser's defender. They urged Hammarskjold to for-get about the *Inge Toft* and the *Astypalea* and make a new start.

These early months of 1960 also witnessed the most serious outbreak of fighting between Israel and the Arabs since the Suez hostilities. It was a clash on the Syrian frontier, involving artillery, jet fighters, duels, big military actions on the ground and disquieting Egyptian troop movements in the strategic in-vasion triangle just south of Gaza.

The crisis dissipated as a result of strenuous activity by Hammarskjold, the UNTSO and a singular assist from the Soviet Union. *Izvestia* suddenly called for a relaxation of tensions and a calming of passions on both the Arab and Israeli sides. The Soviet government newspaper accused both Israel and the

United Arab Republic of violating the 1949 Armistice Agreement.

Izvestia's call for quiet on the borders was much appreciated on the thirty-eighth floor which tended to view it as a response partly to Hammarskjold's press conference plea for "reactions and actions" in support of the UN line.

In conflicts of interest between Israel and the Arab states, Hammarskjold said at the time: "The UN has to speak for the law—the law there is—and the UN has to speak for objectivity when it comes to the facts." But there were conflicts so great that statement of the law and facts by the UN to the parties was insufficient. Then the weight of political opinion had to be placed back of the law and facts in the form of a Council or Assembly decision or actions by UN members.

Hammarskjold does not believe in any other peace in the Middle East except one on the basis of the status quo. It does not make any sense to discuss whether the 1947 Assembly decision partitioning Palestine was right or wrong. But he also believes that acceptance of the status quo requires recognition by Israel of its responsibility toward the 900,000-odd Arab refugees and he is critical of UN bodies for their failure to tackle the refugee problem.

On the basis of paragraph 11 of the 1948 resolution he believes the refugees must have a free choice of compensation or repatriation. Unless the refugees have such a free choice, the Arabs will always have a grievance which will be a continuing psychological obstacle to good relations. But while he urges the Israelis to indicate their willingness to abide by paragraph 11, he assumes that only a minimal number of refugees would opt for repatriation.

In 1959 he made a major effort to get something started in the way of a settlement of the refugee problem. The mandate of the UN Relief and Works Agency for Palestine refugees was due to expire in 1960. The chief contributors to UNRWA, including the U.S., felt that some better system had to be devised than a "dole" approach to refugee relief.

Although Arab spokesmen insisted that no study was needed, that it must be "repatriation, and nothing but repatriation," the

Assembly asked Hammarskjold to report to the 1959 session on recommendations for the future.

Hammarskjold's report was a striking economic analysis, not only of the problem of absorbing the refugees into productive employment, but of what had to be done regionally to make such absorption possible. He linked refugee integration to the economic development of the Arab host countries and a rising standard of living. Reintegration of the refugees into the productive life of the region was "perfectly within reach," he wrote, provided $1,500,000,000 to $2,000,000,000 outside money was invested in the area in the next five years. This, together with capital likely to become available from the oil-rich Arab countries, he estimated would permit the Arab host countries to absorb with a rising per capita income both the refugees and the increase in labor force that will result from natural growth of population.

This approach, if implemented with specific blueprints, would have meant that a country like Jordan in the process of absorbing its refugees would also be assured of general economic development.

The report reaffirmed the right of the refugee to choose between repatriation and resettlement. Hammarskjold could not realistically see a solution of the refugee problem short of regional economic development, but he did not advance economic development as able alone to solve the problem. It was a necessary but not a sufficient condition for a solution.

Although this economic approach to the refugee issue had been cleared with the Arab leaders before Hammarskjold circulated his report, under pressure from the extremists, they shot it down in the General Assembly. The 1959 session adopted a resolution continuing UNRWA for another three years but omitting any reference to the economic absorption sections of the report.

Hammarskjold is confident the approach is not dead, and that the Assembly will, in the end, have to return to it.

Today the Middle East is strewn with UN operations and agencies—UNEF, UNRWA, UNTSO, and special missions—

which increase or diminish as the need occasions. Hammarskjold retains personal command over this "UN presence." He interests himself in all details—uniforms, rations, morale, rights and privileges of UN personnel. He reads a daily summary of the press of the area. On the thirty-eighth floor there is a special shelf for plans, background and working papers on the various facets of the complex Middle East problem.

His policy line on the Middle East might be summarized as follows: to keep the truce; to take the area out of the cold war; to make the peace.

He hopes that in time a situation will evolve where co-existence between the Arabs and Israel becomes possible.

One instrumentality by which this might be done is a great power agreement, especially a Soviet-American, to encourage such a development.

Before the Soviet attack on him, he envisaged a Soviet-American agreement through the Security Council with the Secretary-General as executive agent, on the basis of a Soviet-American common interest in preventing a war in the area which might entangle them. Hammarskjold never believed the *tripartite* policy of Britain, France and the U.S. of trying to deny the Soviet Union a voice in the Middle East was workable.

He favors a substantial program of economic development, perhaps through a Middle East Development Fund. The UN would help to bring it about, but it should be accomplished by the Arabs helping themselves.

There has been a cooling off in his relations with the UAR. While he continues to regard it as the leading force in Arab nationalism, long talks with King Hussein, and visits to Jordan, which brought him close to "pure Arabism," bolstered the conviction that Arab nationalism did not mean subordination to Nasser and the UAR, or that what Nasser told him was necessarily what the Arabs thought. In talks with Arab leaders he speaks of a "commonwealth" approach to Arab unity, citing Scandinavia as an example of ethnic unity and national diversity. He has an abiding faith in Fawzi, but is aware he is an agent and not a maker of policy, who suffers periods of eclipse.

He envisages a continuing and reinforced UN presence in the

Middle East. In an atmosphere of general distrust where at any moment an innocent move can trigger off a chain reaction, his formula remains the "time-honored one . . . to strengthen the hand of the UN and for the UN to stick to its guns."

Returning from one of his quick trips to put out a fire in the Middle East, he described his assignment by citing a quotation from Arthur Waley on what early Chinese historians had to say about the philosopher Sung Tzu and his followers, some 350 years B.C.:

Constantly rebuffed but never discouraged, they went round from State to State helping people to settle their differences, arguing against wanton attack and pleading for the suppression of arms, that the age in which they lived might be saved from its state of continual war. To this end they interviewed princes and lectured the common people, nowhere meeting with any great success, but obstinately persisting in their task, till kings and commoners alike grew weary of listening to them. Yet, undeterred, they continued to force themselves on peoples' attention.

To one who works in the UN, it struck a familiar note, commented Hammarskjold dryly.

11

Preventive Diplomacy

[The Security Council needed only a few minutes in September 1957 to agree on recommending his reappointment to a second five-year term as Secretary-General, and the vote in the General Assembly was equally unanimous. Israel, which was absent because of the Jewish New Year, sent in a letter in order to have its affirmative vote registered.

He is "surely our supreme international Civil Servant," said the president of the Assembly in welcoming the decision, a man of "scrupulous objectivity" and "self-effacing" in the performance of his task. But these words could have been used with equal justice about Hammarskjold in 1953. They did not reflect the change and growth in the man. His missions to Peking and the Middle East had conferred extraordinary authority on this unobtrusive civil servant. He used the occasion of his reappointment to announce that he intended to use that authority to the full on behalf of the Organization and its purposes.

In 1953 he had described the Secretary-General's role as that of "an instrument, a catalyst, an inspirer." Now he enunciated a doctrine regarding the Secretary-General's powers and responsibilities that came much closer to the concept of leader than instrument.

Within the limits set by the Charter and the decisions of the main organs of the UN, he considered it his "duty to use his office and, indeed, the machinery of the Organization to its utmost capacity and to the full extent permitted at each stage by practical circumstances." He should not be asked to act if there were no guidance for his action to be found either in the Charter or UN decisions.

"On the other hand, I believe that it is in keeping with the philosophy of the Charter that the Secretary-General should be expected to act also without such guidance, should this appear to him necessary in order to help in filling any vacuum that may appear in the systems which the Charter and traditional diplomacy provide for the safeguarding of peace and security."

It was a characteristically Hammarskjoldian understatement. Its significance only became apparent ten months later and such a "vacuum" appeared during the Council's consideration of the Lebanese question. When the Soviet veto of the Japanese resolution prevented the Council from taking measures that appeared to be essential to stave off further deterioration, Hammarskjold enumerated the steps he intended to take to strengthen the UN operation in Lebanon. They were essentially the steps which had been proposed in the vetoed resolution. He would, he added, "of course accept the consequences" if members of the Council disapproved. No one did.

He thus provided a "fallback" position. If in a crisis the Council and Assembly were to be formally stalemated, he would be prepared to act on the basis of his reading of the "consensus" underneath the deadlock.

But the philosophy of acting without a formal decision was to be carried a step further. Member states which found themselves in difficulties could invite the Secretary-General's "good offices" and he would respond without formal decision by any other organ of the UN. Cambodia and Thailand became embroiled in a border dispute which led to a rupture in diplomatic relations. After discussions with the Secretary-General they directed parallel invitations to him inviting him to appoint a special representative to help them get over their difficulties. Hammarskjold informally consulted the members of the Council and then appointed Ambassador Beck-Friis with whose help diplomatic relations were resumed and the way paved to a general improvement of relations between the two countries.

"You can see how much more effective and smooth-working such a technique is than the regular one, which involves all the meetings and debates, and so on," he commented.

This was a dispute involving two countries. Another kind of "preventive diplomacy" was his response to the invitation of Guinea to appoint a Special Representative. At the end of 1958 Guinea had cut itself loose from the French Community, and France in reprisal pulled out all its technicians and administrators. The country found itself isolated politically and economically. The Special Representative's job was to see in what way the UN family could help Guinea face "all the economic, social and administrative problems natural in the first phase of its new independence," said Hammarskjold.

In the Introduction, dated August 29, 1959, to his Annual Report to the Assembly, Hammarskjold supplied the rationale for these initiatives without instructions. They fell within "the competence of his office" and were "in other respects also in strict accordance with the Charter, when they serve its purpose." And, "as a matter of course, the members of the appropriate organs of the UN have been informed about the action planned by the Secretary-General and were given an opportunity to express views on it."

The Charter did indicate "working methods" to achieve its objectives, but these were not "limitative." They could be "supplemented by others under the pressure of circumstances and in the light of experience if these additional procedures are not in conflict with what is prescribed." Such new methods of approach might, after "thorough testing," become a part of "a common law of organized international cooperation."

A crisis in the tiny landlocked kingdom of Laos in 1959 showed how far Hammarskjold was ready to go in pushing this common law development. Signs of trouble had begun to appear in this drowsy country of mountains and lush jungles early in 1959. The Geneva agreements ending the Indochina war in 1954 had provided for a Laos which would be neutral internationally and semi-divided internally with the two provinces in the northeast, adjacent to communist North Vietnam, left under Pathet Lao (Communist) control. The arrangement was to be supervised by an International Control Commission consisting of India, Canada and Poland.

In 1958 Prince Souvanna Phouma, a non-Communist, sought to overcome the country's division by establishing a coalition government which included the Pathet Lao, represented by his half-brother Prince Souvannavong. The U.S. was unhappy over this arrangement, fearing it might lead to a complete Communist takeover and under its pressure the coalition was disrupted. Fighting broke out in which the King and the newly installed anti-Communist government were supported by the U.S. and SEATO, and the Pathet Lao forces were actively aided by North Vietnam, Communist China and Soviet Russia.

Scenting trouble, Hammarskjold, in line with his concept of preventive diplomacy, during a trip to southeast Asia in March 1959 had spent several days in Laos talking with the King and other Laotian leaders. The visit resulted in a continuing and close contact with Laotian representatives and discussion of what the UN might do to smooth out the kingdom's increasing difficulties.

He felt a special solicitude for countries like Laos, which he described as groping to find their place on the political world map. Having emerged from colonialism, "they have to find their way back to a national tradition and, on the other hand, they have to adjust themselves to the present international life." A disinterested UN could help these countries as they tried to find the right mix between national tradition and their international position.

By July 1959 the Laotian Government was charging that "foreign troops" had invaded the country from North Vietnam, supported by artillery fire from there. It wanted the Secretary-General to send an "observer team" in the hope that might discourage foreign intervention. Hammarskjold replied that he could only do so if the request came from North Vietnam as well as Laos, or, alternatively, from the co-chairmen of the Geneva Conference, Britain and the Soviet Union.

"If it were a case of one of these fairly newfangled initiatives of the Secretary-General acting without authorization or without a formal decision of any of the other organs, he can never permit himself to act, so to say, in a legally ambiguous way."

He would have to take into account "the most conservative views" about the validity of the Geneva agreements. "He could never override them on the basis of the Charter."

In effect, what Hammarskjold was telling the Laotians, and the U.S. which was backing their request for an observer team, was that he could only be helpful on the basis of a policy line that was acceptable to both East and West, which meant neutralization, internal reconciliation, and reactivation in some form of the adjourned International Control Commission, as the Communist capitals were demanding.

While Hammarskjold was discussing these matters, the ball was taken out of his hands. A note arrived from the Laotian Government requesting the UN to dispatch an "emergency force" to halt the aggression. This was a matter for the Security Council. Hammarskjold asked that body to meet to hear a report from him on his discussions with the Laotian Government and to transmit its request for a UN force. There was not the slightest prospect that either a force or an observer group would escape a Soviet veto. A message from North Vietnam called the Laotian charges of intervention "fabricated," accused the U.S. of trying to transform Laos "into an American military base" and called for reactivation of the International Control Commission. It was against any kind of UN intervention. "Any maneuver designed to replace the International Control Commission is really aimed at abolishing that body and cancelling the Geneva agreements regarding Laos," Hanoi warned.

In order to get around the Soviet veto, the U.S. proposed that under Article 29 (2) of the Charter, authorizing the Council to set up subcommittees, it establish a four-nation fact-finding group to go to Laos and investigate the charges of intervention. Soviet Russia voted against the proposal, insisting its negative vote was a veto. But the Council, by another overwhelming vote, upheld the Council president's ruling that it was a procedural matter and not subject to the veto. Specialists in the Charter are still arguing whether the Western move was legal.

Hammarskjold kept out of this argument, but he was hostile to the subcommittee proposal on other grounds. He did not believe there could be an imposed solution in Laos. It would have to be one that was acceptable to the Soviet Union. Nor did he think the UN could promote Laotian unity and independence or nourish it economically if the dispute was turned into a cold-war issue at the UN.

He moved into the background as the four-nation fact-finding group—Argentina, Italy, Japan and Tunisia—went out to Laos for a month. The subcommittee, while it found evidence of outside Communist support of the rebels in the form of arms, supplies and other help, found little to confirm Laotian charges of "flagrant aggression" by North Vietnamese forces. It thus failed to provide a political or legal basis for further Council action.

At this point—November 1959—Hammarskjold recovered the ball, much to the distress of those elements in the U. S. Government which opposed his line of neutralization and internal reconciliation. Brushing aside the Council's subcommittee, to the irritation of some of its members, he informed the Council by letter he intended to accept an invitation to visit Laos again and that he intended to leave behind him a UN presence in the form of a personal representative.

"The task of this representative would be to report to me as appropriate on such further developments and conditions as might be of importance in the light of the obligations of the Secretary-General," he wrote.

"The legal basis for a decision to leave a personal representative in Laos, apart from the consent of the government of Laos," he wrote further, "would be the general responsibilities of the Secretary-General regarding developments which might threaten peace and security, combined with his administrative authority under the Charter."

This reflected Hammarskjold's view that his authority derived not only from the specific mandates given to him by the other UN organs but from the Charter as a whole, his position in the UN system was analogous in this respect, he felt, to that of the President in the American constitutional scheme who in his view, in addition to being "constitutionally responsible alone for the execution of legislation" also had authority "derived from the constitutional instrument directly." The U. S. Presidency had, in fact, served the authors of the Charter as a model in framing the powers of the office of the Secretary-General.

The visit to Laos would be "independent" of any action by the Council, he made plain.

The Soviet Union appeared to like this even less than the grumblers in Washington. Its delegation wrote a letter to Hammarskjold saying so, and permitted the letter to leak to the press. His impending visit, the Russians warned, and the proposed stationing of a personal representative "as well as any other action on the part of the UN on this question can only further complicate" the situation.

Hammarskjold had talked with the Russians before sending his own letter to the Council. He wanted to find out whether their protest was one intended for the record, to assuage Chinese feelings rather than to intimate any withdrawal of confidence. He tried to get Dobrynin to give him some kind of lead, but Dobrynin left him on his own. He decided to go anyway. It was a carefully calculated political risk.

During this visit to Vientiane he worked out with the King and Prime Minister a policy line of neutrality, internal reconciliation and UN-aided economic development. He summoned to Vientiane Sakari Tuomioja, Finnish Secretary of the UN Economic Commission for Europe, to blueprint a UN aid program. This appointment evoked only a mild protest from the Soviet Union. On his return to headquarters, Hammarskjold apprised members of the Council, at the monthly luncheon given by the outgoing president, of the way he saw the Laotian situation. This time there were no objections from any side.

By mid-December Tuomioja's recommendations for co-ordinated UN aid to Laos were ready. They called for help in the fields of agricultural development, education, health, transport and communications and public administration. Laos would require "considerable foreign assistance for many years to come," Tuomioja said. As a follow-up, Hammarskjold stationed a small technical assistance mission in Vientiane under Edouard Zellweger of Switzerland. Besides being a specialist in the problems of underdeveloped countries, Zellweger was an experienced diplomat and lawyer. When Hammarskjold described this modest technical assistance mission at the monthly Council luncheon, Sobolev twitted him that the mission under an economic hat would also serve political functions, but he did not object to the program.

This precarious arrangement was almost scuttled in January 1960 when a group of anti-Communist generals ousted Premier Phoui Sananikone, charging him with "appeasement of communism." By this they meant that Premier Phoui was going too far in pushing Laos toward neutrality and that internally he was showing too much leniency toward the jailed Pathet Lao leaders. Hammarskjold had been urging the release of these leaders, including Prince Souvannavong, and if that were not possible, at least the postponement of their trials.

Informed of this alarming development while he was in Brazzaville in Africa, Hammarskjold quickly sent off a letter to the King cautioning him against steps that might jeopardize UN efforts to help his kingdom. In his campaign to get the generals to release their stranglehold over the government, the King permitted this letter to leak out.

"Remembering the wise counsel which I received from you, Sire," wrote Hammarskjold, "and which has guided my efforts to give a new direction to the support accorded to Laos by the UN, and taking note of the propitious beginning of these efforts as well as the favorable result of the presence of the Organization in Laos, I would like to be permitted to express the hope that the line of independent neutrality and democratic effort for the economic progress and the integration of the population be firmly maintained."

The next day the King named a nonpolitical elder statesman to lead a provisional regime of civilians pending the holding of new elections for the National Assembly. Those elections were completely rigged by the right and led to renewed fighting in which the Pathet Lao gained the upper hand and produced a new East-West crisis, with the UN pushed again to the sidelines.

Both the U.S. and the Soviet Union blew hot and cold about Hammarskjold's intervention. The U.S., remembering East Europe, was afraid of coalition governments that included Communists. At least some of the agencies of the government, such as the CIA, tended, as in the case of Lebanon, to equate neutralism with Communism. The U.S. did not want the UN around when its clients seemed to have the upper hand, but when the tide turned and military developments were not in the West's favor it turned a more benevolent eye toward the UN.

Similarly, Soviet leaders tolerated a UN presence when they wanted to damp down the chances of a wider conflict and their clients were on the run. But, basically, they considered Laos none of Hammarskjold's business. If the Geneva accords regarding Laos were to be changed to give the UN a role, there should be consultation between the parties concerned. The Soviet Union should not be faced with a *fait accompli*. It considered Hammarskjold's intervention as only helping those who did not want consultation and who opposed the spirit of the Geneva agreements.

It turned into another black mark in the Kremlin's ledger against Hammarskjold.

As for Hammarskjold, his concern was with preventing a brushfire war which might pull in the others. His concern also was with the well-being of Laos. These newly independent countries were "wide open to the winds of the present world." The UN could be of help—"we can screen off a little of those winds."

In 1961, when President Kennedy assumed office, the U.S.

at long last fully embraced the policy toward Laos which Hammarskjold had been urging. But by that time the Soviet Union was in full cry against Hammarskjold and his concept of preventive diplomacy. It didn't want small countries like Laos screened off from the winds, at least those blowing from the East.

12

The UN and the Cold War

At one of the first news conferences after Hammarskjold was notified of his selection as Secretary-General, he was asked whether Soviet agreement on his candidacy was a sign the Soviet bloc intended to end the cold war.

"I can't put any such interpretation on my appointment," he answered carefully, "but I think I can interpret it as a sign of a more cooperative spirit on the part of the Big Five."

When he assumed office he considered the supreme, inescapable challenge facing the UN to be the peaceful resolution of the conflict between the Communist world and the West. Speaking to the UN staff in Geneva, he commented that "where our predecessors dreamt of a new heaven, our greatest hope is that we may be permitted to save the old earth."

The year 1953 was a time when powerful forces in both camps regarded coexistence as a form of appeasement Hammarskjold soon ran afoul of the U.S. intransigents on this issue. With an armistice in Korea close at hand, he spoke sympathetically of "a war which ends without victory for any party" but only for the principle of collective action against aggression, an armistice which should be followed "by a peace without vengeance."

Some people found that contribution "rather defeatist," he remarked wryly a few days later.

"Look anywhere in the world today. Is there any solution in sight except peacefully negotiated agreements?" he asked, bearing in mind the growing nuclear stalemate. The only alternative would be to try to establish "one world" by force of arms, "and that is no alternative. Such an attempt would lead to a catastrophe just as fatal to the presumed victor as to the vanquished."

With the death of Stalin and the ending of the Korean War, East and West began to move gingerly toward high-level negotiations. Some equated such parleying with appeasement. He had been brought up to think of negotiation, he told a university audience in California, the home state of Republican Senator Knowland, "not as something immoral but as a responsible and sensible activity—as a process of working out a mutually satisfactory arrangement with someone I had to live with. To negotiate with someone never meant to me I had to like him or approve of him, much less that I was willing to sell out my principles."

Time was a great healer and playing for time was to be preferred to moving toward an apocalyptic showdown. "Terrible wars have been fought in the past because people thought they could not live in the same world together, or because they thought their beliefs were in head-on collision with their neighbors. Then, with time, they found it was not only possible but necessary to make a working compromise that allowed for the differences. They found that it not only was possible but necessary to accept the principle of diversity in human society."

The fanatics and moralists on both sides made him uneasy. He disliked Dulles' sermonizing and propensity for making a religious war out of a power-political struggle.

On one occasion Dulles called for more emphasis on moral judgments in the General Assembly and more condemnation of Communist actions. Hammarskjold was asked whether the

UN might have a greater impact if there were more emphasis on moral condemnation of wrongdoers.

"I am perhaps not a moralist," he replied.

If UN decisions did not register moral judgments, what is their purpose? another newsman asked. "They register judgments and I hope they are moral," the UN chief came back crisply.

This was a cynical reply to a cynical question, he explained later, but he considered it "preposterous for anyone or any country or any group of countries, whether in a majority or not, to claim the right to be the final moral arbiter."

He could never share the implication in Dulles' view that any nation, race, political system or alliance has a monopoly on the values of spirit and mind.

"The conflict between different approaches to the liberty of man and mind or between different views of human dignity and the right of the individual is continuous," he said in a speech at Cambridge University, but this conflict "does not coincide with any political or geographical boundaries." In language reminiscent of Boris Pasternak's "The issue is between civilization and the cudgel," Hammarskjold went on to say, "The ultimate fight is between the human and subhuman.

"We are on dangerous ground if we believe that any individual, any nation or any ideology has a monopoly on rightness, liberty and human dignity." Mankind's need was on the basis of this insight "to re-establish full human contact and communications across geographical and political boundaries." This is an indispensable condition if humanity is to move toward "true world community."

Once when he had returned from a trip to the Middle East, newsmen asked him about his meetings with Prime Minister Ben-Gurion, President Nasser and King Hussein. He wanted to add, Hammarskjold interposed, "one out-of-the-way tourism with a strong personal accent, and that was that I had the pleasure of paying a call on Professor Martin Buber (in Jerusalem), for whom I have a sincere admiration." He intended to translate into Swedish some of Buber's essays from *Pointing the Way* in which Buber discusses "Genuine Dialogue and the

Possibilities of Peace." In that essay the influential philosopher and religious thinker with great cogency developed the need to set up a dialogue between statesmen and nations that would be inspired by the will "to understand and be understood" rather than to unmask or score debating points.

At UN headquarters, Hammarskjold noted, among the permanent representatives, "there are contacts which in themselves are a denial of the state of absolute frozenness, because they do represent human contacts, they do represent, at the least, an attempt at a meeting of minds, and they are, I think, very often imbued by and inspired by a spirit of personal confidence, even if the general temperature may be low in the sense that it is characterized by, so to say, official lack of confidence."

The proper role of the UN in regard to the cold war was "primarily as a center of reconciliation." The UN, in a dangerously divided world, could neither enforce peace nor impose political settlements. But it could function effectively as a center "for harmonizing the actions of nations" in the attainment of common ends. It could bring to bear upon differences and conflicts of interest "month in and month out, the overriding common interest and to do this in terms of the principles and purposes of the Charter."

The UN should be used for a diplomacy of conciliation, not for waging the cold war. Hammarskjold pleaded for less rattling of verbal sabers and greater emphasis on using the UN to negotiate settlements. This was not too palatable either to the Russians or the Americans. Henry Cabot Lodge's way of selling the UN to the segments of U.S. opinion which had been hostile to it was to demonstrate its opportunities for keelhauling the Russians. He declined to allow himself to be publicly photographed shaking hands with Soviet diplomats and never permitted a Soviet speech criticizing the U.S. to go unanswered. There were times in the early years when Hammarskjold considered Lodge something of a bull in a china shop.

The Russians were even more reluctant to forego the propaganda potentialities of the UN. They were angry with Hammarskjold when he reported U.S. and British intentions to with-

draw their troops from Lebanon and Jordan in a way that made
it impossible for them to raise a storm over Western "in-
terventionism" in the Assembly.

Soviet diplomats preached ending the cold war and the need
for peaceful coexistence, but clearly regarded these themes as
forms of struggle against the West. Like disarmament, it was
often difficult to ascertain whether their interest was in disarming or in making propaganda about the need to do so.

Hammarskjold became the apostle of "quiet diplomacy."

Public debate—or conference diplomacy—had a place in the
negotiating process. It served to shape public opinion, subjected national policies to the "sharp tests of world-wide appraisal," and could educate and guide. But essentially the value
of public debate could be measured "only by the degree to
which it contributes to the winning of agreement by the proc-
esses of diplomacy. If public debate contributes to winning
consent either immediately or in the long run, if serves the
purposes of peacemaking," he agreed.

The danger in public debate was "the temptation to play to
the gallery at the expense of solid construction." There was the
additional risk "that positions once taken publicly become
frozen, making compromise more difficult." Hammarskjold was
equally skeptical of the value of voting victories at the UN. "The
legislative process in the UN is not a substitute for diplomacy.
It serves its purpose only when it helps diplomacy to arrive at
agreements between the national states concerned.

"It is diplomacy, not speeches or votes, that continues to
have the last word in the process of peacemaking."

His concern for results rather than prestige and propaganda
victories produced behind-the-scenes differences with both the
U.S. and Soviet Union on how the question of the peaceful uses
of outer space should be handled in the UN. He told the U.S.
it was unwise for it to push through the 1958 Assembly a
resolution establishing an Outer Space Committee that was unacceptable to the Soviet Union.

The latter had wanted a committee representing the "two
sides" in the field of space achievements, based on the principle

of "parity" which they at that time interpreted to mean a committee equally divided between Communist and neutral nations on one side and pro-Western countries on the other. When the U.S. rejected this "bloc" approach, the Soviet Union began a boycott of the eighteen-nation committee.

This became a test of strength between the U.S. and the U.S.S.R. The Soviet Union was determined to show that the committee could not work without its support and persuaded two of the neutral members—India and the United Arab Republic—not to participate.

Hammarskjold suggested to both the U.S. and U.S.S.R. that it would be better under these circumstances not to have the committee meet but instead get the outer space work started through technical studies by the Secretariat or his Scientific Advisory Committee. These would be submitted to the next Assembly and form the basis for an agreed decision.

The U.S. rejected Hammarskjold's suggestion because "if we accepted his view it would mean the General Assembly would do nothing unacceptable to the Russians." The latter also turned him down. They were out to demonstrate publicly that the committee would be a non-starter without their support.

The ill-starred eighteen-nation group, minus five of its members, did meet and adopt highly useful—and noncontroversial—recommendations and reports addressed to the 1959 Assembly. But the Soviet Union made its point. The 1959 Assembly set up a twenty-four-nation committee consisting of seven Soviet bloc countries, five neutrals and twelve nations allied with the West. The unanimously approved resolution suppressed any reference to the work of the previous committee.

It also authorized the convening in 1960 or 1961 of an international scientific conference for the exchange of experiences in the outer space field. The conference was proposed by the Soviet Union and was to be modeled on the historic scientific conference on the peaceful uses of atomic energy which had been initiated by the U.S. and organized by the Secretary-General. Hammarskjold had always considered that first atoms-for-peace conference in 1955 as one of the most important events in the postwar world. It opened the door to the expansion

of East-West cultural ties, especially the exchange of scientists.
It was a turning point in the whole East-West approach to
atomic matters. In the opinion of I. I. Rabi, the Nobel
physicist and U.S. representative on Hammarskjold's Scientific
Advisory Committee, the atom test ban negotiations flowed
from that conference.

Rabi felt the UN and Hammarskjold had done such a good
job organizing the atoms-for-peace conference, the space conference should be managed the same way. He was enthusiastic
about the way Hammarskjold worked with the Scientific Advisory Committee, which included the top nuclear physicists
of the world: "He was patient and fair. He listened to both sides.
When he made a decision he expressed it in such a way we
accepted it as an end of the matter and it left no bad feelings.
He did things a less skillful man presiding would have botched
by his way of phrasing an issue and of getting to the point.
Many issues were resolved because of his intervention which
might otherwise have become entangled in East-West arguments. He is not a scientist, but was able to grasp the issues
involved."

But in the case of space, neither the Soviet Union nor the
U.S. wanted to place too much authority in the hands of Ham-
marskjold. Their prestige was so involved in the space com-
petition, they wanted to keep a tight control over developments.
The twenty-four-nation committee never met and the plans for
the international conference were stillborn. The U.S. and
U.S.S.R. could not agree on the chairmanship of the committee.
There was jockeying for the best jobs in the space conference.

A U.S. official commented, "When the Russians proposed a
conference we should have said good, let's turn it over to
Hammarskjold. But our people reasoned—the Russians want a
conference. Good. We have a chance to wring some political
concessions. The Russians reasoned—they want a conference
this year [1960]. Good. This is a chance to wring some concessions out of them."

Hammarskjold publicly deplored the delays, but without effect. It was his view that outer space regulation and agreement
would be easier to achieve in the period when the U.S. and

U.S.S.R. were only beginning their activities. It had been his hope that there could be an agreement in these early years "on a basic rule that outer space, and the celestial bodies therein, are not considered as capable of appropriation by any state" and that international machinery would be established reflecting "the overriding interest of the community of nations in the peaceful and beneficial uses of outer space."

An East-West quarrel over "parity" also paralyzed UN disarmament negotiations. Shortly after the Soviet Union launched its first Sputnik, thus giving a stunning demonstration of how far it had advanced in the field of military technology, it walked out of the subcommittee on disarmament which up to then had consisted of the U.S., Britain, France, Canada and the U.S.S.R.

This deadlock hardened at the 1957 Assembly. Although the parent Disarmament Commission was enlarged from twelve to twenty-five members, this did not satisfy the Soviet Union, which insisted on a commission equally weighted between the West on the one hand and East European and "neutral" states on the other. It declared a boycott of this body, too, and proposed the convening of a summit meeting to deal with ways to bring about a resumption of disarmament talks.

As in the case of outer space, Hammarskjold's objectives in this deadlock were to get negotiations going again and to keep the disarmament issue "on the UN rails."

When, therefore, in the spring of 1958, the Soviet Union announced a unilateral suspension of nuclear testing and invited the U.S. and Britain to do the same, Hammarskjold stepped in publicly and hailed the Soviet decision as "a step which I welcome." Asked whether he would welcome similar action by the U.S. and Great Britain, he answered: "Let me reply in this way: I am all for cessation of tests; I am all for the proper inspection of the cessation of tests; and I am all for the stopping of production." Hammarskjold's statement produced dismay in those quarters in Washington which opposed a halt in nuclear testing. The U.S. at that time was linking a test ban with an agreement to end the production of fissionable materials for weapons purposes as well as with adequate controls.

A few weeks later, Hammarskjold, in his concern to get the disarmament baselines advanced, incurred Moscow's displeasure. The Soviet Union had complained in the Security Council that the "alert" operations of the U. S. Strategic Air Command in the Arctic Zone, involving flights on which atomic and hydrogen bombs were being carried "in the direction of the Soviet Union," were a danger to peace. The Soviet Union wanted the Council to condemn these flights and call for their cessation.

The U.S. acknowledged the element of risk in the flights and said the way to eliminate the risk was to set up an Arctic zone of international inspection. It requested the Council to consider such a proposal designed to safeguard against surprise attack.

Hammarskjold intervened in the Council's debate, a rare occurrence at that time. He urged that the U.S. proposal be treated "in good faith." He paired it with the Soviet move to end nuclear tests which, he said, should also be treated in good faith. He appealed to the great powers "to get all the positive value they possibly can out of any positive initiative taken by any government" towards making "a dent" in the disarmament problem. Peoples everywhere were looking for leadership to bring the world "out of the present nightmare," and, he added, the government "taking a fruitful initiative will be hailed as a benefactor by the peoples."

Hammarskjold's intervention provoked the Soviet Union to its sharpest manifestation of public displeasure since he took office. "The joining of Mr. Hammarskjold's voice to the chorus of representatives of NATO countries and their allies praising the American propaganda maneuver did not change the nature of that maneuver and in no way made it more attractive," said Sobolev in the Council. *Pravda* was harsher. It accused Hammarskjold of seeking to "curry favor" with the U.S. and of "forgetting that he holds the post of Secretary-General of the UN and not Secretary-General of NATO."

Hammarskjold did not back away. He had "a sense of urgency" that the arms race was getting out of hand and because of human "impatience" or "failures" could result in a collision no one intended. "I wanted to bring the situation into the open."

There was "no foreseeable time limit" when a collision would become inevitable, but the arms race "makes it impossible to look with equanimity upon the diplomatic game" being conducted in which governments "discuss and write letters" and people are misled into assuming everything is all right. "There is a point in the development when every time an initiative is taken in good faith and its possible consequences, possible values, are not fully explored, I have the feeling we have missed the bus.

"We should not be too sure that the road will remain open for buses all the time in the future."

He minimized apprehensions that his intervention in the Council might "affect the position of the Secretary-General in his relationship to one of the big powers." He did not "for a second believe" that stating his views on a key UN problem would shake governmental trust in "my independence, my sincerity, my impartiality and my sense of responsibility."

Hammarskjold was correct. *Pravda* suddenly published a telegram he had sent several weeks earlier to Khrushchev thanking him for his hospitality in Moscow. There was no withdrawal of confidence, but the episode was remembered.

Although UN disarmament negotiations remained interrupted, East-West experts and scientists met in Geneva in the summer of 1958 and agreed that a test ban was susceptible of control and agreed also on the technical requirements of a control system. Hammarskjold thought the success of the experts might provide a way out of the UN deadlock on the larger problem of general disarmament. He suggested to the 1958 Assembly that it consider separating the political and nonpolitical elements in disarmament and authorize technical studies by experts, which, while they would not bring about disarmament, would help improve the atmosphere and prepare the ground. But his memorandum on the subject was publicly ignored and privately criticized by Gromyko. The only agreement emerging from the 1958 Assembly was that the Disarmament Commission should thenceforth be composed "of all members of the UN."

The decision on when to convene this unwieldy group was left to Hammarskjold. He thought it premature to call it together before the great powers, who were then moving towards a foreign ministers' meeting on Berlin and disarmament, expressed their views.

When the Big Four foreign ministers did meet in Geneva in late spring of 1959, Hammarskjold went to all four separately to discuss how disarmament negotiations could be resuscitated. An eighty-two-nation disarmament commission could neither negotiate nor even agree on the composition of a smaller negotiating body, he agreed. It would be better if the Big Four gave a lead on the matter. At least they should agree on the need for a negotiating subcommittee, he argued.

Gromyko's response, according to U.S. officials, was to insist on "hard parity," that is, an equal number of NATO and Warsaw Pact countries, as the precondition for a resumption of negotiations. Hammarskjold urged "soft parity," that is, the addition of two noncommitted countries. The U.S. was agreeable to this on the understanding that no votes would be taken. But it did not fight very hard, if at all, for the inclusion of noncommitted countries. Both sides were, in fact, uneasy about "neutral" participation and preferred to keep the UN at arm's length. As a British official commented, "Disarmament is complicated enough with five great powers." And the basic Soviet attitude was even more exclusive, according to James J. Wadsworth, the U.S. representative under President Eisenhower in the test ban talks. It was "You and I can get together and fix this whole thing."

East-West disarmament negotiations finally did get under way again on March 15, 1960, when the Committee of Ten met in Geneva, but, for the first time in UN history, they were outside of the framework of the UN. The UN was permitted to supply the housekeeping services and Hammarskjold to submit statements. He invoked this prerogative to remind the opening session that the four Foreign Ministers in setting up the Committee of Ten explicitly recognized that "ultimate responsibility for disarmament measures rests with the UN" and that the committee's deliberations would prepare the way for discussions in the UN.

The Committee of Ten did not go very far into the issues

when a new anxiety arose for the UN. With arms control debate centering on a comprehensive disarmament treaty, the plans of both sides began to deal with the nature of the control organization that would carry out and supervise total disarmament and the nature of the international police force that would be needed to maintain peace in a disarmed world.

Hammarskjold was aghast that even Western plans for such an organization and force envisaged only a loose connection with the UN. The Committee of Ten recessed on the eve of the summit meeting in Paris. Just before it did, Hammarskjold flew to Geneva to unburden himself in rather forceful terms on the interrelationship of disarmament with the pacific settlement of disputes and action against breaches of peace.

Chapter VII of the Charter, he noted, linked the regulation of armaments with peace enforcement provisions under which member states would make available to the Security Council armed forces to be managed by a Military Staff Committee. These provisions had been dead letters because of the great power split, but were there now to be agreement on a substantial measure of disarmament, they could become "of crucial significance" and would have to be dealt with within the Organization. He was equally emphatic that the disarmament control organization should be an organ of the UN "because all the experience up to date indicates that it is extremely difficult indeed to get the proper kind of policy integration when an organ is independent not only administratively but also politically."

He urged the delegates to think in terms of "an administratively independent organ which, however, would be politically under the final responsibility of the UN." In the aftermath of the Paris summit fiasco the Committee of Ten never resumed serious negotiation, but its successor will have to face up to the issues posed by Hammarskjold. There were signs the Kennedy Administration was more sympathetic to Hammarskjold's views in this regard than its predecessor.

The UN organ that was the chief victim of the cold war was, of course, the Security Council. The postwar split paralyzed that body which was supposed to carry the main responsibility for peace and security. Some thought the way to shake off the paralysis was to abolish the veto. Hammarskjold did not agree. "What is needed is not a revision of the Charter," he cautioned. "What is needed is a revision of the world situation" leading to resort to the veto.

The paradox of the veto issue was that "on the day that we can get rid of the veto, there will be no need to get rid of it, because at that time there will be such a measure of unanimity and agreement among the major powers that the veto rule will be completely innocuous."

Since Council decisions could involve heavy responsibilities for all members of the UN in the field of military and economic action, the veto was of importance to *all* members of the UN. Stated positively, it was a guarantee that Council decisions would be unanimous.

Hammarskjold was less concerned with the veto in the Security Council than with persuading the great powers to use the Council for a diplomacy of reconciliation rather than recrimination. There was no reason why the great powers, when they sat down to negotiate seriously on major cold war issues, should move outside of the UN orbit. That had been the case when he first became Secretary-General with the Berlin foreign ministers meeting and the 1955 Geneva summit meeting; it was still the case in 1960. Failure to use the UN on those matters for which it had been given special and primary responsibility could only reduce the influence and effectiveness of the Organization.

He thought the Security Council could be resurrected as an instrument of quiet and businesslike diplomacy if it would meet periodically as it was permitted to do under Article 28 (2) of the Charter. These could be informal sessions behind closed doors where the whole range of problems which the Secretariat follows on a day-to-day basis could be reviewed. Such informal discussions would prepare the ground for public debate "when we come to a point of crisis and the question is formally raised before the Security Council."

Hammarskjold was never able to persuade the Council to

adopt this procedure but a variant was instituted. This was to use the monthly luncheon of the Council. The presidency of the Council rotates on a monthly basis from one member to the next in alphabetical order. By custom the outgoing president gave a party at the end of the month to all members of the Council. They had become deadly affairs. Sir Pierson Dixon and Ambassador Alphand of France established the precedent of having a luncheon instead and inviting the Secretary-General at these luncheons to bring the Council up to date on what he was doing (and thinking) in the field of preventive diplomacy.

Hammarskjold hoped another precedent was established in the way the Laotian crisis came before the Council in September 1959. The Laotian letter requesting a UN emergency force was brought to the Council's attention in the form of a personal report from the Secretary-General rather than a request for a meeting from Laos or a member of the Council.

The Charter gives the Secretary-General the explicit and unconditional right under Article 99 to ask for inscription of an item when he thinks a situation is likely to endanger peace. But Hammarskjold did not ask that a Laotian item be inscribed; he simply requested the right to report personally to the Council. "I did so without any precedent, and without explicit support from the Charter."

The Soviet Union expressed doubts about this procedure. Sobolev said, "The Soviet delegation yields to none in giving its due to the Secretary-General" under the heading of his right to make communications to the Security Council. But this was on the condition that they related to a matter that was "under consideration" by the Council. In the case of the Laotian letter, there had been no Laotian item on the Council's agenda.

Hammarskjold did not consider Sobolev's doubt to be a "reservation." The precedent "opened doors to a method by which the Secretary-General can, in the most official, solemn and responsible form, report to the Security Council on a situation, or a question, without any substantive item so far being inscribed on the agenda."

He hoped to use this precedent of reporting to the Council without an agenda item in connection with periodic, closed-door meetings where there could be a full and free exchange of views before disputes had reached a point of public explosion. It was another device by which he hoped to strengthen the diplomatic role of the Council, but no second occasion has arisen to test its acceptability to the Council.

Hammarskjold's constitutional resourcefulness and political doggedness were taxed to the full in suggesting how the Council might be used for a summit meeting. Correspondence on the subject of a summit began in late 1957, when Premier Bulganin proposed such a meeting as the way to revive the suspended disarmament talks. In 1958 Chairman Khrushchev proposed a summit conference to handle the Jordan-Lebanese crisis. And in 1959 he wanted a summit to deal with his demands that Berlin be transformed into a "demilitarized free city" and a peace treaty with Germany signed.

Diplomats were surprised by the outspokenness with which the Secretary-General moved to stake out a role for the UN in the Berlin negotiations. He was spurred to a bold line of action by the danger of the UN's being sidetracked in a period of intense international negotiations. Prime Minister Macmillan, echoed by statesmen in the U.S. and U.S.S.R., had broached the idea of periodic summit meetings, perhaps every six months. This suggestion was not unlike the periodic meetings of the Council envisaged in Article 28 (2) of the Charter. Hammarskjold feared that if such a continuing international discussion were to be organized outside of the UN, the Organization's role in world politics would become dangerously peripheral.

He decided to make a public exposition of the advantages of holding a summit meeting within the framework of the Security Council. He picked as his audience the Students Association in Copenhagen, and a date a few days before the Big Four foreign ministers met in Geneva to deal with the Berlin crisis.

Hammarskjold blandly disavowed any intention of having his Copenhagen speech constitute a "concrete proposal" for a UN role in the forthcoming East-West negotiations. His speech, he insisted, was "just a balanced statement on what possibilities are available for negotiation," adding that "it is up to others to put forward definite proposals in this matter."

A Security Council framework would provide the summit with "a firm procedural foundation." It would also provide a "clearly defined legal frame" and thus eliminate "elements of uncertainty concerning principles and purposes." When a meeting is held within the UN framework "it means that the UN Charter as a whole emerges as the background of the deliberations. It means that the negotiating parties, without it having to be openly stated, accept as guiding them those basic rules of international coexistence of which the Charter is an expression."

Despite all his comings and goings and his public and private expositions of the usefulness of a UN framework, de Gaulle's hostility to the UN and the natural preference of the great powers to settle the world's affairs among themselves, brought about the decision to meet in Paris in May 1960, away from the UN.

Hammarskjold swallowed his disappointment and placed as good a face as possible on the development. "I do not recognize that there is any tendency among the big powers to lift major problems out of the UN. They have done so in cases where I myself recognize that their special position, their special responsibility with respect to these problems is such that discussion in a smaller group, before the matter is brought up on an 82-nation basis, is useful and perhaps necessary."

That this was making a virtue out of necessity became clear from his comments after the disastrous breakup of the Paris parley. The problems which would have been taken up in Paris "remain with us and require as much of our honest efforts as ever," he said in a prepared statement. He hoped that all would use the UN "to the full in order to overcome a setback which might otherwise threaten to tie us down for a long time ahead."

He reminded the diplomatic corps that the UN provided a framework for public and private diplomacy at any level desired. "It does so as part of a regular procedure without the building up of both expectations and problems." Within the

UN, moreover, there was "the mediating influence of the participation of all those who are vitally interested in peace, while free from an immediate involvement in the issues at stake in terms of prestige or national interest."

The UN as
a Third Force

The attitude of the permanent members of the Security
Council towards Hammarskjold's enlargement of the powers of
his office blew hot and cold depending on how their interests
were affected.

France became disaffected with both the UN and the Secretary-General at the time of Suez. French diplomats who prided
themselves on having discovered him felt he should have treated
the French case on Suez more sympathetically. Although the
Quai D'Orsay "buried the hatchet," as Hammarskjold put it, so
far as he personally was concerned, its attitude toward the UN
did not mellow correspondingly. "There is a collective neurosis
in France about the UN and it will continue as long as the
Algerian business goes on," one knowledgeable French diplomat
explained. The accession to power of the fervently nationalistic
Charles de Gaulle only increased French estrangement from
the UN.

Except for the Russians, the French always were the most rigorous "strict constructionists" in interpreting the UN Charter. They regarded warily Hammarskjold's concept of "preventive diplomacy." They resented his initiatives, not because they were his, but because they distrusted any enlargement of UN powers.

De Gaulle's aim has been to restore France to the ranks of the great powers. Hammarskjold takes a dim view of such strivings. He has noted that Sweden's position as a great power in Europe came to an end in the eighteenth century and that its prestige in the world has depended since then on men like the great naturalist Linnaeus rather than its soldiers. This kind of national maturity, he thinks, must be achieved by the great Western nations now that the growing power of Asia and Africa is pushing Europe as a whole out of its dominant position. It is futile for Europe to react by "sterile self-assertion," he has said, when spiritual greatness is called for.

This doctrine had little appeal to de Gaulle in search of "grandeur." Believing that France's claims to a directing voice in world affairs have a better chance of recognition outside of the UN, he derided and belittled the world organization. He snubbed it when he came to New York and his permanent representative's dispatches exercised little influence on government policy.

The UN no longer resembles what it was or ought to have been at the start, said de Gaulle in April 1961. The Security Council, which was supposed to have been, he claimed, an "executive council" of the UN, consisting of the Big Five, had let its powers be pre-empted by a disorderly General Assembly. France did not wish "to contribute her men or her money to any present or eventual undertaking of this organization—or disorganization."

De Gaulle spoke scornfully of what he said was the UN ambition "to intervene in all kinds of matters." And added, "This is especially true of its officers."

The British were the staunchest advocates of using the UN for a summit meeting, more, perhaps, because of their desire for a summit meeting than because of a devotion to the UN.

While their military power was paramount in the Middle East they did not welcome moves to build up Hammarskjold and the office of the Secretary-General and were only persuaded to go along because they had no answer to the U.S. argument: "Do you have an alternative?" Nevertheless, as a diplomat he rated highly among the professionals in Downing Street. Confidence in him did not waver even during the Suez crisis. That was an operation anyway at which the Foreign Office looked askance. British policy immediately after Suez was to use the UN "with discretion."

But there has been an evolution in British foreign office thinking about the UN which has paralleled the progress of British colonial territories toward independence. Foreign office officials connected with colonial policy still groan when they think of the Assembly's Fourth (Trusteeship) Committee. "But as we free our colonies we become increasingly supporters of the UN," a British UN official noted. "As we don't run the Middle East any more, but have great interests there, we welcome ways of keeping peace and stability in the area."

The more British officials envisaged an important role for the UN, the more they welcomed Hammarskjold's development of the concept of "preventive diplomacy." As British officials looked around the world and made their projections of crises coming up, they thought of a UN presence and Hammarskjold's getting into the act in a way that would not have been conceivable before Suez.

In the Soviet Foreign Office, as in every other, Soviet officials are divided in their views about Hammarskjold and the UN. There were strong forces in the Foreign Ministry who were against using the UN too much. The U.S.S.R. had suffered too many defeats there. Gromyko was presumed to be the chief exponent of this group. But this changed with the influx of Afro-Asians into the UN and the more flexible policy pursued by Khrushchev in the unaligned areas of the world. The Soviets sensed that they could make headway in the UN, especially on the colonial issue. Khrushchev, as a leading advocate of a more imaginative and vigorous approach to Asia and Africa, was not unfavorably disposed toward the UN, although as a power-oriented leader he shared some of de Gaulle's disdain for international organizations.

The mixed feelings about the UN were illustrated the night that Hammarskjold spent as Khrushchev's guest in Sochi on the Black Sea in March 1959. Gromyko was there and Anastas Mikoyan, another member of the Presidium.

Turning to Hammarskjold as the evening wore on and pointing at Gromyko, Khrushchev said, "You know if I had listened to that fellow, you would not be here now. He thinks you're a Western agent and should not be permitted in the Soviet Union." Mikoyan chimed in to observe that in Marxist theory there was no such animal as a Secretary-General of the UN because Marxist theory does not recognize any such entity as a disinterested person. "Everyone is an agent, even if he comes from Sweden."

With characteristic agility, Hammarskjold lifted his glass. He drew a comparison with Soviet Russia's "famous Sputnik," observing: "True, I was launched in Sweden, but once in orbit I do not come close to any country."

Did Hammarskjold make headway in his talks with Soviet leaders, especially Khrushchev, in persuading them to use the UN as an instrument of East-West negotiation? A high Soviet official commented that Khrushchev was no easy man to convince one way or the other. "He has his own opinions, definitely, and he is very frank about his point of view."

Soviet diplomats at the UN gave different answers to questions about Hammarskjold's impartiality and objectivity.

Some gave a qualified judgment. There was no "simple answer," they said. They cited Soviet differences with Hammarskjold but called them "differences on political matters" over which one could disagree "in a good spirit." Soviet officials who commented this way cautioned they could not speak for all Russians at the UN. "People who don't have personal experience with him feel quite differently," one warned.

The latter spoke scornfully of his alleged impartiality. They cited Laos, the surprise attack episode and his alleged reluctance to employ Soviet nationals on the UN staff.

They were of the school which denies there is any such thing as a neutral man.

Of all the great powers, the U.S. has the greatest respect for Hammarskjold and his office. "We want to keep in step with Dag's views," said a member of the delegation. "He doesn't say 'don't do this or that' but manages to make it clear there is another and better way." The relationship with Henry Cabot Lodge did not start out smoothly. But later, from about the time of the Suez events, they became good friends. Lodge was extremely helpful in selling the UN point of view, which meant the Hammarskjold point of view, in the higher echelons of the government. The U. S. Mission in New York would often warn the State Department in Washington that a policy line "doesn't make sense up here."

In the tensest moments of the Berlin crisis, Francis Wilcox, then Assistant Secretary of State for International Organization Affairs, commented: "I have more confidence with him there, realizing you can turn to him when the chips are down. As time goes on it is quite possible the occupying powers in Berlin will find a role for him to play."

But U.S. affection for the Secretary-General and the UN was not unwavering. Wilcox, and his able aide, Joseph Sisco, very often had rough going in persuading their high-level colleagues to include the UN as a major element in foreign policy formation. The men heading the regional desks looked at the UN and the Secretary-General through regional eyes. The psychosis with which France viewed the Algerian problem "rubs off on the French desk," commented a State Department officer. The Far Eastern section saw the UN exclusively in terms of the Chinese representation issue. And since all Scandinavian countries recognized the People's Republic of China, Hammarskjold as a Scandinavian automatically came under suspicion.

Sometimes Hammarskjold offered a convenient way by which to duck out of responsibilities. When the U.S. wanted to disengage, giving it to Dag was an expedient way of doing so while giving the world the impression of energy and dynamism. The Suez and Hungarian crises caught the U.S. without a program. Dulles ran to the UN for help, not hesitating to evade disagreeable responsibilities by dumping them into Hammarskjold's lap. At that time Dulles kept few secrets from Hammarskjold and made few moves without consulting him. Yet a few months later, when the Russians on the heels of their first Sputnik began to press for a summit, Dulles went to a summit meeting of NATO without even telling Hammarskjold what was going on, although much of the agenda was of direct concern to the UN. He showed little disposition to deal with issues like Berlin and disarmament through the UN.

Hammarskjold's relations with Dulles were businesslike and correct, at times amiable but never warm. Dulles often would call Hammarskjold, and even oftener Lodge would call Dulles and say, "Foster, call him." Hammarskjold never quite escaped the feeling that for Dulles he was a convenient instrument. Not that he minded this concept of the Secretary-Generalship, but he did mind the way this was made evident to him. The two were never intimate, but most of the time had a useful working relationship.

Relations with the Kennedy administration began auspiciously. During the years the Democrats were out of office Hammarskjold would occasionally spend an informal evening exchanging ideas with men like Adlai Stevenson and Dean Rusk. In the first months of the Democratic Administration he had somewhat easier access to President Kennedy than to President Eisenhower. Rusk was in favor of such contacts, whereas Dulles jealously shielded Eisenhower from all independent foreign policy viewpoints.

But the Kennedy administration, just as the Eisenhower, was of a divided mind toward the UN and Hammarskjold. Men like Rusk, Stevenson and Harlan Cleveland, the Assistant Secretary of State in charge of UN affairs, had a coherent doctrine about building the UN. They wanted to develop the UN's executive capacities, to make "internationalism operational," as Cleveland put it. Stevenson saw the UN as "the only institution which offers an alternative to imperialism" in a period of collapsing empire in Africa.

But there were also strong unilateralist tugs in the Kennedy administration. These centered in Kennedy's advisers in the

White House, where there was skepticism that either the UN or Hammarskjold could be relied on to promote Western interests and de Gaulle's views were regarded not unsympathetically.

When Lodge had started out at the UN he tended to consider that what was good for the U.S. was good for the UN. By the time he left, he was a strong preacher in Washington of the line that "what was good for the UN, was good for the U.S." His speeches often concluded with a quotation that he picked up from Hammarskjold on the relationship of national to international interests.

It came from a memorandum written in 1907 by Eyre Crowe for the British Foreign Office. Britain's best safeguard for the future, wrote Crowe, would be a national policy that is "so directed as to harmonize with the general desire and ideals common to all mankind, and more particularly that . . . is closely identified with the primary and vital interests of a majority, or as many as possible, of the other nations."

This was a doctrine that Hammarskjold recommended to Democrats as well as Republicans, and there were times, when among some of his aides, a nostalgia for Lodge was evident.

Early in 1960, as the great powers were preparing for the Paris summit meeting that was scheduled for May, Chancellor Adenauer visited President de Gaulle. They had many problems on their agenda, notably Berlin, disarmament, de Gaulle's project for massive help to the underdeveloped countries.

All involved a decision on whether to bring the UN in or not. The French leader pulled a sheet of paper from his pocket and handed it to the German Chancellor. It was a projection and breakdown of growth in UN membership in the next few years. It showed a large-scale influx of new African states which before too many years would give the Afro-Asian plus Soviet blocs between them two thirds of the vote in the General Assembly.

Adenauer was enormously impressed with the tabulation and asked to keep it. It was a dramatic forecast of the way the balance of power was shifting in the UN out of the hands of the West. De Gaulle's conclusion was that the less Europe had to do with the UN, the better off it would be. The Afro-Asians might not gang up with the Russians against the West, but de Gaulle saw little possibility of carrying through a coherent Western policy in an organization that represented "nothing but anarchy."

The view that the small powers, especially the new states, were irresponsible shocked Hammarskjold. He did not believe that they had less "of an understanding of the central political problems of concern to the whole world than those who are more closely related to them and who traditionally wield greater influence in international councils." He could not share the view that their influence was dangerous "in any context."

If there was irresponsibility, during the Berlin crisis, for example, it lay more in the way the great powers prepared to fly at each other's throat inevitably pulling the smaller states with them but without those states having any voice in their fate.

The Big Four had a special position when it came to political responsibilities, he acknowledged, but no four can ever speak for the other seventy-eight, he noted. This was in 1959 when the UN membership was eighty-two.

He was delighted when King Hussein, in a visit to UN headquarters in April 1959, toasted the UN as "the summit meeting of the small nations." He adroitly called attention to this toast when asked to comment on a possible role for the UN in great power consideration of the Berlin crisis. Hussein's expression, Hammarskjold explained, "reflected very widespread feelings in a majority of nations in the UN. . . . That is the way the UN is looked upon in many, very many countries indeed. I think it is an extremely natural attitude. I think it does create responsibilities for the UN, and I think it does indicate an important aspect which should be kept in mind when you discuss the relations between the UN and big power negotiations."

Misgivings about the impact of the smaller nations on UN policy focused on the General Assembly. Small nation spokesmen, like Abba Eban of Israel, saluted that body as the place "where small peoples achieve their fullest dignity." But great power officials considered it a cockpit of disorder, confusion and unpredictability. The U.S., sponsor of the "Uniting for Peace" resolution, had been the main advocate of using the Assembly to get around the veto-bound Security Council, but with the influx of new nations and an increasing difficulty in mobilizing Assembly majorities for its policies, it, too, began to have a change of heart.

A report to the U. S. Senate by Senators Mansfield (D-Mont.) and Hickenlooper (R-Iowa) on their work as members of the U.S. delegation to the 1958 Assembly reflected these reservations. The Assembly's "'one nation, one vote' formula produces little relationship between the desire to act and the responsibility and capacity for action," they concluded. This divorce produces dangerous parliamentary tendencies "to busybody, to scramble for votes, to log-roll, to water down resolutions."

A British diplomat put it more bluntly: "What possible advantage, it is said, can there be to the greater and more experienced powers in taking part in an institution where their vote is worth no more than that of the smallest states in the Middle East or Latin America, and where states which between them contribute less than 2.5 per cent of the total revenues can command a simple majority?"

This was a "good question," he commented.

Hammarskjold did not dismiss these doubts about the Assembly and the way it functioned. He was always searching for ways by which to improve its methods of operation. He was delighted to be able to report to the 1960 Assembly that there had been a further return of the Security Council, where the great powers held a special position, to its central role as the organ of the UN which assumes the primary responsibility for peace and security. But he saw no practical alternative to the "one nation, one vote" system in the Assembly. He doubted the possibility of finding a formula for weighted voting with which everybody would agree. Such a formula, moreover, would go against "a very basic idea in the Charter, which is the equality of sovereign states." It would tip the balance in favor of a few countries and take away from the rest the feeling that the UN is just as much their organization and their platform.

Criticism of the Assembly arose out of a misconception of its role, especially the significance of its votes. It was not a world parliament, he emphasized. Representatives who spoke in the Assembly were not comparable to individual legislators. They were not elected. They were ambassadors of their governments, reflecting rather than shaping policies. And most important of all, Assembly decisions did not have "the force of law." They were recommendations "to independent and sovereign governments." Only Security Council enforcement decisions made under Chapter VII of the Charter had a mandatory character.

The Assembly under the "Uniting for Peace" resolution could make decisions where the Council was deadlocked, but these were recommendations. The Assembly, as he put it, "can decide on a *recommendation* of measures which the Security Council can impose."

The demands for weighted voting reflected a lack of confidence in the newly independent states which was not warranted by UN history, Hammarskjold argued. "Neither size, nor wealth, nor age is historically to be regarded as a guarantee for the quality of the international policy pursued by any nation."

In the heady days of the Suez and Hungarian crises, with the Assembly meeting day and night, Professor Bokhari, then one of his top aides, exulted that the domination of the UN by the great powers was over, that the Security Council had become a "museum piece" which no longer reflected the real relationships of power in the postwar world, and that henceforth the Assembly acting as Parliament would make policy, led by the Secretary-General as executive.

Hammarskjold considered his aide's views overenthusiastic and imprecise. His constant effort was to bring the Security Council back to its central role in the maintenance of peace and security, to discourage General Assembly majorities from overreaching themselves, and he shied away from suggestions that the Secretary-General represented some third line in world policy.

But he also felt that the influx of new nations, most of them uncommitted as between East and West, had outmoded the Yalta concept, shared by Roosevelt, Churchill and Stalin, that the great powers as permanent members of the Council would constitute "a kind of 'built-in' directing group for the world community as organized in the UN."

Until 1955 the split in this great power directorate not only had polarized and paralyzed the Security Council, but it had done the same to the Assembly. However, the ending of the deadlock over the admission of new members in 1955 brought an influx of nations, mostly from Africa and Asia, which in five years raised the UN's total membership from sixty to ninety-nine. It also caused power in the General Assembly to shift on many issues to a kind of center party representing the middle and smaller nations.

The "fire brigades"—the groups of middle-sized powers led by Canada, Norway, India, Ireland, Tunisia, Nigeria, Yugoslavia and Mexico, which worked with the thirty-eighth floor —were a dramatic embodiment of this shift. Lester Pearson was particularly ingenious in coming up with solutions. So was Krishna Menon of India. Unfortunately, the latter's attitude toward Hammarskjold was always "jealous and grudging," as a former Canadian diplomat has noted. "He was only a note-taker" was Krishna Menon's comment on Hammarskjold's role in the talks on the Suez Canal that took place in his office on the thirty-eighth floor. In the Congo crisis, especially during the period Tunisia was on the Security Council, Mongi Slim was an invaluable ally in crystallizing a consensus among the African nations.

In the Emergency Assembly on Lebanon, Engen described the middle-power resolution he sought to get through as staking out "the middle ground, the ground of mutual accommodation, the ground of conciliation and mutual sacrifice." That was the only ground on which the Secretary-General could operate, he added.

The shift in power in the Assembly to the center made it possible to speak of an "independent position" of the UN.

Because all states were represented at the UN, said Hammarskjold, parties to a dispute including the great powers had to meet not only "the arguments coming from the other side" but "the judgments and reactions expressed by states which, even if not directly engaged, are interested." Within the UN disputants were forced "to confront their stand with that taken by states for whom the principles of the Charter may weigh more heavily than direct or indirect partisan interests."

This augmented Hammarskjold's own responsibilities. The Organization was taking up an "independent position" which was based on "the existence of an opinion independent of partisan interests and dominated by the objectives indicated in the UN Charter." To a considerable extent the Secretary-General was the spokesman for this independent position. The requirement that the Secretary-General should be elected by the Assembly on the recommendation of the Council, which meant the concurrence of the great powers, placed him in a uniquely advantageous position to reflect the "independent judgment" of the Organization.

Hammarskjold saw the UN as the main platform and the main protector of the small and middle powers, who looked to the UN for leadership and support "as a spokesman and as an agent for principles which gave them strength in the international concert."

A British official, after hearing Hammarskjold expound his views on the UN as the protector of the smaller nations, said it reminded him a little bit of small boys in school who, not wishing to side with either of two bullies, banded together in a mutual protection society of their own. He was not sure whether this concept of the UN as a third force was good or bad.

An astute French diplomat put it a little differently. "When peace and security were supposed to be maintained by the Big Five," he said, "the Secretary-General's main job was to keep in touch with those Five, whereas his policy now is to keep in touch with the non-committed in order to keep the Big Five in line."

But Hammarskjold was too much of a realist to believe he could be the instrument, not to mention instigator, of a policy that basically was not acceptable to the great powers. His line was to work with, not against, the great powers. And it was tenable only on the assumption that both sides genuinely were seeking to achieve a basis for peaceful coexistence.

After the Paris summit fiasco in 1960, Hammarskjold, while quick to point out that the UN offered "special possibilities to handle even the most touchy situations," emphasized that UN diplomacy and action had greater chances of effectiveness "when we deal with matters which are not what is called cold war issues. . . ."

With brushfires threatening everywhere, he thought the most useful function of the Organization would be to keep newly arising conflicts, for example, in Africa, outside the sphere of bloc differences. In conflicts marginal to the cold war, for example, in the Middle East, the UN aim should be first to localize and then lift them out of the cold war orbit.

He envisaged a division of responsibilities in which the UN protected "the setting and atmosphere" of the summit talks where the great powers would be tackling the basic issues splitting the world.

He had every reason to assume that this division of responsibilities was acceptable to the great powers.

14

A UN Presence

A new kind of diplomatic instrumentality symbolized the UN as a "third force"—the UN presence. In cases like Suez, Gaza, Lebanon and Jordan, Laos, the governments and peoples of those areas preferred to be helped by the UN in their troubles than by the rival great powers. The latter, in turn, tolerated and even encouraged the UN to move in because they did not wish themselves to become embroiled as a result of the competitive effort to gain client states.

"As it becomes harder, and, indeed, far more dangerous," said Sir Patrick Dean in January 1961, "for us all directly to pursue purely national policies, particularly in these so-called uncommitted areas, so we together must be the more ready to work with other like-minded nations of the free world through international bodies and particularly the UN."

The theory of the UN presence was formulated with considerable care and detail by Hammarskjold in the Introduction to his Annual Report for 1960. A basic assumption of the theory was the existence "of a mutual interest among the big powers to avoid having a regional or local conflict drawn in the sphere of bloc politics." The report was dated August 31, several weeks prior to the Soviet attack on Hammarskjold and his whole conception.

Speaking of the entry of the UN into crises in Africa, the Middle East, and South Asia, Hammarskjold wrote: "In all cases, whatever the immediate reason for the UN initiative, the Organization has moved so as to forestall developments which might draw the specific conflict, openly or actively, into the sphere of power bloc differences. It has done so by introducing itself into the picture, sometimes with very modest means, sometimes in strength, so as to eliminate a political, economic and social, or military vacuum."

The world community, said Harlan Cleveland, President Kennedy's Assistant Secretary of State for International Organization Affairs, "can 'intervene in the name of non-intervention' while a single nation, however powerful, cannot." Intervention in the form of a UN presence, whether to serve as a buffer, constable, watchman, tranquillizer or stabilizer, was a product on the one hand of the revolutionary instability of Asia and Africa and on the other of the need to shield these restless areas from the cold war.

The most dramatic embodiment of the "UN presence" concept was the military. As a result of the brilliant success of UNEF, no crisis arose, whether in Lebanon, Laos or Berlin, but there were proposals immediately to handle the situation by some kind of UN military presence.

Hammarskjold's approach to the idea of a UN presence was "completely pragmatic and non-theoretical." For his part "there was a UN presence whenever the UN was present." But he, too, was proud of UNEF and sympathetic to the widespread pleas for the creation of a stand-by UN force. He appreciated, however, the great obstacles in the way of such a force. Hammarskjold's steady effort to implement the stand-by force concept was an elegant example of the way he can weave back and forth on the diplomatic gridiron and yet always move steadily toward his objective.

The authors of the Charter had envisaged that the international law embodied in the Charter would be backed up by an international peace force. This would be controlled and operated by the Security Council assisted by a Military Staff Committee composed of the representatives of the permanent members of the Council.

Because of the great power split, these provisions of the Charter were inoperative from the outset. The first UN force came into existence quite differently than anticipated by the authors of the Charter—by a decision of the General Assembly rather than the Security Council, with direction in the hands of the Secretary-General advised by a committee of small nations. The Military Staff Committee, representing the chiefs of staff of the big powers, continues to hold a ceremonial meeting each month.

Hammarskjold was as eager as anyone to build on the basis of the UNEF experience in the direction of an international force. But he was also aware of the resistance to such an evolution. To obtain Asian-Arab support for UNEF and Soviet tolerance of it, they had had to be assured UNEF would *not* be the nucleus of a permanent force.

The Soviet Union was bitterly opposed to the international force concept because it considered the Secretariat and General Assembly to be organs of the UN that were dominated by the West. Any international force would, therefore, be at the disposal of the West.

Asians and Arabs were almost equally suspicious. They feared such a force would be used to enforce decisions which, under the guise of internationalism, would in fact be interventionist and imperialist. John Holmes, a high official of the Canadian Foreign Office, who was intimately involved in the negotiations to establish UNEF, has called Krishna Menon of India an "arch-propagator" of such suspicions.

"One of the fortunate accidents of history," wrote Holmes, "is that he was stranded enroute by air from Delhi to New York during the days when UNEF was being launched in 1956, and when he arrived at the UN scene to fume against the UN plot he found that it had already been accepted by Messrs. Nehru and Nasser."

Because of Arab-Asian suspicions, Soviet opposition and Latin-American anxieties over the financial burdens a stand-by force would entail, Hammarskjold early concluded that any advance toward a stand-by force would have to be by indirection and easy doses.

He therefore gave the "stand-by" concept a Hammarskjoldian twist. It would not mean forces-in-being but the preparation of a "full set of, so to say, master agreements, master legal texts, master plans for transportation arrangements," so that in a new crisis the UN need not improvise. "We could just press a button and say (with a set of documents approved, I hope by the General Assembly): Would you be willing to do this or that?"

But not even this could get by the Assembly. The U.S. was partly to blame. President Eisenhower, in addressing the Emergency General Assembly on Lebanon and Jordan, called for the creation of a stand-by force so that the UN instead of the U. S. Marines could have moved into Lebanon. "As it was the almost universal conviction of Asians and Africans that intervention in Lebanon was completely uncalled for, the President aroused the worst fears of those without whose support a UN force would be futile," commented Holmes.

One major difference between Hans Engen's resolution at the Emergency Assembly and the Arab States' draft that was finally approved was the latter's silence about a stand-by force.

As a consequence of U.S. overenthusiasm, the regular 1958 Assembly which met a few weeks later declined to go along with even the modest step proposed by Hammarskjold. He had presented a report to that Assembly called "Summary Study of the Experiences Derived from the Establishment and Operation of the Force." This account of UNEF's specific experiences concluded with a set of basic rules and principles which he wanted the Assembly to endorse and which might guide future efforts to set up UN forces.

It was hoped that Soviet and Asian-Arab mistrust would be

allayed by the clear-cut stipulation in these guiding principles that "any such Force, unless it were to be called into being by the Security Council under Chapter VII of the Charter, must constitutionally be a non-fighting force, operating on the territories of the countries concerned only with their consent and utilized only after a decision of the Security Council of the General Assembly regarding a specific case for the clearly international purposes relating to the pacific settlement of disputes which are authorized by the Charter."

But India, at a meeting of the UNEF Advisory Committee, where Hammarskjold sounded out reaction to the basic principles, said that while it fully concurred with them, and supported UNEF and UNOGIL, it would, if it came to a formal vote in the Assembly, nonetheless vote "no." Soviet opposition was much more absolute. It even included an implicit threat of withdrawal of confidence if he did not agree to shelve the proposal.

As a consequence, Hammarskjold's study was not endorsed by the Assembly. But that did not end the matter. The study went to all the member governments of the UN. "It is a kind of handbook for governments," he was saying six months later, and it would be "extremely natural if governments took into account the conclusions we have reached to the extent that they feel that they would like to be prepared to assist the UN were a new situation to arise in which such assistance of a similar kind would be indicated."

He was addressing himself at this point to a proposal of Pearson, who in connection with the Berlin crisis regretted the absence of a force-in-being and asked why should not the middle and smaller powers, "whose credentials and whose motives would be above reproach," implement Hammarskjold's report on their own, and, without awaiting an Assembly decision, agree "to earmark, train and equip certain of their forces for UN action," forces which would be available when called for by resolution of the Assembly.

Such "volunteer commitments" might be a "useful next step," Hammarskjold commented. If the UN were to get such commitments on the initiative of governments, it could create a unit within the Secretariat for the joint administration and registration of such commitments, he added cautiously.

This was where matters stood when the Congo crisis broke. Within thirty-six hours of the passage of the Security Council decision authorizing the Secretary-General to send a force to the Congo, Tunisian and Ghanaian troops were arriving in Leopoldville. The experience of UNEF had been assimilated even if never made a formal part of the record.

Hammarskjold sought to strengthen the Secretariat on the military side. The Congo experience reinforced his view that a standing UN force would be an unnecessary and impractical measure because each new crisis presented special problems in the composition, equipment, training and organization of a force.

But it would be an entirely different matter, he wrote in his 1960 report, if governments would maintain "a state of preparedness so as to be able to meet possible demands from the UN." UN preparedness would also be facilitated by a "qualified staff" capable of quickly and smoothly adjusting plans to new situations. It was a Secretariat weakness that it did not have in its ranks the necessary "military expertise." To overcome this deficiency, at least during the Congo crisis, General Rikhye of India, who had served with both UNEF and UNOC, was brought into headquarters and became the top-ranking military member of the Congo Club.

A "UN force" was only one form of "UN presence." In the case of Lebanon, the UNEF concept would have been "too extreme a measure," commented Hammarskjold. It would not have been possible to interpose a UN force between conflicting parties there, nor could such a force have operated without becoming a party to the domestic political conflict, he thought. At its peak, UNOGIL numbered five hundred "recruited from officers' corps in a score of countries, but no matter how useful their military training" UNOGIL did not exercise even the modest military functions that were accorded UNEF.

There was still another variant of the "UN presence" in Jordan. Before going out to Jordan to establish a "presence" there,

Hammarskjold cautioned newsmen against oversimplification "by always referring to a force or to observers." There was an "infinite variety" of shapes a UN presence might assume. To a reporter from the German Press Agency, he quoted a line from Goethe: *"Name ist Schall und Rauch* [The name is nothing but sound and smoke]." Since the Jordanians believed a UN force might reflect adversely on their reputation as a fully sovereign state, a purely civilian organization of very limited scope was established by Hammarskjold. It was in this case enough simply to show the UN flag.

In the Berlin crisis all kinds of UN presences were suggested, from the UN's garrisoning the city to its taking over the complete administration of the beleaguered community.

Hammarskjold ruled out both extremes as beyond the competence and ability of the UN. A force with military functions in Berlin would require somebody "who can give the proper kind of directives and instructions," he noted. These "would have to be of a very serious political nature." Hammarskjold doubted that any organ of the UN would be entrusted "with that kind of policy decision back of a potentially fighting force." Against whom would such a force protect whom, he asked further, and where could it be recruited on a basis that would ensure its neutrality and effectiveness? Certainly not outside Europe, he thought, "but from where inside Europe?"

But if prudence and realism excluded the more ambitious assignments being proffered the UN in Berlin, that still left a very wide area where some form of UN presence might be helpful. He declined to spell out what this might be in advance of knowing what the Big Four intended to do about Berlin, but he did comment positively on the possibility of a UN team monitoring propaganda activities in Berlin, if the Big Four were to agree on such a monitoring operation. This "in principle falls within the competence of the UN," he said. "Fact-finding activity is nothing new, and I have understood the situation, or the proposals made, as aiming just at a fact-finding operation."

The UN presence was not limited to a military or a political operation. The concept of the UN filling the vacuum left in the wake of decolonization first took shape in the Middle East and while UNEF had been its most striking expression, there were other manifestations of the healing blue and white presence, one of the most useful being the UN Relief and Works Agency for Palestine Refugees. When Hammarskjold left behind him in Vientiane, Laos, a technical assistance mission, Sobolev had teasingly accused him of smuggling in political functions under an economic hat.

The idea of a UN presence primarily to furnish economic and technical aid, which would also have a stabilizing effect politically, was particularly applicable to the newly independent countries of Asia and Africa.

Hammarskjold returned from his trip to South Asia in early 1959 with an overriding sense of the hopes and expectations the countries in that region had in the UN as well as the "insufficiency of our response to those needs." His trip to Africa a year later, one of the most important experiences in his life, a journey which took him to twenty-four African territories, confirmed him in the conviction that a strong UN economic program in Africa would also help reduce political turmoil in that continent as it re-emerged into history.

The UN Charter includes among its objectives the promotion of "higher standards of living, full employment and conditions of economic and social progress and development." Freedom from want was considered to be one of the prerequisites of a peaceful world, but the authors of the Charter in writing this prescription had in mind the experience of the thirties, especially the Great Depression. In creating the Economic and Social Council (ECOSOC) as one of the major organs of the UN, they sought to provide a forum where policies could be concerted internationally to avoid depression and unemployment.

By the time Hammarskjold became Secretary-General, however, there had been a great shift in UN economic preoccupations. The thinking of UN economists, the debates in ECOSOC and the Assembly's Second (Economic) Committee were dominated by the staggering problems of the underdeveloped countries. The executive functions being conferred on the UN in the field of economics were the administration of aid to Asia, Africa and Latin America.

A well-diversified machinery was at the Secretary-General's disposal in the economic field. There was the traditional form of technical assistance. There was OPEX, another idea of Lester Pearson's which Hammarskjold had picked up and with pertinacity promoted from experimental to permanent status in the UN arsenal. OPEX supplied the new countries with experienced administrative, operational and executive personnel. They entered the service of the governments which requested them and became responsible solely to them.

In addition, there was the UN Special Fund, under Paul Hoffman, a hard-headed industrial manager and gifted economic popularizer. The fund concentrates on relatively large pre-investment projects likely to contribute substantially to an underdeveloped country's growth. Its activities include resource surveys, training programs, applied research projects which contribute to increased investment and productivity.

Hammarskjold and Hoffman were tireless preachers of the advantages of multilateralism in extending aid. Hammarskjold had been deeply impressed by the comment of one of South Asia's leading statesmen that he should "fully realize that it can be much more difficult to receive aid than to give it."

The advantage of channeling aid through the UN from the viewpoint of proud nations such as this statesman represented was that it made aid a matter of "international solidarity" rather than charity, he noted. African and Asian leaders preferred aid through the UN because it was their organization, they participated in its life and accepting help from it did not involve them in the cold war.

"We are, of course, as a family, the worst beggars in the world and the worst beggars in world history," Hammarskjold cheerfully acknowledged, but that unpatrician posture did not bother him since it was "in a very good cause."

His trip to Africa bolstered the solid and sound arguments for increased economic aid generally with a powerful brief regarding the beneficial political results that would flow from an augmented UN economic aid program to that continent.

Africa was infested with disputes that might at any moment boil up to a point where they would endanger international peace. Frontiers had been established arbitrarily by the colonial powers without regard often for ethnic or linguistic factors. The slogans of pan-Africanism represented a rebellion against these frontiers; they often concealed dynastic ambitions as well. Split tribes, obscure boundaries, fledgling governments—the continent was littered with enough Macedonias to keep it and the world in turmoil for a hundred years.

A strong UN presence under an economic hat, Hammarskjold suggested, could serve as a factor for political stability internally and as a damper on frictions externally.

The need for help was indisputable. With the coming of independence, the peoples of the new African countries looked to their governments with great expectations. But those governments with the helping hand of the metropolitan power withdrawn, with that power's technicians and administrators going home, and its foreign investors holding back, were often less able than before independence to cope with the administrative, economic and social and educational needs stemming from the rising expectations.

This was a transitional problem arising from the speed with which decolonization was taking place in Africa. "On the continent of Africa," said Hammarskjold, "there is the problem of personnel. There is the problem of money. There is the problem of education, and there is the problem of, let us say, moral support in the reshaping and shaping of a nation."

"Timely" help was the key to a useful UN contribution. "At the moment of transition to independence, new countries often have to make basic decisions which are likely to determine for many years the pattern of their national life as well as their relationship with the rest of the world."

The UN should move in when asked, he said, "as a kind of stop-gap administration" with the assistance needed. The actual amount of additional money Hammarskjold requested for the program was comparatively small—in the range of $2,500,000 to $10,000,000, varying with what he estimated he could get. This additional amount added to the existing resources of the

Special Fund, OPEX and Technical Assistance that were ear-marked for Africa, would, he thought, enable him to meet the most urgent needs, and to station trouble-shooting personal representatives as well as aid teams in such key spots as Togo, which was under pressure from Ghana, Somalia, which had no mutually accepted frontier with Ethiopia, perhaps even the Congo.

Despite the modesty of the program, Hammarskjold had to move circumspectly and prepare the ground carefully. He had come back from Africa with what one Western diplomat de-scribed as "a bagful of ideas." He then began intensive con-sultations and by the time ECOSOC met in the spring of 1960 he had a pretty good idea of what the traffic would bear.

There were all kinds of doubts that had to be answered.

The ex-colonial powers wanted to be sure his programs would supplement, not displace, their own. In talks with the Brit-ish, French and Belgians, he persuaded them that the UN would not work in a way that would lead to a weakening of the network of existing relationships between African countries and the metropolitan powers.

Other regions of the world such as the Middle East and Latin America had to be assured that an "African program" would not divert attention from the needs of their own regions. There was no "special African program," Hammarskjold as-sured them, except in the sense that there were problems "of a basically transitional nature" which should be met by sup-plementary funds, not by taking away funds from other areas.

And African representatives, fiercely nationalistic and proud, were quick to suspect "paternalism" in any program that started from the assumption of a "special responsibility" of the UN in Africa. President Nkrumah was already registering un-happiness that Africa was not being sufficiently consulted.

The U.S. was the chief backer of Hammarskjold's plans. Sec-retary of State Herter promptly gave them the green light. "The more the UN gets into the picture, the better for Africa," was the U.S. view.

The Soviet Union voted for the ECOSOC resolution of April

14, 1960, which urged a "substantial increase" in UN aid to Africa, but it did so hesitantly.

Administrative expenses could be reduced, said Ambassador Sobolev. Some of the countries getting help were not really underdeveloped. Moreover, the new countries of Africa should not be encouraged to expect miracles from the UN. With its limited resources the UN could not play a paramount role in assisting them, he said. Such large-scale aid, the Soviet delegate explained to the Council, could only come through bilateral agreements such as that concluded by the U.S.S.R. with the new state of Guinea.

The resolution was, nevertheless, approved unanimously.

A few weeks later Hammarskjold designated Pier Pasquale Spinelli, director of the European Office of the UN, who had headed up the "UN presence" in Jordan to represent him at the Independence Day ceremonies of the Republic of Togo and to discuss with Premier Sylvanus Olympio the manner in which the UN "can, within its means, best assist in the development of the new state."

Then in June he dispatched Constantin A. Stavropoulos, UN legal counsel, to Somalia, and Dr. Bunche to the Congo to represent him at the Independence Day celebrations.

They will go out for the celebrations, he announced on June 16, and will stay on "in order to plan UN assistance in various respects and report to me when I pass through these two cities [Mogadiscio and Leopoldville]. . . . What may happen after my return to New York from the Congo, I cannot tell."

15

Vox Populorum

"Somewhere during the night I had become what is termed 'newsworthy' and my callers wanted me to 'react,'" Hammarskjold ruefully commented to an editors' meeting a few weeks after he had arrived at UN headquarters.

He had found there a permanent press corps which on dull days numbers close to a hundred and on days of even mild crisis jumps severalfold. This press group attested to the world's interest in what the UN says and does, which often means what the Secretary-General is saying and doing.

The Organization's own massive public information setup—daily broadcasts on a score of frequencies to most of the countries of the world, taped television shows and film shorts, pamphlets and press releases—reflected the view of the founding fathers that, as Hammarskjold himself put it, public opinion in the end is "the life blood of the UN."

This capacious press and public relations apparatus had trans-

formed Trygve Lie into "Mr. UN." It now proposed to do the
same with Dag Hammarskjold, despite the difficulties his last
name presented to headline writers and radio announcers.

But Hammarskjold did not lend himself willingly to such
plans.

As an official of the Swedish Treasury and Foreign Office,
he had had his dealings, and controversies, with the press, but
in general, although the top civil servant in both ministries, it
had been the Minister rather than he who had confronted the
press. A shy, reserved man, Hammarskjold preferred it that
way.

Staying out of the headlines is, moreover, a rule with the
Swedish Foreign Ministry in line with Swedish policy of avoid-
ing frictions and serious clashes. While some small nations en-
joy acting as a kind of Greek chorus, commenting and ad-
vising on all events taking place on the international stage, the
Swedes, when they have the option, enter a "no comment,"
or at most comment with restraint. Hammarskjold considered
this a good rule of thumb for diplomats generally.

Some public men gladly, others sourly, reconcile themselves
to the public's curiosity about their personal lives. But Hammarskjold, completely indifferent to popularity ratings, drew a
sharp distinction between the public and the private man. The
latter was off limits to the press.

At the same time, however, he was tremendously keen to
have his public views and actions correctly understood, especially by his fellow professionals. He did not consider the daily
press the best way of accomplishing this since he was temperamentally and intellectually disposed toward the nuanced
statement rather than the simplification or slogan that fitted
easily into a headline.

"In the process from thinking to public speaking, something
may be lost. In the process from public speaking to the headlines of the world, very much is lost."

But as Secretary-General he was not only the Organization's
chief administrator and diplomat, he was also its spokesman.

His public relations duty, as he conceived it after a few

months in office, was "to explain, interpret and defend the UN
to the peoples of the world." This should not be a propaganda
operation. "He is not out for 'selling' anything . . . but we
feel that what we are doing is something that should have the
support of the simple reactions of plain men, if we manage to
tell them our story in the right way." Public statements by the
Secretary-General should not come in conflict with his obligation as the representative of all member nations. Neither should
he permit himself to become a cause of conflict "unless the
obligations of his office under the Charter and as an international civil servant leave him no alternative."

With these principles guiding what he might say, he experimented with various forms of press conferences at headquarters.
He first tried an informal session with the UN "regulars" seated
around him in armchairs in the Security Council lounge. His
agents had circulated in the press purlieus on the third and
fourth floors and had told him what was on newsmen's minds.
An indefatigable monologist, he then made an extended statement on what he thought newsmen wanted to know. But the
press did not take to this system.

A few weeks later, the prepared statement was dropped and
there was a free flow of questions and answers but with substantial chunks off the record and the other parts attributable
but not to be directly quoted.

By the end of the year, however, he had established the pattern of a fortnightly press conference with everything on the
record. These were held in Conference Room 4 with the
Secretary-General flanked by his aides behind a long mahogany
desk on a raised rostrum facing the correspondents in semi-
circular banks of desks. Photographer and stenotypists worked
in a well in front of the rostrum while the telescopic turrets of
TV cameras jutted out from booths in the rear wall.

These press sessions usually last half an hour with the president of the correspondents' association signaling the end with
a "Thank you, Mr. Hammarskjold." He keeps his rendezvous
faithfully, unless the Assembly or Security Council is in session,
when by custom the Secretary-General is supposed to keep quiet,

or if he wants to go on record publicly, he does so in the Council or Assembly.

Once or twice a year Hammarskjold lunches with the "regulars." He considers the press corps "an absolutely essential part of the operations in this house" and is comforted by the thought that most of the newsmen assigned to the UN "believe in what we are doing, in the value of this experiment in international, organized cooperation." The press, he feels, shares a common aim with the Secretariat "and that is to play our roles in such a way as to help to the extent possible for us to set this poor world of ours on the road which may finally lead to peace, to greater sanity in world affairs."

Hammarskjold's public statements, while addressed ultimately to world public opinion, are meant in the first instance for the world's chancelleries. To use a distinction suggested by Professor Richard E. Neustadt in regard to the U.S. presidency, he is almost indifferent to his popular image, but his "professional image" is all-important. He was rarely troubled about his standing with the public, but he knew that his reputation with the professionals in the field of governing and diplomacy, their appraisals of his abilities and purposes, would be decisive for what he could do.

The transcripts of his press conferences—as, indeed, the texts of his occasional speeches, and the Introductions to his annual reports—were designed to be read and studied in foreign offices and by the diplomatic community generally.

His replies and comments were the despair of the wire service men. "I can easily see what kind of difficulties you must sometimes have," he told newsmen once, "caught between the undramatic character of diplomacy and diplomatic developments and the need for, so to speak, daily drama from the point of view of news."

But that was not the only problem. Developments and initiatives that were decidedly dramatic had to be veiled in hints, allusions and generalities.

"I am the servant of seventy-six nations," he told a crowded press conference in Moscow, "representing the most varied political philosophies and outlooks. This does not of course mean that I am completely neutral and have no point of view of my own. But my position is nevertheless affected by the fact. I should, therefore, also like to say that I am afraid my answers will perhaps strike you as rather general."

A Hammarskjold transcript, like a Dead Sea Scroll, is a disappointment if read as an exchange between Hammarskjold and the general public; it is a treasure house of information and insights if read as part of his dialogue with the diplomatic community.

When Syngman Rhee, in the course of a speech to the U. S. Congress in 1954, virtually advocated a resumption of war against the Communists, Hammarskjold was asked to comment.

THE SECRETARY-GENERAL: "Do you think that I should comment on what a chief of state says in the U. S. Congress? I do not think so."

QUESTION: "If he advocates a war, I should think it would be the prerogative of the Secretary-General to comment on it."

THE SECRETARY-GENERAL: "As to the way in which his statement is to be regarded by the Secretary-General, I think I can only refer you to the Charter, the appropriate articles of the Charter."

QUESTION: "Which articles?"

THE SECRETARY-GENERAL: "You know the Charter very well."

This did not make a wire service story that the Secretary-General had rebuked Rhee or cautioned the advocates of preventive war, but that was its implication and its meaning was so registered in foreign offices.

A few weeks after President Nasser nationalized the Suez Canal and there was great diplomatic activity, Hammarskjold was asked whether any delegations had sought his advice on a dispute which, after all, very much affected his own responsibilities in the Middle East.

"No," replied Hammarskjold, "my advice has not been considered that interesting on this question. I have been informed about certain aspects by the Permanent Representative of Egypt. That is all. We have not discussed it."

Two weeks later the matter came up again:

QUESTION: "At your last press conference you said that your advice had not been sought by anyone on the Suez question. I wonder if that still holds true?"

THE SECRETARY-GENERAL: "If you take the words I used literally—'advice being sought'—it still holds true. If you give it a wider interpretation, if people or delegations or governments have shown an interest in how I analyze the situation and what I feel about it, it does not hold true because the question has come up quite a few times."

One of the people he had talked with after the initial signal was Dulles, who, at the suggestion of the U. S. Mission, had called him.

The more the Secretariat, following Suez, was given executive functions, the more the press conferences were looked to by governments for information on what the Secretary-General was up to. Hammarskjold himself compared them to question time in a parliament. "As we have no other parliament in which I am, so to say, responsible in this peculiar way, I do not mind in any sense."

Sometimes he used his press conference to alert the diplomatic community to do some prodding. This was the case with the stalemated outer space negotiations in 1959 and 1960.

MAX BEER of the *Neue Zuericher Zeitung,* and dean of the UN correspondents group, would ask him: "What about the Outer Space Committee?"

THE SECRETARY-GENERAL: "Yes, what about it, Dr. Beer? I think you grasp fully the significance of my reply."

A few weeks later, DR. BEER went at it again: ". . . not to disappoint you and not to disappoint my colleagues: What about the Outer Space Committee?"

THE SECRETARY-GENERAL: "The last time I echoed your question and I do it again today."

He was adept at picking up a question and turning it to a purpose far from the questioner's mind. A question on Outer Mongolia was turned into a reply that West Germany's observer at the UN was quick to cable back to Bonn. Hammarskjold was asked to comment on a proposal by U. S. Senator Mansfield that he investigate whether there was a reasonable basis for the admission of Outer Mongolia to the UN.

Under "the widest interpretation" of the Charter he had no such authority, Hammarskjold said. His policy on admitting observers from non-member states to UN headquarters, he added, was to do so when the country in question has some form of diplomatic recognition from a majority of UN members.

"The reason for this stand is simply that the Secretary-General should not, through any action of his, prejudge the stand of member nations on such and such a country. That is to say, I put myself in second place when it comes to judgments of this nature."

The reply also constituted Hammarskjold's answer to East Germany, which several times pressed him for observer status at the UN comparable to that of West Germany.

In reply to a question about Laos, he managed to sum up a whole political program in one word. A reporter recalled that a few months earlier, December 1959 to be exact, he had said that one of the things to be achieved in Laos was to imbue the country, torn as it was between conflicting East and West pressures, with a sense of direction.

"Could you now say that the compass points left or right, East or West?" the reporter asked.

"Forward," replied Hammarskjold.

The UN press corps has its quota of actors and gloryhounds. Hammarskjold puts up with them courteously and patiently, only occasionally betraying a mild impatience.

Once after a question that ran on and on, Hammarskjold observed: "Mr. X, that was a very long statement." The reporter apologized, adding that if he apologized for every long statement he made, "I am afraid it would be a long apology."

"But it is a long statement also involving a lot of judgments, and I do not really think it belongs in a press conference or is in the press conference style." Then he went on to answer the question.

A reporter for a Saigonese newspaper, Tran Van Ky, persisted in questioning him about his marital intentions.

QUESTION: "There are reports that you are going to get married."

THE SECRETARY-GENERAL: "From sensation to sensation. First Mr. Gabriel [who had questioned him about a second term] and now you."

QUESTION: "This was stated by a friend . . ."

THE SECRETARY-GENERAL: "It is obviously explained by my general silence. You get so little news that you really have to invent something."

QUESTION: ". . . I will only volunteer to say that if there was a choice between the two, I myself would rather see you a bachelor Secretary-General than being married."

THE SECRETARY-GENERAL: "That is not a very humane approach. After this diversion, may we return to serious matters."

Occasionally a question will anger him. An Israeli reporter noted that on Hammarskjold's return from Egypt in April 1957, he had reported a "gentleman's agreement" with President Nasser. The reporter wanted to know: "How is it possible to make a 'gentleman's agreement' with a person who is not a gentleman?"

"I do not think much of that question," Hammarskjold replied curtly and motioned to the next questioner.

A series of detailed questions by a Danish reporter about the tragic case of Povl Bang-Jensen of Denmark, a UN political officer who was warring with his superiors, brought from Hammarskjold the comment: "It is somewhat unusual to hear a member of the staff speaking with the voice of a correspondent in a press conference, but . . ."

QUESTION: "Well, I must protest . . ."

THE SECRETARY-GENERAL: "I do not criticize you in any way . . ."

QUESTION: "I must protest against that. I did not get these questions from Mr. Bang-Jensen."

THE SECRETARY-GENERAL: "But you could not have put those questions without having direct information from Mr. Bang-Jensen."

QUESTION: "Not direct, sir."

THE SECRETARY-GENERAL: "He is a free man, and I do not criticize in that respect. But it is quite obvious that the questions do belong to the investigation committee and not to a press conference. However, I will say a few words about these various questions.

"As to the first one, the question of evidence, will you please repeat your words?"

Hammarskjold's press conference language is usually undramatic, almost antiseptic in the avoidance of the sentimental phrase. "You use such rather drastic language," he told a questioner, "and my own language, as you know, is rather flat."

This is not always the case. He is able, when he wishes, to state his meaning with a homespun concreteness, as indicated by such phrases as "missing the bus" on disarmament, a "will to peace" in the Middle East, his observation that the UN "took the steep hill of Suez."

The imagery is commonplace, but as one of his aides commented, "Nothing is ever a platitude" with Hammarskjold. There is always a twist to the expression which gives it point and individuality.

Perhaps the most characteristic aspect of Hammarskjold's press conference style is the nuanced statement; his mind plays over and around a subject like sunlight over rippled water, and is as difficult often to net. Thus, at a news conference in February 1959, when the Soviet Union was boycotting the Outer Space Committee, Hammarskjold noted that his Scientific Advisory Committee, on which both the U.S. and U.S.S.R. were represented, and which had worked with him in preparing the two conferences on the peaceful uses of atomic energy, had had its mandate renewed by the Assembly "with some modifications in the direction of widening its functions."

Then, several questions later, he suggested that if the Outer Space Committee should prove unable to meet, its initial task of drafting what the UN might usefully do in the space field, "all the same might be tackled in some useful form." Hammarskjold did not link the two replies but when juxtaposed they were an indication that if the Soviet boycott of the committee could not be ended, its work could be taken over by the Scientific Advisory Committee. He hoped the thought would occur to some of the transcript's readers who would pick up the ball and carry it from there.

There was another way in which the game might be played, he was suggesting most delicately, but it was up to the players to decide whether they wanted to try it.

It is only a step from the nuanced statement to the obscure one. There are frequent complaints about his "Swedish English." Selwyn Lloyd publicly complained of his "ambiguity," and Israel once icily described one of his reports as "an interesting and complex document, whose purport is not entirely clear."

But this obscurity is a matter of diplomatic method. The French have dubbed him "master of the calculated imprecision." This becomes a necessity in a job where saving face is important, where sparring for time is often obligatory because failure cannot be admitted, and where Hammarskjold must probe for openings in situations that have been dumped into his lap because neither the Assembly nor the Council was able to agree on more than the most generalized kind of mandate.

Astute ambassadors generally take along their sharpest political adviser to a meeting with Hammarskjold, for his nuances can be portentous and his vagueness can be an effective device. A close aide once displayed a magnifying glass which he had bought in order to read the Secretary-General's script. "I haven't yet found a similar instrument for the ear," he added.

Hammarskjold's "Swedish English" is only part methodology; it also is the way his mind is cast. Reading obscure poetry is a form of "intellectual calisthenics." He prefers the music of Bach and Vivaldi because "both have a beautiful way of creating order in the brain," and his doctoral dissertation was a semi-mathematical exercise in abstraction, almost to the point of aridity.

A studied optimism is as much a part of his diplomatic

arsenal as is calculated ambiguity. Newsmen taxed him occasionally with excessively optimistic appraisals of situations that appeared to them to be heading for disaster. Every time there was a bellicose speech, an exchange of rifle fire, a reprisal raid in the Middle East, newsmen cruelly flung back at him his "will to peace" dictum.

Optimism was a professional weakness, he confessed once. "I may perhaps have a certain inclination, in view of the fact that bad news is likely to have a greater interest than good news, to underplay the bad news at the expense of the good. I think, subconsciously, we might have that tendency, all of us, when we approach developments in which, after all, we do not want to stir up feelings prematurely or unjustly and where we want, on the other hand, to create an atmosphere as profitable as possible for constructive work for those in responsible positions in various nations."

Asked once what made him hopeful that the leaders of the Union of South Africa would deal with him in good faith on the issue of human rights, he replied: "I have to believe in the good-will of member nations and in their wish to take seriously what are the most serious reactions among member countries in the UN. Sometimes that hope—the hope for that kind of reaction—is frustrated, but it is a hope which is undying."

It was an optimism rooted also in his philosophy.

He took a Bergsonian view that evolution was not only a theory of biology but had its application to sociology and found "its expression in higher and higher forms of society.

"Of course, we are working on the brink of the unknown because we have no idea as to what the international society of tomorrow will be. We can only do what we can now to find solutions, in a pragmatic sense, to the problems as they arise, trying to keep a sense of direction, and then we will see later on what comes out of it."

Hammarskjold's press conferences were only one of several ways by which he projected his views. There were the Introductions to his annual reports on the work of the Organization. These spare, ascetic analyses, ranging from five to ten thousand words, of the major problems facing the UN, are the UN equivalent of the U. S. President's State of the Union message.

There were, in addition, reports he was directed to make either to the Assembly or the Security Council, such as those on the experiences of UNEF and future of the Palestine refugees. Hammarskjold drafts most of his reports himself, dictating at high speed thanks to a phenomenal ability to organize his ideas in advance. "He doesn't need private secretaries," an aide said half complainingly, half admiringly. "He remembers everything."

There are also a half-dozen or so speeches a year, frequently to a university audience, on some aspect of the work of the UN. The titles are indicative: "The Vital Role of the UN in a Diplomacy of Reconciliation," "The Element of Privacy in Peace-Making," "Asia, Africa and the West, the Beginning of a New Synthesis," "Do We Need the UN?" "The Development of a Constitutional Framework for International Cooperation."

Asked about this last speech, he said: "If you want to use such preposterous and 'highfalutin' words as 'creed' or 'confession of faith,' you might apply them to that speech, because I made an attempt there to set out my philosophy regarding the UN and the work we are all of us pursuing, you as well as I, within the framework of the UN."

Some of his speeches are studded with poetic imagery, especially those that touch on Sweden or nature. His address to the Swedish Tourist Association on the avoidance of "complacent provincialism" on one side and "a rootless cosmopolitanism" on the other contained some very personal statements about his feelings about Sweden, characteristically objectified.

His feeling for language and style is suggested by the following comment on Flaubert. "When I was studying law at the university I took to reading Flaubert as a kind of counterbalance. There is not a sloppy line in Flaubert."

His delivery of speeches remains the despair of his associates. He shrinks from what he considers staged effects. The idea of rehearsing a speech or artfully stressing key words fills him with mild horror. He is still no showman.

But if his delivery has not become more forceful, he has

become bolder and more outspoken in stating his views. In his 1959 Copenhagen speech, he came close to enunciating a *vox populorum* concept of the Secretary-Generalship. The Secretary-General was the spokesman of the Organization "in its capacity as an independent opinion factor," he declared. There was such an "independent opinion" building up, he insisted. It reflected the reaction, judgment and evaluation of that vast majority of member nations not directly involved in a dispute for whom the principles of the Charter weighed more heavily than direct or indirect partisan interests. This suggested that the Secretary-General was beginning to speak for a kind of "third force" in the international debate, but such statements were always strictly subordinated to the diplomatic operations in which he was engaged. If the UN could be heard in "the inner councils of nations" he was willing "to pay the price of being less visible to the public," he said soon after assuming office, and six years later he was still of the view that it was more essential in the long run for the sound development of international cooperation "to achieve de facto successes, even if they are unknown to the public, than to endanger a de facto success because of too great a willingness to 'sell' the UN."

He was, moreover, skeptical of the impact of dramatic public appeals. They might help to concentrate attention on the UN, but if not backed up by an effective follow-up, bounced back and revealed "weakness and shallow pretensions." Or such appeals might just be ignored. In the spring of 1960 he journeyed to Geneva to make a statement to the Ten Nation Committee on Disarmament on the need to fit the control and peace force aspects of any disarmament plan into a UN framework.

"Those of you who are interested in press statistics," he told his news conference a few days later, "may care to look at the coverage of that statement in Europe as in the U.S. I regard it as a piece of very public diplomacy, but I do not think the public is very aware of this move."

Newsmen wanted him to comment on French A-tests in the Sahara. He declined. In his time, the office of Secretary-General had added a new dimension—"a negotiation job." If he were rash enough to try to establish himself "as a kind of arbiter passing judgment on what is being done and how it is being done, I think I would definitely take a step which would kill the value of the development that has taken place and eliminate the role of the Secretary-General for diplomatic purposes and in negotiation contexts."

But a month later, when the nuclear test talks in Geneva again showed signs of bogging down, he would not exclude a public effort to get them moving forward again. "If a situation would develop in the case of the test talks where an open stand by the Secretary-General could in any way be of use, I would feel that I would certainly be remiss if I did not use that opportunity."

Elected by the General Assembly on recommendation of the Security Council—which meant the concurrence of the five permanent members—the Secretary-General held a "constitutionally objective position," Hammarskjold pointed out. He could interpret that position to mean he should keep quiet and preserve the neutrality of his office or speak up and "express what may be called the independent judgment of the Organization."

This did not mean speaking up publicly. For the Secretary-General to exercise a "positive influence politically" on behalf of the Organization's independent line, he had to have "the full confidence of the member states, at least as to his independence and his freedom from personal motives." He also had to accept "the limitation of acting mainly on inner lines without publicity."

Public appeals over the heads of government would in nine cases out of ten destroy the Secretary-General's chances of exerting an independent influence. "Only in rare exceptions—in the tenth case, one might say—this is what the situation requires, and then he must of course be prepared to see his future value as a negotiator endangered or even lost.

"In the latter case, he ought, naturally, to resign from his post."

16

The Sources of His "Power"

The Secretary-General does not represent any center of power, said Hammarskjold. He represents an abstraction—the international community. And yet, at the beginning of 1960, the year of the Congo and Khrushchev, his office was vested with the weight of a major power in international affairs.

The sources of this influence were legal, political and, above all perhaps, personal.

Legally his powers rested on a few brief clauses in the Charter. Article VII describes the Secretariat as one of the "principal organs" of the UN on a par with the General Assembly and the three Councils—Security, Trusteeship and Economic and Social. The Secretary-General is represented in Article 97 as the "chief administrative officer of the Organization." Article 98 states that not only shall he "act in that capacity" at meetings of the Assembly and the three Councils, but that he "shall perform such other functions as are entrusted to him by these organs."

Above all, Hammarskjold noted, it was Article 99 which transformed the Secretary-General "from a purely administrative office to one with explicit political responsibility." This Article authorizes the Secretary-General to draw the attention of the Security Council to any situation which may threaten peace or security. In line with this Article, the rules of procedure of the Council stipulate that the Council cannot refuse to take up a matter presented by the Secretary-General under Article 99.

This means the Secretary-General can start the whole UN machinery moving on the basis of his own subjective judgment regarding what is a threat to peace and security. But this is the extreme or limiting boundary of what he can do. Therefore, he can do anything to prepare for this step, anything up to the point of taking the step.

In the case of Laos, Hammarskjold did not say it was a threat to peace and security but that it might be, and how could he know, how could he decide whether to take the very serious action of putting into motion Chapter VII of the Charter, without looking for himself. Article 99 obligates him to know; therefore, the Secretary-General, in a potential case of 99, can send observers to an area of tension.

This reasoning caused the Russians to open their eyes like peacocks. They thought it a very dangerous interpretation.

A second consequence flowing from his reading of 99 was that if he found that a situation might become a threat to peace, he was definitely entitled to raise the issue with the government concerned to see whether it was possible to avoid the dangerous developments. He did not have the right to butt into China's domestic affairs in the case of the sentenced American fliers or those of the Union of South Africa in regard to its racial laws, but the possible international repercussions of these domestic events did make them a legitimate object of concern of the Secretary-General.

What this amounted to was the assertion that the Secretary-General can act unless there is an explicit decision to the contrary. When the Soviet Union vetoed the Japanese resolution on expanding UNOGIL, Hammarskjold said he would act anyway; the veto only meant he had no explicit instructions to guide him.

In cases where he did act on the basis of a Security Council request, he carefully noted that he would have had the right to act anyway, independently of the Council's request.

These were far-reaching dicta on how the Charter should be construed legally. That they were accepted by the big powers, or at least tolerated, reflected not so much the legal as the political necessities and, above all, his great personal authority.

The balance of forces in the Security Council and the General Assembly was such as to shift the emphasis to the Secretary-General. The cold war and the great power veto had paralyzed the Council; "swirling majorities" in the Assembly, which shifted with every issue, permitted it to reach decisions of only a most generalized character.

Increasingly greater responsibilities were thrust on Hammarskjold as the only way by which the Organization could preserve operational effectiveness and the capacity to have some influence over events.

Thus the Assembly in 1954 asked him to obtain the release of the American airmen "by the means most appropriate in his judgment." In the 1956 effort to shore up the Palestine armistice regimes he was instructed by the Security Council "to arrange with the parties for the adoption of any measures" which he thought "would relieve existing tensions along the armistice demarcation lines." In the Suez crisis he was directed by the Assembly to "obtain compliance of the withdrawal of foreign forces," to submit a plan for a UN force to "secure and supervise the cessation of hostilities" and "to take all . . . necessary administrative and executive action to organize the Force and despatch it to Egypt." In 1958 the Council requested him "to despatch urgently an Observation Group . . . to Lebanon so as to insure" against illegal infiltration across Lebanese borders and the Emergency Assembly directed him to make "such practical arrangements as would adequately help in upholding the purposes and principles of the Charter in relation to Lebanon and Jordan."

These generalized mandates were handed to the Secretary-General because required majorities were not available in either the Council or Assembly for more specific and detailed instructions.

"The Council with some vague sort of consensus asks him to do a job," a British diplomat commented, "or the Assembly passes some procedural resolution. They can do so because everyone knows perfectly well he has a good scheme of his own."

But it was a technique only possible with Hammarskjold, he added. "His reputation is such that our first disposition when he does anything is to consider it a very serious move." The Council and Assembly did not have to entrust its missions to the Secretary-General, Dr. Francisco Urrutia of Colombia, and an old UN hand, has noted. Alternative methods were available to them such as "the *ad hoc* appointment of someone other than the Secretary-General to serve as a UN mediator, or as UN representative on an important problem; the appointment of inter-governmental committees or commissions; and the use of the President of the Security Council or of the General Assembly to undertake negotiations."

The increasing use of Hammarskjold, the ascendancy that he established over the entire network of diplomatic relationships converging on the UN above all turned upon his personal endowments. Professor Michel Virally of Strasbourg University summed up Hammarskjold's personal ascendancy as a kind of "moral magistracy."

His authority was rooted in integrity and sheer intellectual power. Hugh Gaitskell had spoken of his "razor-sharp mind." Secretariat activities were no flaccid sprawl; they reflected his purposeful intensive intellectual direction. He is a man who insists on subjecting all issues, irrespective of their emotional and ideological content, to rigorous intellectual analysis. These analyses are remarkably impersonal and objective. Delegates regularly cable back his appraisal of events.

Hammarskjold uses his vantage point to have at all times

"a most complete and objective picture of the policies and difficulties of member states." Having seen "a little bit from the inside the working of the mind of the other party in this story," he said on his return from Peking, enabled him to form more definite and mature views of Far Eastern problems generally; it also increased "the possibility of saying the right word at the right moment."

Ambassadors and Ministers moved in and out of his office with almost conveyor-belt regularity. But to be the trusted confidant of governments meant that "private talks must remain private."

It also meant that his suitcases were always packed. He has never added up the total mileage of his travels but no doubt it exceeds that of the late John Foster Dulles.

To keep in personal touch with the world's leading statesmen he has gone rowing on the Black Sea with Khrushchev at the oars, breakfasted with President Kennedy, and sipped swallow's nest soup with Chou En-lai.

He is a gifted listener. A personal contact need not be a prolonged one, he said. "If it is established in the right spirit, it is fantastic how much you can get the feel of the situation and atmosphere and personality, and the whole approach, in even twenty-four hours."

The main qualities an international civil servant required, he once said, were "a heightened awareness combined with an inner quiet . . . also, a certain humility which helps you to see things through the other person's eye, to reconstruct his case, without being a chameleon."

He does an immense amount of preparation. Before he makes a move he talks a line out with his closest aides. Then he will test the line out on the delegations whose support he needs, making the changes that his enormously keen antennae tell him are necessary. He senses what the shift has to be, working around to it gradually, without seeming to make concessions. By the time he makes his move publicly he has touched all bases and knows he is on the way home.

This requires great physical as well as intellectual energy. "He has a physical stamina," commented President Eisenhower admiringly during the Suez crisis, "almost unique in the world." This was a man, the President went on, "who night after night has gone with one or two hours of sleep and worked all day intelligently and devotedly."

His dedication to work is almost monastic in its concentratedness. He sometimes gives his aides the impression they should not have families because they interfere with getting the job done.

He is tremendously realistic and pragmatic. One must have the courage to face the facts. "In a cold climate you do not ask for apples in the spring or daffodils in the fall." He combines inexhaustible patience with a sure sense of timing. When the Arabs shot down his refugee plan in the Assembly, he did not rush out and cry "betrayal," although the proposals had been cleared with the Arab delegations at headquarters. But neither did he abandon his proposals; he is sure that in time the Assembly will have to come back to them.

Perhaps not in the same form. He does not believe in frontally attacking thorny problems, as best shown, perhaps, by his approach to a stand-by force.

But realism does not mean abandonment of objectives. "Politics and diplomacy are no play of will and skill where results are independent of the character of those engaging in the game. Results are determined not by superficial ability but by the consistency of the actors and by the validity of their ideals. . . . Apparently easy successes with the public are possible for a juggler, but lasting results are achieved only by the patient builder."

There are more than a half-dozen resolutions on UN books which are being flouted. "I must watch my possibilities to do something that helps in the right direction," he said with regard to those on Hungary. On his visit to Moscow in March 1958 he called Khrushchev's attention to these resolutions. Khrushchev blew up, stormed around the room reaffirming Soviet Russia's views on Hungary, including its insistence that UN consideration of the issue was illegal.

When Hammarskjold saw there was nothing constructive to be accomplished, he dropped the subject. His attitude is never that of judge or prosecutor; he does not point the accusing finger. His approach is always positive—a suggestion for a step forward.

Not even in his statement to the Security Council when Britain, France and Israel invaded Egypt "did I condemn any party," Hammarskjold has noted. "I explained that I wanted to act on the basis of the Charter, of the law as I understood it and of the facts as I knew them. And my proper reaction is a reaction in action, not by words of moral evaluation."

He does not go in for tongue-lashing, but he can be very precise in indicating what under a resolution is required of a particular government, all the while using diplomatic language. "If your government is running counter to a resolution, you don't have an easy time with him," a diplomat on the receiving end during the Suez crisis commented.

Sometimes the firmness is wasted because delegates are not capable of following his subtlety. "Dag sometimes told me he had been very firm with some delegate, but when I talked to the delegate in question he was unaware of any special firmness," a senior delegate commented.

It is not Hammarskjold's policy to "fight" for something. He tries rather to persuade nations to do what he wants them to do by showing them how it is in their own interest. An old-style diplomatist, he does not believe in forcing an issue. Dr. Goldmann once complained he could not get a simple "yes or no" from him. "Diplomats no more than women should allow themselves to be so cornered," he replied.

"Diplomacy is also a form of chess with him," comments Charles Cook, a Lodge aide, "double-guessing what the other fellow guesses you will do—relating what the fellow said to what a person in his position would have to say and to what he could not say and yet mean."

Above all, Hammarskjold's influence rested on his reputation for probity. He has said he commands only the influence members are willing to give him in the light of his independence, impartiality and objectivity.

But can the Secretary-General maintain the trust and confidence of all member states, he has asked, without paying the price of "a self-effacement to the point of emasculate neutral-ism?"

His experience proved the opposite, Hammarskjold said in some extemporaneous remarks at a luncheon in Mexico City given by the Mexican Foreign Minister. "It is not by suppress-ing his views, but by forming his views on an independent basis and by consistently maintaining them that a Secretary-General can gain and maintain the confidence on which he is dependent.

"Following such a line of independence he may antagonize one group today and another group tomorrow, or a third group the day after tomorrow, but that is nothing to worry about as member governments come to realize they have much to gain and little to lose through such independence of the Secretary-General in international conflicts."

Of course, he cannot incur the continuing hostility of any group of states or harbor grudges. After the Suez crisis, he sought systematically to rebuild his relationships with Britain and France as well as Israel. He brought onto his staff a senior member of the British diplomatic service, Sir Humphrey Tre-velyan, as a sign of the reconciliation and there was a state visit to Britain where he was feted by the government and the heads of all of Britain's political parties. He flew across the Atlantic for luncheon with President de Gaulle, who afterwards acknowledged to associates that here was a man of quality, but who did not moderate his hostility to the UN as an organization.

The creation and maintenance "of the right relationship to member states," said Hammarskjold, "is not destructive of the integrity of the Secretary-General. On the contrary it depends on his integrity."

A West European diplomat complained during the Suez crisis: "I do not know what system of values he is loyal to." Hammarskjold's reply was that the "Secretary-General is, in his reactions, cut off from his allegiance to any one country—I think, of course, in the first instance, of his native country.

"Again, it is natural to ask how this is possible without a draining of the spirit which might seem to be an unavoidable result of such de-nationalization. The reply is simply that to the extent that he, in truth and spirit, can eliminate all such allegiances and fall back on himself, he will find a new home country which is everywhere in the sense that he will find open doors wherever he goes."

There were some who saw the enlargement of the Secretary-General's powers as a grasp for personal power.

But this was distinctly a minority view. His patient and persistent efforts to build up the power and authority of his office were not regarded as personal empire-building. "He is without vanity and desire for magnification of his public personality," commented Lodge. "He cultivates a cult of impersonality," an aide despairingly said. The UN stage which overnight can transform an unknown official into a world figure has its share of diplomatic grandstanders and power-grabbers. Hammarskjold is not considered one of them. He never thrusts himself forward as the indispensable mediator.

His persistent knocking on the doors of the world's chancelleries demanding that "attention be paid" to the UN was not a matter of institutional parochialism or self-aggrandizement. He was always ready to acknowledge that the UN was a means to an end, not an end in itself, and might be superseded. It was, nonetheless, mankind's current expression, born of the bitter experience of two world wars, of the realization that "at this stage of human history, world organization has become necessary." Admittedly imperfect, the UN was nevertheless an indispensable instrument whose reinforcement and adaptation should be the solicitude of all foreign offices, and, of course, of the Secretary-General.

Far from trying to displace the Security Council or the other main bodies of the UN, he was constantly lecturing statesmen on how the Council and Assembly could be better used for a diplomacy of reconciliation. As Secretary-General he was as much concerned with realizing to the utmost the peacemaking and peace-keeping functions of those bodies as well as his own office.

Better than anyone, he realized that his own continuing authority, wrote John Holmes, depended on the maintenance of consensus. Of all his talents, this, perhaps, was his greatest—a conciliatory spirit matched with a brilliant gift for evoking unanimity.

In situations where the policy-making organs of the UN gave him only the most general directives, he used the Advisory Committee both to clarify his own thinking and the intentions of the Assembly or Security Council. Or he would report directly to the members of the Council or Assembly on his intentions and leave it to them to challenge what he was doing.

He did everything possible, Holmes concluded, to make his authority legitimate.

As the critical year of 1960 began, there was a kind of magic to the Secretary-General's operation. He had fashioned a mantle of authority out of the most insubstantial of materials.

17

The Private Man

Except in times of crisis, Hammarskjold shuts up shop around 8:00 P.M. Generally he goes home to his bachelor apartment in the East Seventies and a variety of civilized interests. These are mirrored in the furnishings of the capacious eight-room apartment.

There are the stacks of books sent him by the Swedish Academy and some of the rare editions which he has been collecting for a long time. There is a small but select record collection. The climber's alpenstock given him by the Sherpa guide Tensing hangs over the fireplace. By his bedside table there is a French devotional work. Some samples of his amateur photography adorn the walls of his study and a few Swedish paintings are discriminatingly hung in the soft white living and dining rooms. The most important piece of furniture in the study is a spacious writing table designed for him by the Swedish architect Andreas Bjorklund, on which his Swedish housekeeper Nellie always has a few flowers. Guest rooms are furnished with the same fastidious care for detail, and the dining room is planned for formal entertainment.

The apartment reflects the life-style of the man. Nothing is accidental, casual or there simply because convention requires it. The furniture was handmade by Swedish and Danish craftsmen to his specifications and the fabrics and rugs handwoven. Whether practicing diplomacy or furnishing his apartment or writing or listening to music he is fully committed and involved.

His interests are not compartmentalized. All flow from a single center at the core of which is a Schweitzerian reverence for life, where life is more than the antonym of matter. Spirit and matter are both manifestations of a central life force, or energy, which finds expression in painting, music, literature, friendships, nations and international society, and which, along with the Jesuit philosopher Pierre Teilhard de Chardin, he believes is moving mankind by evolution toward new types and higher degrees of social organization.

Public service, the life of the spirit, self-realization are to be found and harmonized in self-surrender to this life force, in the courage to say *yes* to its every demand. "The important thing is to be engaged," he frequently says.

Reading, therefore, is not simply a diversion and relaxation. It is a challenge. "To submit to the discipline of a writer with an extremely mature mind who also is a master of language keeps your sense of human values acute," he commented to a Secretariat News interviewer in 1958. "If one read only UN reports, one would develop a rather curious mentality."

He tries to get in "at least one hour a day" of reading, "even if it has to be late at night. I take it as a necessary mental exercise, a kind of intellectual calisthenics." As a member of the Swedish Academy it is his obligation to keep in touch with Swedish literature and to read the works of the candidates for the Nobel Prize. He also tries to stay abreast of what is published in the U.S.—from the beatniks to Steinbeck. He shares his literary enthusiasms with the aides who are close to him, passing on to them books in French, German and English which have interested him, as for example, James Baldwin's *Nobody Knows My Name*, Jean Genêt's *Les Negres*, Heinrich Böll's *Wo Warst du Adam* and Steinbeck's latest book, *The Winter of Discontent*, which he rated more highly than most of the book's reviewers.

Literature and diplomacy commingle. His speeches, press conferences and diplomatic talks are interlarded with citations from the poetry of all cultures. He corresponds with Ben-Gurion about Buddhism and was responsible for opening the eyes of many Israelis to the importance of Martin Buber. A favorite form of gift to diplomatic colleagues and statesmen is a book —*Dr. Zhivago* to Krishna Menon; Teilhard de Chardin's *Phenomenon of Man* to Ben-Gurion; *The Spiritual Espousals* of the Blessed Jan van Ruysbroek, a fourteenth-century Dutch mystic, to his old freethinking colleague of the Swedish Foreign Office, Sven Backlund.

On his 1959 visit to Khrushchev he anticipated that his host might be holding against him his support of Pasternak for the Nobel Prize. To clear the air he himself at his first dinner with the Soviet leaders brought up the fact that he had been a member of the committee which had awarded the prize to Pasternak. There was a moment of startled silence which Mikoyan broke by asking how the Secretary-General of the UN could identify himself with a book like *Dr. Zhivago* which voiced reactionary views, and Mikoyan cited one or two offending passages.

Not the least abashed, Hammarskjold recalled that on a previous occasion Mikoyan had sung the praises of Dostoevsky. Did that mean Mikoyan approved of the killing of old ladies, he asked in a reference to *Crime and Punishment*. Khrushchev roared with laughter. Hammarskjold had made his point that art was something different from propaganda. The Soviet leadership's somewhat mellower attitude toward Pasternak may have dated from that episode.

In the West he was criticized for serving on the committee which sought Ezra Pound's release from an insane asylum. Identification with the spirit of a writer, he explained to critics, does not mean endorsement of his views.

He is a writer as well as consumer of literature. Together

with his friend Karl Ragnar Gierow, director of the Royal Dramatic Theatre in Stockholm, he translated Djuna Barnes's verse play, *The Antiphon,* which was then produced by Gierow. Was it worth doing? a puzzled Swedish press asked. He also translated *Chronique,* the latest volume of poems by Saint-John Perse. He was Perse's chief backer for the Nobel Prize and reveres the poet, partly for abandoning a worldly diplomatic career and living in obscurity in order to write poetry. Swedish reviewers of Hammarskjold's translation said it showed he was quite a poet himself, and Perse commented that he knew from the questions Hammarskjold had asked him that he was a true poet.

As a collector he specializes in old Swedish and English books. He has all of Linnaeus in first editions. Lapland is a great love and he shows with affection rare books about this wild, trackless region. He has always been a collector but after he became Secretary-General he had more funds with which to indulge this hobby. He often sends his acquisitions for binding to his friend Uno Willers, the Royal Librarian.

During crises when he is too tired to read he turns to music. "I must say that listening to Bach's Sixth Brandenburg Concerto is, in a way, like reading an extremely good book or poem." Bach and Vivaldi are composers he returns to "again and again," Mozart "in smaller doses," and Brahms' "Alto Rhapsody" and later works but "not the tumultuous Brahms." Mahler's *Das Lied von der Erde,* Franck's "Piano Quintet" and some of Stravinsky are also high on his list. And of course Beethoven.

A portable stage which the industrialist Thomas J. Watson donated to the UN permits the cathedral-like General Assembly chamber to be transformed into a concert hall. Foreign dance ensembles, dramatic troupes and famous symphony orchestras perform there at Hammarskjold's invitation. There are at least two concerts a year with Hammarskjold taking an active part in deciding the program and usually saying a few words about the significance of the music during the intermission.

There is the same productive approach to painting and sculpture. Dorothy Miller of the Museum of Modern Art recalls

that very soon after he arrived in New York he inquired
whether it would be possible to borrow paintings from the
museum. "We were very pleased and thought perhaps he
wanted to leave the selection to us. But quite the contrary—he
had a great deal of knowledge, very definite tastes and a very
good one. He came himself and did the choosing. I went along
to the UN to help him hang them. I didn't know whether he
was going to leave that to me. But again he had his own
ideas, very good ones, quite definite ones. So we hung them
together.

"He chose very good French things—Picasso, Braque, Gris,
Matisse. He was also interested in certain Americans. He took a
long time here to go through all our storage racks. He is very
interested in Fritz Glarner. We didn't offer it. He found it himself in our storeroom. 'Oh, I like that,' he exclaimed. 'What
is it?' "

Museum officials were so impressed with his knowledge that
he was invited to be the guest speaker at its twenty-fifth anni-
versary. He accepted and, after consulting Bo Beskow, delivered
an address in which he described modern art as engaged in an
"agnostic search, based on a re-evaluation of all values" that
expressed "the spiritual situation of our generation."

He is always on the lookout for paintings to cover the vast
wall spaces at the UN. He is proud of the Picasso he acquired
for the Security Council Lounge, deplores some atrocities he
inherited, but admires the two Fernand Leger abstractions on
the side walls of the Assembly, which leave most visitors un-
moved.

The placement of a work of art can involve as much of his
diplomatic skill as weightier disputes. A huge bronze figure on
a horse now standing in the UN gardens was the gift of the
Yugoslav Government. The sculptor, a friend of Marshal Tito,
wanted to situate it at a spot UN officials considered "ghastly."
The matter was solved by Hammarskjold's picking a site and
pointing out that it was on an axis with several UN buildings
and neighboring spots of interest. This proved acceptable to
the Yugoslavs.

He is an accomplished enough photographer with his Swedish

Hasselblad camera to have been invited by a professional jour-
nal to write his views on the subject. He did so in a piece
entitled "The Camera Has Taught Me to See." To see means to
take into account "the play of line, the division of light, the
balance of detail and totality." He described some of the pic-
tures in which he takes pride—"an evening motif with a
thunderstorm over the Chartres plainland . . . shows the play
of forces around the Cathedral which, despite its hugeness, by
human measure, disappears as a futile detail in the shadow of
the cloud; a poor Burmese woman sitting in devotion in front
of a reclining Buddha; a bare oak branch where the lines reflect
the balance between force and nervous sensitivity that Nature's
own creations can so often display."

On a trip to Nepal the King placed his plane and pilot at
Hammarskjold's disposal and with Hammarskjold in the co-
pilot's seat taking photographs, they went hedgehopping among
the eastern ranges of the Himalayas. The expedition produced
some striking shots of the Himalayas never before photographed
from the air. Lodge saw them and enthusiastically put the
editors of the *National Geographic Magazine* onto them. They
came in for a look, were delighted and reproduced them with
a graphically poetic commentary by Hammarskjold.

There are other forms of relaxation. Apart from official
entertaining he enjoys small parties of intellectually and artis-
tically compatible people. The day after Pablo Casals' UN Day
concert, Hammarskjold had a small luncheon at his apartment
for the Casals, the Fritz Kreislers and the Leonard Bernsteins.
Swedish friends who are passing through town are often his
guests, poets and writers like Perse, Mistral, Sandburg, the
Steinbecks and political analysts like George Kennan and Barbara Ward. Mrs. Eugene O'Neill, Djuna Barnes, the sculptress
Barbara Hepworth have graced his table, as have Lotte Lenya
and Greta Garbo. At the request of Gierow he made the first
approach to Mrs. O'Neill that resulted in the posthumous
production of *Long Day's Journey* and *A Touch of the Poet*.

He cannot bear ambitious, pretentious or aggressive women.
His Swedish friends twit him over his gallantry toward old
ladies and toward one or two great romantic actresses of the

thirties. But he is at ease with women only if the relationship is confined to the level of wit, intellect and chivalry.

Queen Elizabeth asked him why he had never married. He explained that having watched his mother suffer so much from his father's absences on public business he did not feel he wanted to subject a woman to such a life. Hammarskjold's sense of public duty is even more highly developed than his father's. A friend observed that he had never met a man with such an "alarming" capacity to subordinate the requirements of the private man to public duty.

Hammarskjold shuns formal "society" and avoids invitations in order not to acquire obligations. Yet he is tremendously correct about protocol. He frequently reviews the arrangements made by his Chief of Protocol, and his instinct is absolutely sure. At home he sees to it that his table is set with intimacy and elegance, and with his housekeeper Nellie and Bill Ranallo, who is also something of a cook, is always on the lookout for some new and interesting recipe.

He has a Swedish butler, but on nights when both the housekeeper and butler are off, does the dishes himself. With his brothers he used to help set and clear the table at the old castle in Uppsala and cannot bear the thought of a messy kitchen. When staying with Ben-Gurion at Sdeh Boker, he cheerfully accepted Paula's invitation to help peel the potatoes.

Browsing through bookstores and art galleries and an evening of talk in a restaurant with one or two people is a favorite form of recreation when abroad. He considers the "working breakfast" a slightly barbarous institution. An official who insisted on one found himself unable to break in on a brilliant monologue on existentialism. He loves the theater and goes often if circumstances at the UN permit. Belfrage recalls attending six or seven plays during a two-week stay with Hammarskjold.

He has a tiny hideaway in Brewster, New York, essentially a place to sit in the garden, and he goes there to sleep, read and take walks at a pace which leaves his companions breathless and which they describe as "mammoth" but which he calls "some hiking during the weekend." In Sweden he would drive for half an hour out of town "and then walk straight across the country by the compass for six hours or more. Here, of course, that can't be done."

There is a small shelf of books at Brewster dealing with the birds and the flora and fauna of the area. Occasionally he will poke a fishing rod over the pond at Brewster but he is a most absent-minded kind of angler. Before Suez he played squash regularly, enjoys an occasional game of badminton and has experimented with archery. Cordier once took him to a baseball game, but it reminded him too much of schoolboy stuff, and when Ralph Bunche at the end of the day will ask whether anyone had seen the ninth inning of such and such a game, the response does not come from the SG.

To many of his UN associates he is an aloof, almost intimidating figure, especially when the telltale flush signals the approach of anger which is no less frightening because it is controlled. Even high-ranking officials and diplomats find it something of a chore to be with him and prefer dealing through Cordier or Bunche. Dobrynin would tease his colleagues asking them, "What are you afraid of," but he himself would alter a subordinate's memorandum, explaining, "The SG doesn't like it this way."

The withdrawn quality, "the devastating impersonality" as *Time* described it, reflects neither snobbery nor unfriendliness. He cannot bear the idea, as one observer put it, "of being matey." Beneath the icecap is a genuinely nice man, although he tries his best to disguise it.

With a few friends and aides he engages in horseplay, exchanges highbrow jokes, makes up mischievous nicknames for the cast of characters that frequent the UN stage, and, says one of his friends, gives the impression "he's really giggling inside all the time."

He is most at ease with old friends from Sweden—Beskow, Belfrage, Lind, Gierow, Willers—perhaps because they treat him as a human being rather than a demigod. His attachment to them reflects also the strength of his feeling for Sweden, a feeling conveyed by the Swedish poet Verner von Heidenstam in the lines he quoted to the Swedish Tourist Association.

". . . I yearn for the ground,
I yearn for the stones where as a child I played."

Every summer he hopes for some time off from diplomatic
duties in order to get to his summer house that overlooks the
sea and moors in Löderup in the south of Sweden. It is a 150-
year-old farmhouse built around a courtyard with its old
beams still intact. It was brought to his attention by Beskow
who owned the place right next to it.

When Hammarskjold is at Löderup he and Bill Ranallo,
whose assignment is to be with him whether in Peking, the
Congo or New York, often take their meals with the Beskows
and Hammarskjold insists on doing his share of the chores.
Just as often Bill will cook them all a meal of antipasto,
spaghetti and meatballs. Hammarskjold is a connoisseur of
schnapps, wines and good food, but also can get along con-
tentedly on bread and cheese.

Hammarskjold is very sweet with the Beskows' two-year-old
daughter Maria, as he is with the three children of his Swedish
aide, Wilhelm Wachtmeister, when they come to Brewster. His
older brother Bo recalls that "Uncle Dag was a great favorite"
with his children when they were young. But he never shows
off with children, says Bo Beskow. He never campaigns with
them.

He tries to get to Stockholm for Christmas, usually on the
way to Gaza to be with UNEF or to Africa. On such occasions
there will be a meeting of the Swedish Academy, meals with
old friends, usually at the home of the Belfrages and then bare-
headed through the snow to Beskow's studio for a midnight
party with Bo opening tin upon tin of Sils and pouring the
aquavit. In Stockholm, among his friends, he is completely at
home and content. There is a palpable air of sadness about
him when the next day he is obliged to say his good-by at the
airport.

Yet he regards the period in which he has been Secretary-
General as the best time of his life. America and the calls of
his office have changed him, broadened him as a human being
and brought him closer to people as people.

But even with his Swedish friends, there is always one part of him withheld. There is warmth and genuine affection but always some distance. Perhaps this is the price of leadership and responsibility.

Speaking of the political unpopularity that was the fate of his father as World War I progressed and the difficulties multiplied, Hammarskjold said: "A mature man is his own judge. In the end, his only firm support is being faithful to his own conviction. The advice of others may be welcome and valuable, but it does not free him from responsibility. Therefore, he may become very lonely. Therefore, too, he must run, with open eyes, the risk of being accused of obdurate self-sufficiency."

In the middle of the Suez crisis he found time to have a pet project completed—the remodeling of the UN Meditation Room. Under Hammarskjold's guidance this became "a room of stillness" dominated by a six-ton rectangular slab of Swedish iron illuminated by a single shaft of light and behind these symbols a Beskow abstract "opening up the room to the harmony, freedom and balance of space."

Stillness is needed, says Hammarskjold, because "when we come to our own deepest feelings and urgings we have to be alone, we have to feel the sky and the earth and hear the voice that speaks from within us."

18

The Congo — Precedent or Fiasco?

The Congolese surge toward independence may have caught Belgium unaware but not Hammarskjold.

Almost from the first day he assumed office he had been alive to the new stirrings in Africa and their importance to the UN.

To a Danish cabinet minister who visited him in those early months, he commented how odd it was that of thirty-five hundred members of the Secretariat "only a handful are concerned with Africa." Philippe de Seynes of France, in charge of economic and social affairs, recalls that Africa was one of the first topics brought up by Hammarskjold when de Seynes talked with him in 1954 about taking on the job of Under-Secretary. He was already aware of the utility of the economic approach.

Four African states were members of the UN in 1953 when he took up his duties. By the end of 1960 the number was twenty-six. With the movement toward independence reaching flood tide, Hammarskjold embarked, at the beginning of 1960, on a memorable six-week tour of African capitals south of the Sahara. He was accompanied by Wieschhoff who had made his first trip to the Congo in 1928 and was his chief adviser on Africa; Bill Ranallo, his bodyguard; and Wilhelm Wachtmeister, his personal aide.

Everywhere, the red carpet was out for the man who personified the UN. He met with cabinets, and with nationalist leaders just out of jail and about to join cabinets, including, in Leopoldville, the cast of characters which a few months later was to dominate the UN stage.

Everywhere, he sensed dangers—of balkanization, of great power clashes, of nations being rushed into decisions they were not prepared to make—and everywhere he sensed also opportunities for the world community, acting through the UN, to help these fledgling states.

He returned with another basic conviction. He could see Africa revitalizing the Security Council, if its problems could be kept out of the cold war orbit.

The initial welcome given his proposals to establish a network of UN presences under economic hats bolstered his belief that the nations principally concerned with Africa—the colonial countries which were moving out politically, the U.S. and U.S.S.R., each of which suspected the other of planning to rush into the resulting vacuum, and especially the African states themselves—shared his view that Africa's engulfment in the cold war would be a tragedy.

Then, in April, the Security Council handed him an African mission that many diplomats considered the nastiest he had ever been given. He took it on willingly to show that the UN could act and achieve some easing of a situation, even one that to many appeared insoluble.

In the wake of the Sharpeville massacre in the Union of South Africa in which sixty-eight Africans were killed during a protest against the "pass laws," the Council by a vote of 9 to 0, with Britain and France abstaining, asked the Government of the Union "to initiate measures aimed at bringing about racial harmony based on equality." It also requested the Secretary-General to consult with the Pretoria authorities in order "to make such arrangements as would adequately help in upholding the purposes and principles of the Charter in the Union of South Africa."

Hammarskjold's first problem was to establish some sort of working relationship with the Union Government on the issue —a difficult matter since the Union Government rejected the Council's intervention as contravening Article II (7) of the Charter. This prohibits the Organization's intervention in the domestic affairs of member states.

Hammarskjold got around this difficulty by invoking the "Peking formula." The Union Government's relationship to the Security Council was its affair, just as Hammarskjold's relationship to the Council was his own affair. But the business he had to transact with the Union Government flowed from his general powers under the Charter.

South Africa agreed to hold consultations with Hammarskjold "on the basis of the authority of the Secretary-General under the Charter." It agreed further to discuss the Security Council's resolution with him, without its entailing, however, prior recognition of UN authority.

The ingenious formula was his "card of entry." The next problem was to work out with Foreign Minister Louw a basis for discussion of his government's racial policies, in view of its rigid insistence that those policies were its own business. He would not be concerned with the policies, he told Louw, but with the international impact of those policies and the arrangements he wanted to make would relate only to the international aspect. Thus the "pass laws," which required persons of African origin to carry passes and which precipitated the mass demonstrations, would not arise as a matter of the Union's internal policies but only insofar as they produced international friction.

It was a face-saving formula for Pretoria, but it worked, and, in practice, meant the Union's agreement to discuss appropriate safeguards of human rights.

This all-important preliminary of opening the door was achieved by the middle of May. Some easing of the situation seemed a real possibility. Asians and Africans, who for a decade had unsuccessfully tried to get Pretoria to pay some heed to the UN, were delighted.

When Hammarskjold left for Geneva and the summer session of the Economic and Social Council on July 8, he was planning to stay there until July 23 and then visit the Union of South Africa in connection with his Security Council assignment. Then he would go on to newly independent Somalia and the Congo.

But there already were danger signals from the Congo indicating that he might have to revise his travel plans.

Bunche's cables from Leopoldville were becoming more foreboding by the hour. Bunche had gone to the Independence Day ceremonies anticipating that the fragile republic, with only a handful of trained native administrators, might need a strong infusion of UN technical experts and advisers to supplement Belgium's post-independence aid.

When the messages started to arrive from a beleaguered Bunche about a mutinous *Force publique,* panic in Leopoldville, and talk among diplomats of a UN force, Hammarskjold's reaction, as he left for Geneva, was that technical assistance would have to be on an unprecedentedly large scale.

On July 10, with the rampaging *Force publique* in full cry against its Belgian officers, with Belgian administrators fleeing the country and Belgian paratroopers moving back in, UN thinking changed somewhat. Bunche, on the phone with Cordier in New York and Cordier with Hammarskjold in Geneva, advised them on the basis of his talks in Leopoldville with President Kasavubu and Premier Lumumba of the urgent need to provide the Congolese Government with assistance that would help it bring its Army under control, instill it with some sense of discipline and train a corps of native officers.

Hammarskjold suggested to Bunche that he get from the Congolese Government a formal request for "technical assistance in the security field." Armed with this he would proceed to raise a sizable force of officers and NCOs to advise and assist the Congolese Government in reorganizing its Army.

He canceled his African plans and returned to New York to

discuss the program with the permanent representatives of the African states. He was thinking of a Security Council meeting, but primarily to finance the program he had in mind, and to break free from the paltry $5,000,000 to which he had been limited for his African program.

The morning of July 12, Hammarskjold met with the representatives of Ethiopia, Ghana, Guinea, Liberia, Libya, Morocco, Sudan, Tunisia and the United Arab Republic. The UN was at once opening up a technical assistance office in Leopoldville, under a "resident representative," he informed them. Its mission would be to work out, together with Dr. Bunche, a detailed program of aid. But, in the meantime, there were "high urgency" needs for security personnel to train the Congolese forces and for public administrators. He asked the African representatives quickly to canvass their governments on officials and officers who could be assigned to such a program.

But even as Hammarskjold was consulting members of the Security Council on his technical assistance plans and awaiting the formal request from the Congolese Government, a cable came in from President Kasavubu and Prime Minister Lumumba that changed everything. It requested the "urgent dispatch" of military assistance.

This was the first request to the UN for military aid. The day before, several cabinet ministers, headed by Vice Premier Gizenga, had requested the U. S. Ambassador in Leopoldville, Clare Timberlake, to transmit to the U.S. an appeal for three thousand American troops to help the Congo get the Belgians out. Timberlake told them he was certain the U.S. position would be that aid would have to come through the UN. President Eisenhower instructed Secretary Herter to inform Hammarskjold of the request and the U.S. reply that such aid should be channeled through the UN and not be given unilaterally.

This was also the view of the Ghanaian delegation in Leopoldville. President Nkrumah considered Lumumba his protégé and hoped that the newly independent Congo would ally itself with him in the intra-African struggle. The Ghanaians were practically encamped in Lumumba's house. They made a fast trip to Luluabourg—Kasavubu and Lumumba were then rushing furiously around the country trying to re-establish the authority of the government—and the appeal for UN help came soon afterwards.

The Kasavubu-Lumumba cable and a subsequent clarification said that the unsolicited intervention of the Belgian troops was an "act of aggression," accused Belgium of instigating the secession of Katanga, said the purpose of the military aid that was being requested was *not* to restore the internal situation in the Congo but "to protect the national territory of the Congo against the present external aggression which is a threat to international peace." The UN force should consist only of contingents from neutral countries, the clarification said. And the cable ended with a typical Lumumba flourish. If the UN did not provide the assistance "without delay" the government would appeal to "the Bandung Treaty Powers."

Bunche in Leopoldville, operating out of Room 410 in the Stanley Hotel with a single telephone and fitful cable service, knew nothing about this request. Messages that came from Hammarskjold requesting clarification Bunche thought referred to the request for technical assistance which the government had finally formulated and dispatched. But with anarchy and chaos spreading, his messages on the thirteenth spoke of the desirability of a UN military presence. And whatever was sent, he implored, should be sent swiftly and should be equipped with a saturation supply of blue and white UN flags and emblems.

Hammarskjold, on the thirteenth, made the fateful decision to respond affirmatively to the Congolese appeal for military help. Kasavubu and Lumumba had not asked the Council to meet; neither did any member of the Council. It was Hammarskjold who made the historic decision to reply affirmatively to the newborn nation's plea. He invoked his right under Article 99 to convoke a meeting of the Council. He did so after consulting the African delegations and informing the members of the Council of his intentions.

The Council met that evening. It stayed in session until the next morning. In an opening statement Hammarskjold said the only durable solution for the Congo was to render the army and police capable of handling their duties. That was the purpose of the technical assistance program. But that would take some time. There was an "intermediary period." Belgian forces were in the Congo stating that they were there to protect life and maintain order. That could not be "accepted as a satisfactory stop-gap arrangement." The UN should accede to the Congolese request for UN military aid as "preferable to any other formula." It was understood the Belgians would then see their way clear to withdrawal.

If the Council authorized such military aid, which he hoped it would do that night, his action would be based on the principles set forth in the report he had made to the 1958 General Assembly on the experiences of UNEF. He specifically mentioned that the Force would not be authorized to shoot except in self-defense; would not become a party to internal conflicts; and would exclude the troops of the big powers.

A resolution authorizing Hammarskjold to proceed along the lines he had outlined was piloted through the Council by Ambassador Mongi Slim, the permanent representative of Tunisia. Slim, the only African on the Council, played a role in the Congolese crisis comparable to that of Hans Engen's in the Lebanese and Lester Pearson in the Suez. He was in touch with Hammarskjold and his aides, especially Wieschhoff, and with the African group. He was also in touch with other members of the Council, some of whom wanted a specific reference to an "emergency international force" and to methods of financing.

But there were fears of how the Soviet Union and Poland might vote. If they had abstained, as Britain, France and Nationalist China did, the resolution might have failed. The Soviet delegate wanted to delay a decision, but he was pressed hard by the Africans, who, along with Hammarskjold, insisted that the Council act that night.

After the Council adjourned, Hammarskjold, Cordier and Wieschhoff went up to the thirty-eighth floor. There was a talk with Walter Loridan, the Belgian representative, about withdrawals. Slim spent a half-hour analyzing the situation with Hammarskjold. A long cable was sent off to Bunche.

Hammarskjold decided to name the operation ONUC, the French initials standing for "Organization of the UN in the Congo" and embracing both the military and civilian aspects. Bunche had urged a quick showing of the UN flag, and orders were drafted for blue-painted ONUC helmet-liners, berets and armbands.

Messages were dispatched to a balanced group of African states requesting troops. Even before the meeting Hammarskjold had been assured of contingents by Tunisia, Ghana, Morocco and Guinea. Cordier was on the phone with U.S. officials about airlifting these troops. In another office, problems of personnel, finances, logistics were being worked on under David Vaughan. On the basis of the Suez experience, they thought they would need a staging area like Capodochino in Naples. The British agreed to make Kano in Nigeria available. There was a food and fuel crisis in the Congo and messages went out to UN members for emergency contributions.

By 6:30 A.M., when they quit, the basic organization had been set up and UN wheels were in motion everywhere. It was a characteristically speedy operation on the executive side.

It was a climactic night, a rare moment of high consensus in the Security Council, appearing to vindicate Hammarskjold's belief that Africa would revitalize the Council and that the UN could be the instrument for insulating fledgling nations like the Congo from the cold war and nurturing them through the take-off stage.

It was a case of the world community's being able to "intervene in the name of non-intervention" while single nations, however powerful, could not.

The story of the Congo from a UN viewpoint is the story of an almost superhuman effort on the part of Hammarskjold and his collaborators not to allow the UN intervention to be used for selfish, parochial interests, neither authorized by the Council nor sanctioned by the Charter. At one point or another almost every country that was a party to the original consensus, and almost every Congolese politician, broke away from the agreement in an effort to bend the collective effort to their special purposes.

The aims and principles underlying the consensus were defined in the Council's resolutions of July 14, 22 and August 9, all adopted with the concurring votes of the U.S. and the U.S.S.R., Hammarskjold's initial statement and his first report to the Council on the implementation of the July 14 resolution, both of which were endorsed by the Council.

The key paragraph in the July 14 resolution was taken by Slim almost verbatim from Hammarskjold's initial statement. It authorized him "in consultation with the Government of the Republic of the Congo, to provide the Government with such military assistance as may be necessary until, through the efforts of the Congolese Government with the technical assistance of the UN, the national security forces may be able, in the opinion of the Government, to meet fully their tasks."

Although this paragraph was later to become a major subject of contention, Hammarskjold, in the same initial statement, explained its purport and no member of the Council demurred.

What this meant, said Hammarskjold, was that the protection of law and order, whose breakdown the Belgians said had brought their troops back in, would be taken over by ONUC, thus paving the way for Belgian withdrawal, and that the UN would carry on until the Congolese were able to take over.

The principles laid down by Hammarskjold, and accepted by the Council, emphasized in the first place that ONUC would maintain a position of scrupulous neutrality in relation to all domestic political problems. It would not be permitted to become a party to any internal conflict.

It followed from this principle that neither the Force nor the civilian operation could be used to promote any person or faction or specific political solution.

With respect to the Force, he laid down additional principles that were also approved by the Council. While the Force was dispatched to the Congo at the request of the government, it would be under the exclusive command of the UN, vested in the Secretary-General under the control of the Council. The

ONUC operation "must be separate and distinct from activities by any national authorities." Joint operations were excluded.

The Force was not entitled to act except in self-defense. It could not take the initiative in employing armed force.

In regard to the Force's composition, the great powers would be excluded and the first contingents would be drawn from "sister African nations as an act of African solidarity." But there would also be units from Asia, Europe and Latin America, as was natural and essential for an international organization whose hallmark was universality.

With such aims, principles and means, the operation was launched. Within forty-eight hours the first contingent of Tunisian troops was disembarking at Ndjili airport as a welcoming Bunche murmured a prayerful "thank goodness." By July 18 the Force numbered 3500—460 Ethiopians, 770 Ghanaians, 1250 Moroccans and 1020 Tunisians.

An equally energetic build-up was taking place on the civilian side. "The Congo in July," said Brian Urquhart, a sparkling, quick-witted British aide of Hammarskjold's, "was like the *Marie Celeste*—a large, fully equipped ship from which the crew had vanished and in which fear and utter disorder had already caused the breakdown of many essential services." A summons had gone out to all the specialized agencies and throughout the Secretariat's thirty-eight floors for volunteers for Congo duty. Offices and departments were denuded of all but the most essential staff.

By July 20, when the Council met again, Hammarskjold could report that "the UN has embarked on its single biggest effort under UN colors, organized and directed by the UN itself." The Belgian withdrawal had begun and the operation was off to a flying start but "we have in no way passed the corner." He was going to have to ask member states for much, much more but there should be no hesitation "because we are at a turn of the road where our attitudes will be of decisive significance, I believe, not only for the future of the Organization but also for the future of Africa. And Africa may well in present circumstances mean the world."

The Council unanimously commended the Secretary-General

"for the prompt action he has taken to carry out the Council's decision" and the president of the Council praised him for his "magnificent work . . . as the Council's agent." Yet within a few weeks the unanimity was shattered. The Congolese Government in Leopoldville split into three competing governments, the African powers divided, the great powers roared and thundered, the Belgians played a cat-and-mouse game with the UN. The Secretary-General was pulled down from his pinnacle of influence and the UN was shaken to its foundations.

It probably would not have happened if Patrice Lumumba, the dominant figure in Congolese politics had been politically more experienced, and temperamentally less volatile. Had he co-operated in "good faith" with Hammarskjold, had he been willing to abide by the principles on the basis of which UN aid was being furnished, the other players in that fateful game would have had little alternative but to conform.

But Lumumba was a dictatorial, self-intoxicated nationalist politician, who could say to associates, "I am the Congo." He was impatient, unpredictable, swift in change of mood—one moment uttering the direst of threats, the next purring placatingly. It is difficult to envisage a greater contrast with Hammarskjold.

The day after the Council voted to send a force, he was already handing Bunche an ultimatum to clear out all Belgian troops in seventy-two hours or he would call in "Soviet Russian troops." There were to be many problems with the Belgians, but their military withdrawal began within a week of the Council's first decision and, compared to the Suez experience, the withdrawal under UN prodding was a speedy operation.

Lumumba himself, while he found the Belgians a convenient public whipping boy, privately was not dissatisfied. It was an amiable Lumumba, full of congratulations, who arrived at UN headquarters on July 25 for two days of conference with Hammarskjold. Their discussions centered around technical assistance and went into great detail about the kind of experts and administrators needed. What was agreed to in effect was a kind of UN shadow administration which would work arm in arm with Congolese officials in the nonpolitical field.

The issue over which the public break was to occur two weeks later, Katanga, was scarcely mentioned.

Lumumba went on to Washington, looking for some hard cash, and it was only when Hammarskjold arrived in Leopoldville, on July 28, that Congolese officials headed by Vice Premier Antoine Gizenga told him they expected the UN to move into Katanga at once.

Hammarskjold had not underestimated the importance of the Katanga issue to the Central Government. A province with two million inhabitants, it produced 60 per cent of the Congo's revenues.

Even before Congolese independence, the independent states of Africa had been in touch with him about secessionist intrigues in Katanga, emanating from Belgium and the neighboring Federation of Rhodesia and Nyasaland. Secession may have been Moise Tshombe's idea, but the fact that it was proclaimed on July 11, just after the arrival of Belgian paratroopers, stamped it indelibly in the eyes of African nationalism as a Belgian plot.

The more anarchy took over in the Congo, the more erratic Lumumba's behavior, the more Tshombe and his Belgian supporters wanted to cordon off Katanga and convert it into a bastion of Western interests. If it could not be done by secession, then it might be accomplished by confederation. While secession had few supporters outside of Katanga, resistance to Lumumba's project of a highly centralized government was widespread, starting with President Kasavubu.

In his July 20 statement to the Security Council, Hammarskjold had specified that Belgian's obligation to withdraw included Katanga. The Force would move in, he informed Tshombe, but he noted also that it could not become a party to an internal conflict and its presence in Katanga would not be used to settle the constitutional issue.

Hammarskjold's policy and intent regarding Katanga were clear when he arrived in Leopoldville, but the timetable he had in mind called for consolidating ONUC's position in the rest of the Congo before tackling Katanga. Again he was guided by the Suez precedent where negotiating the Israeli withdrawal was deferred until after the Anglo-French evacuation.

But on his arrival in Leopoldville he was greeted by a crowd of two thousand who mingled an ovation with shouts of "Down with Tshombe," and Gizenga's first question to him was when would ONUC move into Katanga. And in New York, Lumumba, returning from visits to Washington and Ottawa (where he had also closeted himself with the Soviet Ambassador), sent a formal letter to the president of the Council bitterly complaining about the slowness of the Belgian withdrawal and calling particular attention to Katanga.

Hammarskjold and his aides decided the Katanga move would have to be made immediately. He sent Wieschhoff on a secret overnight mission to Brussels to persuade the Belgian Government of the necessity for co-operation. Wieschhoff, a hard-headed, unsentimental civil servant, came away from his meeting with Foreign Minister Wigny persuaded that the Belgians would place no obstacles in the way of UN entry.

Hammarskjold announced that Bunche on Friday would fly to Katanga to pave the way for ONUC's entry the following day. At a dinner given in President Kasavubu's honor, Hammarskjold assured his Congolese guests there never had been any question that Belgian withdrawal and ONUC entry applied to Katanga, but the UN was obliged to give every undertaking "a good diplomatic preparation." The UN, he added, had carried out all that it had promised to do, "and it has carried it out with all possible speed." Paraphrasing Franklin D. Roosevelt, he suggested to his Congolese listeners that "the only thing we have to mistrust is mistrust itself."

Despite the impression given Wieschhoff in Brussels that the green light was on, Bunche was given a hostile reception by Tshombe. He warned him that entry of ONUC "would be opposed by all the force Katangans could bring to bear." Bunche flew back to Leopoldville and advised Hammarskjold that entry of ONUC as scheduled would require the use of force.

Since it was a basic principle of ONUC that force could not be used except in self-defense, Hammarskjold canceled the operation and flew back to New York to consult the Council and get its backing for another attempt. In a report to the Council he advised it that in light of Tshombe's attitude, the Council could change the character of ONUC and transform it into a fighting force. He was opposed to this, noting among other things that the basis on which governments had contributed contingents was that they would not be called upon to shoot except in self-defense. Alternatively, the Council could make it clear to Tshombe that UN entry would not mean submission to Lumumba or weighting the constitutional dispute in favor of a unitary rather than a federal solution. Were the Council to do this, it might "open the door" to speedy fulfillment of the resolution.

Hammarskjold's decision not to force his way into Katanga provoked a storm. The Soviet Union denounced him for perfidy and accused him of "a capitulation before the colonialists." From Conakry in Guinea Lumumba telegraphed Kasavubu to call the ministers together "and take a cabinet decision to renounce the services of UNO." He had been assured of direct military aid by countries like Guinea and Ghana and "we will settle the Katangan problem for ourselves."

At the August 7 Council meeting, Hammarskjold protested Belgium's lack of co-operation in Katanga. He reproached Ghana and Guinea, without naming them, for threatening to take matters into their own hands, "breaking away from the UN Force and pursuing a unilateral policy." But his sharpest censure was directed at the Central Government whose impatient response to his desire to act responsibly was to incite the population against the UN effort.

While the Soviet Union and Poland demanded that he shoot his way into Katanga, insisting he already had the authority to do so, Slim, with the support of the Africans, said Hammarskjold was right to come to the Council to have his powers clarified. He favored authorizing Hammarskjold to use force if necessary against Katanga, but his soundings showed him he could not muster sufficient support in the Council for such authorization.

The resolution Slim and Ceylonese Ambassador Sir Claude Corea introduced, with the concurrence of the African caucus, called on Belgium to withdraw its troops from Katanga, declared the necessity of the entry of ONUC into Katanga, and, in a gesture toward Tshombe, reaffirmed that ONUC "will not be a party to or in any way intervene in or be used to influence the outcome of any internal conflict, constitutional or otherwise."

No order to shoot his way into Katanga would have mustered a majority in the Council, nor did Hammarskjold want such powers given him. He believed the methods of negotiation and conciliation would work. He believed, further, that UN use of force would turn the Congolese population against ONUC and transform it into an army of occupation.

"I do not believe," he said in an exchange with Kuznetsov, "that we help the Congolese people by actions in which Africans kill Africans, or Congolese kill Congolese, and that will remain my guiding principle for the future."

Justin Bomboko, who, as Foreign Minister, headed the Congolese delegation to this Council meeting, begged the Council "on behalf of the Congolese people . . . to accept the position taken by the Secretary-General as the only one that will permit us to break the deadlock."

Break the deadlock, Hammarskjold did. Fortified with the Council's resolution, Hammarskjold conferred with Wigny, Kuznetsov and the Congolese delegation which included Gizenga. He informed Tshombe that he would arrive in Katanga the next day at the head of two companies of Swedish troops. He had chosen the Swedish contingent because there was a large European population in Katanga and because his countrymen would respond instantly to his orders. At one in the morning he left New York in a Boeing 707 placed at his disposal by the U.S., conferred with Nkrumah during a refueling stop in Accra, touched down in Leopoldville to link up with his Swedish contingent and flew on to Katanga to achieve what he called a "breakthrough." He was referring to the vicious circle in which the Belgians had argued they could not leave Katanga until ONUC came in and ONUC was kept out because Belgian-advised Tshombe threatened violence. Three days after the Council acted, Hammarskjold, General Kettani of Morocco, the

Deputy Commander of the Force, and the Swedish unit were in Elisabethville.

But this success, instead of placating Lumumba, infuriated him. Back in Leopoldville, on "that famous Monday" as Hammarskjold's aides refer to August 15, there was an extraordinary exchange of letters starting with Hammarskjold's suggestion that he report to Lumumba and his ministers on the Katanga breakthrough. Instead, in three letters Lumumba snubbed this offer, said he could not accept Hammarskjold's "unilateral" and "personal" interpretation of the Council's resolution of July 14. The Council had not intended to have the UN in the Congo act as a "neutral" organization but to place itself at "the disposal of my government," including assistance to "subdue the rebel government of Katanga." His dealings with Tshombe violated the resolutions of the Council and made him a party to the conflict between Tshombe and the Central Government. He charged Hammarskjold further with having used Swedish troops because Sweden had "special affinities with the Belgian Royal Family," scolded the UN chief for not having consulted with him before entering Katanga and declared his government had lost confidence in the Secretary-General.

The "personal" and "unilateral" interpretation to which Lumumba objected was Hammarskjold's memorandum setting forth his understanding of the Council's stipulation that ONUC should not become a party to internal disputes. Hammarskjold noted the Congo was not the first time the Council faced a crisis "where elements of an external nature and elements of an internal nature had been mixed." There was the Lebanese precedent when the constitutional president, Mr. Chamoun, faced with a domestic rebellion, had called for UN aid alleging the rebellion was fomented from abroad.

In that civil war situation, UNOGIL was deployed on both sides in rebel- and government-held areas but was concerned solely "with the possibility of intervention from outside in assistance to the rebels." In line with the Lebanese precedent he argued that ONUC "cannot be used on behalf of the Central Government to subdue or to force the provincial government to a specific line of action."

This was his own interpretation. Since Lumumba challenged it, the arbiter was the Security Council. Several times that day, while the "lively correspondence" was going on, he indicated his readiness to meet with Lumumba and Gizenga. He waited until ten that night without any reply "and without having received the guests whom I had invited and whose invitations I had not cancelled."

Hammarskjold left Leopoldville that night a thoroughly aroused man, convinced that Lumumba was an incipient dictator who in his drive for power was prepared to wreck the Congo and the UN.

As for Lumumba, since he could not bend the UN to his purpose of mastering Katanga and the Congo, he would drive it out. UN headquarters were raided and UN personnel arrested. Anti-UN incidents multiplied, especially against white personnel. Canadian signalmen were mauled. Crew members of a U.S. transport plane were badly beaten by a mob at the Stanleyville airport under Lumumba's eyes. A campaign was launched against "Belgian spies disguised as UN personnel."

The Council met on August 20 to deal with Lumumba's challenge of Hammarskjold's interpretation. Opening the discussion, Hammarskjold noted that the operation had come under Lumumba's "severe criticism" at the moment when the objectives of Belgian withdrawal and preservation of the country's unity were being achieved. He had been obliged to act with "great firmness" in regard to many parties, but he had never "failed in courtesy."

As for advance consultation with the Central Government, the Congolese delegation headed by Bomboko and Gizenga had been briefed on his Katanga plan and had raised no objection just as Gizenga and his cabinet at an earlier stage had approved Bunche's going to talk with Tshombe.

On the key issue of the role of the Force, if members of the Council disagreed with his interpretation they should give expression to the correct interpretation in a resolution. If the Council in offering military assistance to the Congo had intended it should also be used to subdue Katanga, it would have been necessary for the Council to say so explicitly, and the Council would have had to invoke Articles 41 and 42 of the Charter relating to enforcement measures. It had not done so.

In his first report he had said the Force would be under the exclusive command of the UN and its authority could not be exercised in a joint operation with the Government. No Council member had dissented.

Kuznetsov, aware that Lumumba's position commanded only Soviet support, said Hammarskjold's interpretation to have legal force should have been approved by the Council. Hammarskjold replied that implementation means interpretation. As the Council's agent, he interpreted, and, if challenged, referred back to the Council. "I have the right to expect guidance," but if the Council said nothing, "I have no other choice than to follow my own conviction."

Kuznetsov did not submit a resolution. As for the Afro-Asians, their spokesmen on the Council, Mongi Slim and Sir Claude Corea, publicly rebuked Lumumba. Slim said Hammarskjold deserved congratulations, and Sir Claude said it was "clear that the only role which can be played is the role of neutrality."

What had happened to Lumumba? What was he up to? President Bourguiba of Tunisia, who was following Congolese events closely since twenty-five hundred of his troops were in the Congo and who had conferred with Lumumba on the latter's way back from the U.S., remarked on Lumumba's inconsistency. "Mr. Lumumba shifted his rifle from one shoulder to the other and became the sworn enemy of the UN. Henceforth, nothing but words of invective and insults for Mr. Hammarskjold fell from his lips.

"A people has proved incapable of managing its affairs; its leaders unable to assume their responsibilities," Bourguiba commented sadly.

From the very beginning Lumumba alternated between cooperation with the UN and threats to throw it out and turn to the Russians and left African nationalists like Nkrumah and Sekou Touré.

Diplomats believe his meeting with the Soviet Ambassador

in Ottawa may have been the turning point. In his meeting with Hammarskjold before Ottawa he could not have been more amiable. But then Washington and Ottawa turned down his plea for hard cash, telling him their aid would be channeled through the UN. It was a disillusioned Lumumba, with a soft spot for the Russians, on whom the Soviet Ambassador called. When Lumumba returned to New York and conferred with Cordier on his way home his anti-UN line had become pronounced, even to the point of accusing Hammarskjold of siding with the Belgians.

From that point on, he behaved and spoke like a man who had decided that, with the Belgians on the way out, his own ambitions of creating a centralized Congo under his control would be better served by relying on the Russians and the left nationalists. He tried to push the UN out of the airfields so that Soviet planes could fly in unfettered. He lost interest in technical assistance from the UN, believing he would get a better deal from Moscow. He sent Moscow a list of his requirements. He sought to place UN operations in the Congo under a committee of Afro-Asians sympathetic to his ambitions.

Lumumba's renunciation of the UN was of critical importance, especially as it encouraged the Soviet Union to bow out of the consensus.

The Russians had gone along with the original resolution setting up ONUC hesitantly. Sobolev wanted to delay a decision but the Africans insisted on action that night. Moreover, with Britain and France abstaining, a Soviet abstention would have rendered it an accomplice in the eyes of Africa in stopping action designed to get the Belgians out.

While the Russians were delighted to use the UN as a lever with which to evict Western interests from the Congo, they were also probing for ways by which they could move in. Already, on July 15, Khrushchev had promised the Congo "any assistance" in reply to a message from Kasavubu and Lumumba begging him to "watch hourly" over the situation. Alone of all the powers contributing food in response to the UN appeal, the Soviet Union furnished it directly to the Congolese Government rather than through the UN. And one of the first Soviet planes flying in food also brought in Andre Fomin, a top Soviet political expert on Africa, to direct Moscow's on-the-spot operations. Fomin went around Leopoldville openly telling the Congolese they were foolish to expect technical help from the UN; they would be much better off to follow the pattern of Guinea and make a direct deal with the Soviet bloc.

Within a week of the Council's first decision, talk of direct Soviet military intervention was so widespread that the U.S. felt obliged to announce formally in the Council that "with other UN members we will do whatever may be necessary to prevent the intrusion of military forces not requested by the UN."

At this stage, the Soviet delegate at the UN was emphasizing that the main purpose of the Council's decision was to get Belgian troops out. It did not authorize the UN to intervene in Congolese domestic affairs, he insisted.

There were mild Soviet criticisms of Hammarskjold in July. In August, however, in synchronization with Lumumba, Moscow stepped up its campaign, accused Hammarskjold of dragging his feet in favor of the U.S. and the colonizers. If the UN Command was incapable of getting the Belgians out, it should be replaced, Moscow said.

The Soviet press worked itself into a fury over Hammarskjold's "disgraceful role" in dealing with Tshombe, greeting him and shaking his hand. On August 20, the Soviet Government rejected Hammarskjold's proposals for the organization of a UN Civilian Operation in the Congo which Lumumba had accepted when he was in New York. They would infringe upon Congolese sovereignty, the Soviet Union claimed, reduce it to a "trusteeship," and since most of the experts would be recruited from the U.S. and its allies, would, in effect, place the Congo under U.S. domination.

By the end of August, Soviet "technical assistance" to Lumumba included at least seventeen Ilyushin twin-engined turboprop transports complete with crew and maintenance and a special gift of an Ilyushin complete with crew to Lumumba for his personal use, a hundred Soviet trucks and several hundred Soviet bloc technicians.

In July, Hammarskjold had inquired about Ilyushin 18s that the Soviet Government had placed directly at the disposal of the Ghanaian Government, rather than the UN Command, to ferry Ghanaian troops from one point in the Congo to another. The Soviets did not reply to this inquiry.

On September 5, Hammarskjold asked for information about the Soviet planes being placed at Lumumba's disposal, noting that ten of them were being used for military purposes. Hammarskjold pointedly recalled Soviet Russia's own protest on July 19 against the arrival of twenty U.S. soldiers in the Congo to help with the airlift of UN supplies and troops.

Soviet Russia reacted on September 10. The Security Council resolution, Moscow said coldly, did not restrict the right of the Congolese Government to get aid wherever it wished, nor did it give UN officials the right to control aid given the Congolese Government. Nothing was going to stop the Soviet Union from giving aid to Lumumba if it wished.

A major reason for the intervention of the UN in the Congo was to assure the nonintervention of the great powers. Now this appeared to be threatened. In Washington, President Eisenhower warned that if the Soviets insisted on acting unilaterally "this would indeed be serious."

The issue was squarely drawn at the series of Security Council meetings and the Emergency General Assembly in September, just before the arrival of Chairman Khrushchev.

A resolution by Ceylon and Tunisia which would have had the Council state explicitly "that no assistance for military purposes be sent to the Congo except as part of the UN action," was vetoed by the Soviet Union. This provision, the Soviet Union maintained, would violate "a basic principle of the UN—respect for the sovereign rights of all states—it would mean the imposition of a UN trusteeship on the Republic of the Congo."

From the Soviet ship *Baltika,* which was en route to the U.S., Chairman Khrushchev wired the *Daily Express* in London that "the colonialists and imperialists are carrying out their policy through the hands of the UN Secretary-General, Mr. Hammarskjold." He was doing this "consciously" and "the zealous defense by Mr. Hammarskjold of his proposal that assistance to the Congo should come through his hands only is explained by the same desire to uphold the interests of the colonialists."

A few days later, when the whole Soviet operation was ordered out of the Congo by Colonel Mobutu, who had seized power, the Soviets angrily decided their best course was to comply.

Soviet Russia's rupture with the original UN consensus on the Congo was now almost complete. Kuznetsov, whose private talks with Hammarskjold throughout this period of deteriorating relations had been reasonably cordial and his line moderate and impersonal, had returned to Moscow, his place taken by Soviet Deputy Foreign Minister Zorin. The debate in the Soviet foreign office and ruling circles had ended. Khrushchev had thrown in with those advocating a tough line toward the UN.

The explanation can only be speculative. The decision partly was a corollary of the breakup of the summit and Khrushchev's determination to lock horns with and harry the U.S. throughout the world. It also reflected the bitter ideological struggle with Peking, where Khrushchev was under attack for "revisionism," especially a failure to pursue a sufficiently militant policy in revolutionary and unstable areas like Africa. Peking was contending the original Security Council decision on the Congo was a gross error and "opened the door for the imperialists." And, clearly, Khrushchev was furious over being balked by the UN just when it appeared the Congo lay wide open for the taking.

Henceforth, the Soviet Union in one way or another sought to undermine, harass and destroy the UN operation, including refusal to pay its share of the heavy Congo budget, and, beginning with the end of November 1960, publicly called for liquidation of the operation. Its argument was always the same —the perfidy of the Secretary-General and his alleged violation of UN decisions—an argument that was time and again rejected by both the Assembly and Security Council—notably in the 70–0 vote of the Emergency Assembly of the Congo, just before Khrushchev's arrival; in the February 1961 Security Council vote which strengthened and clarified the basis of UN action in the Congo; and the 83–11, with five abstentions, vote at the resumed session of the General Assembly in April 1961, which was on a direct vote of confidence challenge.

Hammarskjold's line of neutrality and scrupulous adherence to the aims and principles of the UN brought him into conflict with West as well as East.

If his difficulties with the Russians seemed greater than with the Americans, he remarked to a visitor at the end of 1960, it was only because the former were publicized. It appeared as if he were in a great quarrel with Lumumba; whereas, in fact, he had had a one-month quarrel with Lumumba and a three-month wrangle with the Belgians.

Belgium was part of the original consensus. It publicly agreed to withdraw its troops on condition that they would be replaced by the UN force. But in a variety of ways it sought to evade its obligations under the Security Council and Assembly resolutions.

Hammarskjold's first experience with Belgian methods occurred in the negotiations over the withdrawal of Belgian troops from Katanga. He thought he had been assured of the Belgian Government's co-operation, but then Tshombe and his Belgian advisers threatened to prevent UN entry with force. This might have reflected Brussels' lack of control over its people in Katanga, but when the Council sternly enjoined it to comply, Brussels was able to get its local representatives to co-operate.

Belgium proved equally evasive in regard to its pledges to withdraw all military forces by August 31. On August 30 Hammarskjold was expressing surprise at the discrepancy "between the information received from Brussels and the facts observed on the scene," regarding the presence of Belgian military units.

A subsequent note reiterated his "formal protest against the delay and against the erroneous information which I have received. In so doing, I feel bound to add the expression of a keen personal disappointment at the doubtful light this casts on the cooperation afforded by the Belgian Government in the spirit of the Security Council resolution."

A few days later, when the Secretary-General was deeply concerned with Soviet military aid to Lumumba, the Belgians were discovered shipping in tons of weapons to Katanga. To Hammarskjold's outraged protest, the Belgians replied disingenuously that the order had been placed before independence and its execution "was due to the incompetence of an ill-informed official."

And when Belgian troops were withdrawn, Hammarskjold found himself engaged in a running battle over the evacuation of Belgian military and para-military personnel, who, under the guise of "technical assistance," entered the Katanga forces. Belgium declined to end such "technical assistance," contending it would weaken the forces of order in Katanga "which is precisely what the Security Council's resolutions aim to avoid."

The deepest rift with Belgium (and the U.S., Britain and France) opened up after the Central Government in Leopold-ville disintegrated into rival power groups. This started with President Kasavubu's ouster of Lumumba as prime minister, an ouster that was promptly challenged by Lumumba and produced constitutional bedlam as ministers, parliamentarians and administrators wrangled over who had the right to do what to whom under the *Loi fondamentale*. Into this bedlam, a few days later, strode twenty-nine-year-old Army Chief of Staff, Colonel Mobutu, who proceeded to "neutralize" both the president and the prime minister, closed down Parliament and sought to govern through a so-called "College of Commissioners."

"Strong man" Mobutu was clearly an inspiration of the Belgians with the reported backing of the U.S.

Hammarskjold's orders to the UN Command and to his special representative, Rajeshwar Dayal of India who had just arrived in Leopoldville, were to stand aside from the political and constitutional jockeying and avoid any action which could even remotely make them a party to the conflict or appear to influence the political balance.

But, as Dayal was to note in his first report to Hammarskjold, this involved delicate and complex judgments which produced criticisms from all sides. While it was relatively easy to adhere to when it came to public pronouncements or balancing an interview with one leader by talks with the others, it was difficult for ONUC to exercise the functions assigned to it without having some impact on domestic matters.

Thus, Lumumba's supporters had raised a storm when Cordier and General von Horn, in an action taken without consulting Hammarskjold but subsequently endorsed by him, had closed the airports and silenced the radio. They did so because they feared that the conflict between Kasavubu and Lumumba would erupt into civil war. But the critics contended that this was interference in Congolese internal affairs; interference, moreover, that benefited the opponents of Lumumba.

Thus, it was ONUC's policy to protect all political leaders, including Lumumba, from arrest and violence. When it barred the arrest of Lumumba, Kasavubu protested to Hammarskjold against the organization's illegal interference in the Congo's internal affairs and "conniving at crimes." But when Lumumba evaded his UN protectors, was captured by Mobutu's forces, and Hammarskjold ruled that the UN did not have the right to liberate him by force, he was denounced as an accomplice of Mobutu.

In his second report, Dayal noted grimly that "the same party which has condemned ONUC for 'interference in domestic affairs' not infrequently challenges it to 'intervene' against the actions of a rival."

Dayal's second report was especially harsh in its strictures against Mobutu. It described him as usurper of political power and called his *Armée Nationale Congolaise* "rabble" and the "principal fomenter of lawlessness." Mobutu's rise to power, the report said further, coincided with a systematic return of the Belgians to the Congo and a developing anti-UN feeling.

The only way out was a return to legality. The two institutions which remained with some semblance of authority and law behind them were the office of the Chief of State and Parliament. If the ANC could be brought under control, a "single government of conciliation" might emerge through the medium of these two institutions.

The Dayal report reflected Hammarskjold's policy. They were in almost hourly touch. It bitterly angered Belgium and its allies, not least of all the U.S.

Obsessed with a fear of a Lumumba comeback, seeking frantically for some point of governmental stability around which to end the drift and decay, the West, led by the U.S., wanted ONUC to bolster Kasavubu and Mobutu in their efforts to establish a central authority in the Congo.

The more firmly ONUC insisted on neutrality, the more openly Kasavubu and Mobutu turned against it. Charles ("Chip") Bohlen, top U.S. adviser on Soviet affairs, was then directing U.S. policy at the UN. Accompanied by Wadsworth, he infuriated Hammarskjold with his peremptory demands and pointed reminders that the U.S. was being asked to foot most of the bill for the Congo operation.

Hammarskjold was pressing Tshombe to "circumscribe the Belgian factor and eliminate it and to move closer towards Leopoldville along the path of reconciliation."

The West thought that was a formula for spreading Leopoldville's anarchy to Elisabethville. Hammarskjold requested Belgium to channel its aid to the Congo through the UN. Belgium, in arguments reminiscent of the Russians in the summer, said such prohibitions constituted an attempt "to place a sovereign state under trusteeship." Belgian Foreign Minister Wigny arrogantly called demands that Belgium channel all aid through the UN "stupid even for the UN" and charged that the UN operation in the Congo was "a failure."

Getting nowhere with Hammarskjold who stood firm on the line of a government of conciliation which would include all factions, and a return to legality, meaning the reconvening of Parliament, the U.S. moved, in November 1960, to take matters out of his hands.

It borrowed a leaf from the book of the Afro-Asian supporters of Lumumba. Ceylon, Ghana, Guinea, India, Indonesia, Mali, Morocco and the UAR had introduced a resolution into the Assembly to seat a pro-Lumumba delegation on the grounds that Lumumba still was the legal government of the Congo. The U.S. and its allies decided to employ the same tactic. President Kasavubu suddenly arrived in New York. Addressing the Assembly as Chief of State—his authority as such was not disputed—President Kasavubu demanded the Assembly seat his delegation.

The demand split the Assembly wide open. More importantly, it split the Afro-Asians whose united support for ONUC was indispensable. Motions to adjourn consideration of the credentials issue were supported by such moderates as Sweden, Tunisia, Nigeria, Togo, Ethiopia. Many of the moderates were reluctant to see the seating issue forced because an Afro-Asian Conciliation Commission was about to leave for the Congo and they felt its task would be rendered more difficult by seating Kasavubu.

But all of NATO was dug in behind Kasavubu, as were the vast majority of French-speaking African states which had just been admitted to the UN. The adjournment motions were beaten down. Accreditation was finally voted 53–24 with nineteen abstentions. But it was a costly victory. The African group was splintered. Six opposed the seating of Kasavubu—Ghana, Guinea, Mali, Morocco, Togo and the UAR; seven abstained— Central African Republic, Ethiopia, Liberia, Libya, Somalia, Sudan and Tunisia; two did not vote at all—Nigeria and Upper Volta. The ten which voted yes were French-speaking African states.

The July consensus now was totally disrupted. How much so was indicated just before Christmas 1960, when the Council and Assembly sought unsuccessfully to clarify and bolster the mandate and role of the UN in the Congo. It was perhaps the lowest point in the Congo operation.

Lumumba, after his flight from UN protection, had been caught. Dayal reported, in early December, that he had been badly beaten after his arrest and imprisoned in Thysville in conditions reported to be "inhumane."

Zorin convened the Council, denounced the UN operation as "a failure" and proposed that ONUC "disarm the terrorist bands of Mobutu," effect the release of Lumumba, and that Parliament be reconvened. "The events in the Congo," a Soviet statement said, should "dispel the spirit of patriarchal trust of the age-old oppressors and their lackeys, of Messrs. Hammarskjold, Bunche and Kasavubu type, which is still in evidence here and there."

"We have been accused of servility in relation to the West, of softness in relation to the East," Hammarskjold commented, "of supporting this or that man in the Congo whom one group or another on the world scene has chosen to make its symbol, or for assisting another man to whom another group has chosen to tie their hopes for the success of interests they wish to safeguard."

But his concern was with the welfare of the Congo and the integrity of the UN.

He wanted his mandate clarified but he did not believe in an imposed solution. The way the Congo's problems would be solved, he said, would be by the "normal political and diplomatic means of persuasion and advice, not by the use of force or intimidation." It would be helpful, however, if the Assembly "morally and politically would strengthen the hands of its representatives."

He would use such strengthened authority to promote national reconciliation and a return to constitutionality, including "the reduction of the position of the Army to its constitutional position."

Despite the efforts of middle-of-the-road diplomats like Slim, the plea went unheeded. No resolution was able to muster sufficient votes either in the Council or the Assembly.

This was doubly unfortunate. The U.S.S.R. and Belgium were busily spreading the notion that the operation had failed. Several of the pro-Lumumba African powers were threatening to withdraw their troops from the Force. And a new peril had developed in mid-December when Antoine Gizenga, Vice Premier and leftist lieutenant of Lumumba, declaring himself the rightful heir of Lumumba, withdrew to Stanleyville, and with the aid and encouragement of the Soviet and left African blocs sought to entrench himself there as the legal government of the Congo.

If the UN were forced out of the Congo, Hammarskjold warned, "the consequence would be immediate civil war, degenerating into tribal conflict fought in the most uninhibited manner." The country would break up into fragments with outside support for the different factions. The world would again be confronted with "a confused Spanish War situation, with fighting going on all over the prostrate body of the Congo and pursued for nebulous and conflicting aims."

He was deeply troubled over the "dual failure" of the Assembly and the Council. Its "most serious aspect" was what it revealed "of the present split within the Organization on this issue of vital significance." He would "naturally" press ahead with the operation in the Congo on the basis of his reading of the mandate and the debates but "the outcome here, as it now stands, has not given us the moral or political support of which the operation is in need."

A few weeks after this, President Kennedy took office, and the new Administration began an immediate reappraisal of its Congo policy, moving in that reassessment to a position much closer to the general African view on what should be done in the Congo.

But before dealing with that new beginning, a word is necessary about the alienation of a substantial group of left African nationalist states, symbolized by Dr. Nkrumah, from the original agreement.

Lumumba, before independence, had taken part in a pan-Africa congress in Accra and regarded Dr. Kwame Nkrumah as his friend and mentor. "My brother," Nkrumah wrote him during the September governmental crisis, "we have been setting the pace for quite a while now and we know how to handle the imperialists and colonialists." With the Brazzaville French-speaking African states about to take a hand in African politics on one side, and an independent Nigeria on the other, Nkrumah's brand of pan-Africanism was likely to be swamped unless he could gain the support of a country as strategically placed as the Congo.

When disaster overwhelmed the newly born Congo, he wanted the UN to move in, but he also wanted to use the UN to further his own pan-African concepts and ambitions.

He was quite distressed to learn that Tunisian troops were scheduled to arrive in Leopoldville first and called Hammarskjold about it. Hammarskjold wanted to satisfy him, but this priority was a matter of logistics rather than politics. The contingents were being airlifted by U. S. Air Force troop carriers based in Germany. The logistics plan the U.S. presented to the UN called for a pickup first of the northernmost contingents and the UN accepted the plan.

Nkrumah, nevertheless, was in first using his own aircraft, and, later, in his impatience to have his troops on the spot, asked the Russians to provide transport, which they did; this brought an admonitory message from the Secretary-General.

By mid-summer, when the Katanga crisis broke, Ghana and Guinea were threatening to withdraw their troops from the UN Command and place them directly at Lumumba's disposal. "Ghana would provide this assistance even though it meant that Ghana and the Congo had to fight alone against Belgian troops," Nkrumah said, adding that Ghana and its African allies "would not be without aid and assistance from other countries. . . ."

It did not help the UN, Hammarskjold told the Council on August 8, "if it has to live under a threat of any one—or more —contributing governments taking matters in its, or their, own hands, breaking away from the UN Force and pursuing a unilateral policy."

The root of the difficulty was Nkrumah's belief that there was "one Africa" with himself destined to be its leader, and that he could bend the UN to this ambition.

He wanted the UN to delegate its functions in the Congo to the independent African states. ONUC and the UN Command should be drawn entirely from the independent African states and non-African troops withdrawn from the Congo.

The UN should collect the funds for Congolese technical assistance but the program should be administered by a Committee of Independent African States accountable to the UN.

The Congolese Army should be retrained by the UN but the retraining center should be established in Ghana, and managed by it, with instructors to be provided by Canada.

This was, in effect, the Korean War formula, when the UN established a Unified Command but delegated the responsibility to the U.S.

But Ghana did not have the power and resources of the U.S. The ranking officer in the Ghanaian Army was an Englishman. Canada turned him down on his request for training instructors.

And the UN, under Hammarskjold, had moved a long way from the Korean-type operation.

From Suez on, executive operations in the UN had not been delegated to member states but carried out by Hammarskjold and the Secretariat.

In the Lebanese disorders of 1958 Nkrumah's approach would have meant making UNOGIL an exclusively Arab group commanded by President Nasser.

Since the U.S. declined to support Nkrumah in his pan-Africanist aspirations, he turned to the Soviet Union, believing he could manipulate Moscow to his purposes. But the result was to encourage Moscow to pursue its own aims. African solidarity was weakened and the U.S. was frightened into giving greater support to Belgium than it otherwise might have done.

Fortunately, Nkrumah did not speak with one voice. Despite his public threats of unilateral action, Nkrumah privately was much more conciliatory and constructive. He was the only one of the Casablanca leaders who did not withdraw his troops from the Congo. The Ghana contingent, unlike the UAR's, obeyed the instructions of the UN Force even when those instructions went against Ghana's policy. Nkrumah's permanent delegate at the UN, Ambassador Quaison-Sackey, was moderate and helpful, and this was on instructions from Nkrumah.

Ghana's co-operation was of the utmost importance to Hammarskjold, outweighing Nkrumah's public blasts and even his private advice to Lumumba not to "throw out the UN troops until you have *consolidated your position*. That will be the time to ask them to go."

African solidarity was indispensable to Hammarskjold. Without the united support of the African caucus, the initial resolutions that were approved by the Council in July and August might never have been adopted. Later in August when the break with Lumumba had taken place and the Soviet Union was pulling away from co-operation with the UN effort, and the meaning of his mandate was in dispute, Hammarskjold formalized and broadened his consultations by establishing an Advisory Committee consisting of the nations which were supplying contingents to the UN force. This was a predominantly African group.

The seating of President Kasavubu in November had fractured African solidarity.

The arrest and beating of Lumumba by forces under the command of Colonel Mobutu added to the disaffection of the African radical nationalists with Hammarskjold. They could not understand how, if Hammarskjold's mandate was to restore law and order, he could take a position of neutrality and nonintervention toward Mobutu, whom Dayal had branded a usurper and who had suppressed Parliament and set aside the country's constitution.

Hammarskjold was not wholly unresponsive to this argument. "It is possible to argue in a purely theoretical way that the maintenance of law and order may embrace the enforcement of basic constitutional law, but it is hardly possible to reconcile this point of view with the actual decisions taken by the Security Council."

To "enforce the Constitution" would involve the UN in "coercive action against competing political factions to a degree that was clearly excluded from the scope of its mandate. Moreover, as several delegates have observed, such forcible intervention in internal constitutional and political conflict could not be considered as compatible with the basic principles of Article 2 of the Charter relating to sovereign equality and nonintervention in domestic jurisdiction."

Nkrumah wanted Hammarskjold to take action to disarm Mobutu's forces. He was critical of the ineffectiveness of the UN Command and claimed the *Force publique* could have been brought under control in one week in the first weeks of the mutiny if the Ghanaian Army had been given the job.

Hammarskjold agreed that private armies loyal to individual political leaders had become a principal source of mischief in the Congo and that these armies aggressively challenged the UN force in its efforts to preserve law and order.

But, he asked, "Why were the critics not, at an earlier stage, interested in widening the mandate, as their comments now indicate, including a disarming of the *Armée Nationale Congolaise?*" In September 1960, when Hammarskjold proposed that his mandate be clarified to include a temporary disarming of Congolese Army factions, the Russians refused, scenting a plot to overthrow Lumumba and establish a UN trusteeship.

The Russians would not admit that they had opposed action in September which they urged in December in regard to what they called "the terrorist bands of Mobutu." Nkrumah, however, had the grace to say: "Nor can I imagine that Premier Lumumba would now dispute the right of the UN to re-establish proper law and order."

But the eight-power resolution presented by such supporters of Lumumba as India, Ghana and the UAR to the General Assembly just before Christmas 1960, and which would have authorized the ONUC to get the armed factions out of the country's political life and free Lumumba, was rejected by a vote of 28 in favor, 42 opposed, and 27 abstentions—hardly constituting a mandate to Hammarskjold.

But neither was there a mandate to disarm Kasavubu's opponents. Gizenga had taken control of Lumumba's old stronghold, Orientale Province, and another Lumumba lieutenant, Anicet Kashamura, had taken over in neighboring Kivu Province. With the aid and encouragement of the Soviet bloc and countries like the United Arab Republic, they were in the process of consolidating their positions.

Kasavubu and his Western backers began to press the UN force in early 1961 to help them subdue the "rebel bands of Gizenga and [Gen.] Lundula." Kasavubu's letters, in January 1961, read almost like a parody of Lumumba's, in August 1960, in regard to Katanga. Gizenga and his colleagues were "subversives" who had "usurped" power. Kasavubu was "astonished" at the UN's legalisms and warned Hammarskjold that "it is of the greatest importance that the Government should receive this military assistance within the framework of the UN, for otherwise it will be compelled to seek assistance outside the UN, despite the manifest danger that would entail of the conflict becoming international."

It was easier to fire away at Dayal than Hammarskjold, and

when he, on the Secretary-General's instructions, turned down their demands for help in subduing Gizenga, Congolese leaders accused him of following an Indian pro-Lumumbist line, just as Lumumba and his supporters had charged Bunche with following an American imperialist line.

They demanded Dayal's recall. Hammarskjold refused. Granting Kasavubu's request that ONUC assist him in disarming the pro-Lumumba forces "cannot be done by me or the UN Force short of new instructions from the Security Council," he wrote the Congolese Chief of State.

He recalled that when Kasavubu had been in New York he had presented a similar demand which he had dropped when the Secretary-General told him that he "personally shouldered responsibility for the actions of Ambassador Dayal" to which Kasavubu took exception.

Again Bohlen and Wadsworth backed by Sir Patrick Dean trooped into Hammarskjold's office to back up Kasavubu's demand, now reinforced by Jaja Wachuku of Nigeria, for the withdrawal of Dayal and to insist on all-out backing for Kasavubu, including the disarming of Gizenga. Hammarskjold turned them down and a story was leaked ("dictated" commented Hammarskjold acidly) in Washington to the New York *Times* which reported that Washington officials were "becoming increasingly uneasy over the trend in the Congo and the performance of the UN there." Dayal was portrayed as "hostile to the Kasavubu Administration and to western influence" and Hammarskjold was described as being "under such heavy pressure from the Communist and Asian-African powers that he has been unable or unwilling to correct the situation."

The U.S. was paying most of the bills, the dispatch went on, "but forces hostile to the West are having more and more influence on what the UN does and what it does not do."

Secretary Herter called and offered apologies for the story. It appeared on the eve of President Kennedy's inauguration and as a grace note added that the new Administration would be told by its "political and military advisers that it must act quickly to redress a bad situation."

Adlai Stevenson's first major move on arrival at the UN was

to hold a series of long note-taking sessions with Hammarskjold in order to orient himself. Stevenson conferred in addition with the Africans and with India as well as America's allies.

The result was a new approach to the Congo, keyed on the part of the U.S. to co-operation with the Afro-Asian states. The elements of this new approach had been foreshadowed in a letter from Hammarskjold to Kasavubu—the freeing of political prisoners, political reconciliation, the convening of Parliament, reorganization and political neutralization of the Congolese armed forces, the elimination of outside aid and stern measures to halt the spreading civil war.

Ambassador Slim and Sir Claude Corea had tried to promote a resolution incorporating these principles at the December meetings of the Security Council "but our efforts were strongly opposed by the U.S. and U.S.S.R.," said Slim. "We came to that resolution in February after the death of Lumumba."

The murder of Lumumba almost snuffed out the new beginning. The Russians, intent on getting the UN out of the Congo and destroying its authority in Africa, unleashed a violent campaign against Hammarskjold as "an accomplice and organizer" of the crime. They formally broke relations with him and introduced a resolution calling for his dismissal and the withdrawal of the Force within a month. The regime of Gizenga was formally recognized and "all possible assistance and support" was promised to it.

"It is vain to argue with those for whom truth is a function of party convenience and justice a function of party interest," Hammarskjold commented icily. The friends of Lumumba had sought to get from the Assembly and Council in December an authorization for ONUC to compel the release of Lumumba and had been turned down. It was not the Secretary-General who determined the mandate nor decided on the means he would have at his disposal.

"A single voice does not change the decision of a major organ and no single member is above the Charter."

Taking note of the Soviet threat of direct intervention in support of Gizenga, Stevenson warned that the U.S. did "not intend to sit by" if that happened, adding: "The only way to keep the cold war out of the Congo is to keep the UN in the Congo."

This last was the view of the Security Council also, and of an Afro-Asian bloc united as it had not been since late summer. The resolution embodying the new approach which had been presented by Ceylon, Liberia and the UAR (Tunisia was no longer a member of the Council) was approved by a vote of 9–0, with France and the Soviet Union abstaining. France, like the Soviet Union, wanted the UN out of the Congo. It believed the whole issue would be better handled outside of the UN on the basis of a joint U.S.–British–French approach. Like the Soviet Union, it refused to pay any share of the costs of the operation.

As for the Soviet "dismiss Hammarskjold—quit the Congo" resolution, it alone voted for it.

There had been substantial withdrawals from the UN force by such pro-Lumumbist countries as Ceylon, Guinea, Indonesia, Morocco, Yugoslavia and the UAR. Nkrumah had also threatened to pull his men out, but in the end kept them in the Congo and backed up Hammarskjold's efforts to find replacements for those withdrawn.

After the February 21 resolution was adopted by the Council, Nehru, a prime mover in the new policy, offered to send Hammarskjold five thousand new troops.

The closing of the ranks among the Afro-Asians, their support for Hammarskjold, the healing of the breach between the Afro-Asians and the U.S. did not please the U.S.S.R. Premier Khrushchev, in a message to Nehru, called for the "speediest termination" of the UN operation and the "withdrawal of all foreign troops." The Africans should take over the UN role in the Congo, he added, in "full contact" with Gizenga.

The Khrushchev letter boomeranged. Nehru did not take kindly to this sort of pressure. He sent Hammarskjold the badly needed troops.

In the resumed session of the General Assembly Gromyko and Zorin again attacked, now adding a new count to their indictment, denouncing Hammarskjold for not implementing the February 21 resolution. The ambush had been anticipated.

The Congo Club, which met for hours at the end of each day on the thirty-eighth floor to go over the day's developments, had been broadened to include Under-Secretary Narasimhan of India, in addition to Brigadier Rikhye, Francis C. Nwokedi of Nigeria, Robert Gardiner of Ghana, and Taieb Sahbani of Tunisia.

With such a group working under the Secretary-General, charges of alleged failure to implement the February 21 resolution because of colonialist sympathies backfired. Moreover, in the weeks following the adoption of the resolution, Hammarskjold was in daily consultation with the Congo Advisory Committee on the resolution's implementation. Sixteen of the committee's members were from Asia and Africa.

"I do not remember any case regarding the implementation where we did not reach consensus" in the Advisory Committee, Hammarskjold informed the Assembly. Before the resumed session was over the Soviet Union was obliged to retreat. Its own resolution, one of the mildest since it broke out of the consensus, was silent on the subject of Hammarskjold and the UN's quitting the Congo and emphasized instead the reconvening of Parliament. It drew only perfunctory support.

Armed with the support of his Congo Advisory Committee and the 83–11 vote of confidence at the resumed session, Hammarskjold, a stubborn and resilient man, went ahead with the work of restoration.

There were still problems. Belgium was still putting up obstacles to the evacuation of military personnel and political advisers. There still were secessionist threats from Tshombe on the right and Gizenga on the left. The Kennedy Administration was as importunate as the Eisenhower in its insistence that Dayal be released. It argued that there was no point in having a special representative of the Secretary-General in the Congo whom Congolese would not deal with. It was a logic Hammarskjold could not accept since Dayal had loyally carried out his policies. In the end Dayal, faced with the unrelenting opposition of Kasavubu and his African and Western backers, asked Hammarskjold to relieve him.

But there was also light at the end of the long tunnel.

Despite the Dayal affair there was encouraging co-operation from President Kasavubu. At least one faction in the Congo, and that which had the greatest legality on its side, now looked to the UN. The U.S. was supporting Kasavubu and the UN in their efforts to bring Katanga under central authority. With UN help the nation was moving towards political reconciliation based on federalism. The danger of civil war was abating. There was agreement with Kasavubu on reorganization of the Army. The descent into chaos had been halted.

Were no mistakes made? Hammarskjold has said yes, but appeared to have in mind mistakes of execution rather than policy. He dislikes not being right, and, as a friendly diplomat commented, can "split a hair finer than anyone else to show consistency." When he scents a position has to be modified, his technique is to work around to it gradually without seeming to make concessions.

A firmer hand by the UN force in the early stages of the operation might have prevented the armed factions from playing as much of a role as they subsequently did. But there was the pledge to the countries contributing troops that they would not be involved in shooting except in self-defense.

The seizure of the airports and silencing of the radio, while clearly justifiable in terms of preventing civil war, was difficult to square with the basic UN policy of nonintervention in domestic affairs.

At the beginning of the operation, Hammarskjold and his aides, on the basis that this was a Secretariat operation, in which the Secretary-General was not simply an instrument of the Council but an interested party, got a little out of touch with governments. There *were* intensive consultations. The Advisory Committee was established *by Hammarskjold* and his repeated requests that the Council and Assembly establish a body with which he could consult on interpretation of the mandate went unheeded. Nevertheless, looking back it is clear the Secretary-General would have been in a stronger position if he had used the Advisory Committee from August onwards as intensively as he did after February 21.

The strong infusion of Afro-Asian elements into the Congo

Club, the informal group of top-level officials directing the day-to-day operations, in retrospect should have been done earlier. The Westerners in this group had worked selflessly and disinterestedly, but symbolism had become important.

It was not in character for Hammarskjold to permit himself to lose contact with a principal in the negotiations, as he did with Lumumba, a diplomat remarked who had worked with the Secretary-General very closely. Lumumba gave him plenty of provocation, this diplomat acknowledged, but so had Ben-Gurion and Nasser, yet he went out of his way to ensure that he remained on speaking terms with them.

The most perplexing question relates to his policy of nonintervention in the Congo's internal politics. John Holmes commented: "There was something wrong with this formula for a country whose desperate handicap was the absence of a strong central government."

Even if Hammarskjold had wanted it, he could not have obtained authorization for an "enforced" political solution, divided as the Assembly and Council were between partisans of different Congolese factions.

And Hammarskjold did not favor such powers. "I reject everything that would have a touch of control or direction of the Congo's internal affairs," he said. He had noted with some surprise, in view of Africa's jealous concern for its newly gained sovereignty, the proposals in this direction "from highly authoritative African sources." He did not believe that "the use of military initiatives, or pressure, is the way to bring about the political structure, in terms of persons and institutions, which at present is the first need of the Congo."

Hammarskjold was no doubt right in insisting on nonintervention. The smaller states in the UN would quickly take fright if it became an instrument for imposed solutions, especially in matters relating to their domestic affairs.

"I can understand the reluctance of the Congolese to have more authority given to the Secretary-General," an Israeli commented. "In Israel the UN is like a separate sovereignty that asserts all kinds of rights in our country."

And Krishna Menon, who wanted to "compel" the Secretariat to take a stronger hand in Congolese internal affairs, in the Suez crisis was strident in his demands that UNEF do nothing in Egypt that might infringe upon its sovereignty.

The UN was on trial in Africa. Its newly independent countries were watching to see not only whether the UN could be relied upon to protect them from the cold war and give them disinterested help in the take-off period, but whether it would do so with a minimum of trespass on their newly gained sovereignty.

This was the first time the UN had undertaken an executive operation of such magnitude within the territory of a member state.

"For our part," said President Bourguiba of Tunisia early in the ONUC operation, "we have chosen to side with the UN."

Nine months later, twenty African states meeting in Monrovia voted to stand firm behind UN efforts to achieve stability in the Congo and to advise all African states against interfering or taking sides with rival Congolese factions. They condemned all efforts to weaken the authority of the UN.

They knew by then that the UN's multi-national army of 20,000, along with a civilian operation of several hundred experts and administrators, had prevented civil war and kept the country afloat administratively and economically.

The Congo had developed into neither a Korea nor a Spain.

An international organization had again demonstrated the capacity to act.

Hammarskjold had kept faith.

The record in the Congo shows him and his colleagues to have been guided "solely by the interest of the Congo and solely by the wish to develop the practices of this Organization in a way which may lay a foundation for future international co-operation."

19

Chairman Khrushchev
Pounds the Desk

On August 1, 1960, the hurricane first was sighted. Chairman Khrushchev proposed that the heads of states personally participate in the disarmament debate of the Assembly session that was scheduled to open September 20.

Since Mr. K. only three months earlier had torpedoed the long-prepared Paris summit in a display of calculated violence and rudeness that had shocked the world, the Western leaders cold-shouldered the bid. They judged that what he had in mind was a propaganda spectacle rather than serious negotiations.

The brush-off did not deter Khrushchev. He announced he was coming to the Assembly anyway as head of the Soviet delegation. The Communist party chiefs of East Europe promptly advised they would do the same. Experienced diplomats began to take hurricane precautions. The Muscovite leader sent out an appeal to the leaders of the Afro-Asian states to join him

in New York, and early in September with the party chiefs of
Bulgaria, Romania and Hungary as shipmates he set sail for
New York in the Soviet ship *Baltika.*

The Russians had asked Hammarskjold to invite Khrushchev
to attend the General Assembly. Since the participation of the
heads of states had become an East-West tug of war, he declined, but when the Soviet Government announced that Khrushchev would head the Soviet delegation, he welcomed the visit
"for the possibility it offers for the presentation of views on the
most responsible level regarding some crucial problems which
the Assembly has to face." It was a guarded comment that
concealed strong private apprehensions.

All summer there had been stinging East-West exchanges over
the U-2 and RB-47 incidents. There had been Soviet threats to
intervene directly in the Congo and Cuba and equally emphatic
U.S. "you-had-better-not" rejoinders. Khrushchev was voyaging
to New York against a background of boasts that he would
make the West "dance like fish in a frying pan." It was not an
atmosphere in which a "summit" Assembly would produce constructive diplomatic results.

One obvious inducement prompting Khrushchev to come to
New York was the prospective admission of sixteen new African states, an influx which was bound to alter the balance of
forces within the Assembly.

Hammarskjold had his own views on how the influx would
affect this balance. The Introduction to his Annual Report,
which was written a few weeks before the opening of the
Assembly, spoke of the countries of Africa and Asia as "powerful elements in the international community" capable of chal-
lenging the authority of the big powers, even though lacking
their military and economic strength. The UN was the "main
platform" and the "main protector" of the interests "of those
many nations who feel themselves strong as members of the international family but who are weak in isolation."

But this was not doctrine that commended itself to Khrushchev. Under his leadership there had been a dramatic ex-
tension of Soviet influence in Asia and Africa and, with Cuba,
the establishment of a promising beachhead in Latin America.

Khrushchev was persuaded that the West burdened with a legacy of colonialism and racism would not be able to withstand his challenge in these areas. The UN was another matter. It was a useful crowbar, perhaps, with which to accelerate the eviction of Western power and influence from Asia, Africa and the Middle East, but he was not going to allow that crowbar to be turned into a policeman's club with which to keep him out. That was "neo-colonialism."

The Soviet Union had become increasingly uneasy over Hammarskjold's concept of the UN as a "protector" and "platform" of the small and weak. It had opposed UNEF even though the parties directly concerned, Israel and Egypt, favored it.

It had sharply rebuked Hammarskjold for his intervention in Laos even though it was at the bidding of the Laotian Government.

It liked even less the fact that Assembly majorities working together with a strong Secretary-General had become a way around the veto. It could not do much about the operations of the Assembly without offending the Afro-Asian bloc. The answer might lie in re-structuring the Secretary-General's office. The U.S.S.R. had tried unsuccessfully at Dumbarton Oaks and San Francisco to obtain a semi-veto over the UN's executive operations. Now these plans were taken off the shelf and brought up to date.

Ever since the first Sputnik, Khrushchev had been searching for ways in which to translate the shift in the military balance of power into political terms.

This was the origin of the demands for parity on UN bodies dealing with disarmament and outer space. It was not a big jump to apply the parity concept to the executive organs of the UN. Perhaps it would not have emerged as dramatically and brutally as it did if it had not been for the Congo. But the Congo confirmed Soviet Russia's worst fears.

As the *Baltika* sailed into New York harbor Zorin's personal attacks on Hammarskjold as a colonialist stooge already had brought from the Secretary-General the statement that he did not know how to interpret Zorin's "strong language." But the Assembly knew him well enough to realize that he would not wish to serve "one day beyond the point at which such continued service would be, and would be considered to be, in the best interests of the Organization."

The 70–0 vote in the Emergency Assembly, a vote that was widely interpreted as a setback to Khrushchev knocking him off balance on the eve of the "summit" Assembly, the way the substantial Soviet operation in the Congo was being eased out by the UN, infuriated Khrushchev and his aides. Their tempers were not improved by the U.S. order confining Khrushchev to Manhattan, except for weekends at Glen Cove.

But the Soviet bloc abstention on the resolution and Khrushchev's deceptively mild shipside statement on landing somewhat allayed anxieties.

The fifteenth General Assembly which opened on September 20 was to be history's most raucous if not most productive diplomatic assemblage. The cast of characters included the most powerful leaders of the Communist states except for Mao Tsetung. There were the neutralist Big Five—Nehru, Tito, Nasser, Nkrumah and Sukarno.

With the neutralists turning up in such force, the leaders of the West, except for an immovable de Gaulle, overcoming their distaste for the huge propaganda circus, starting with Eisenhower and including Macmillan, Diefenbaker and Menzies, put in an appearance. Then there was Fidel Castro, stomping angrily out of one hotel allegedly for discriminatory treatment, moving up to Harlem, bear-hugging with Khrushchev, declaiming for 4½ hours.

Khrushchev turned the staid parliamentary traditions of the Assembly into a shambles, denouncing fellow delegates as "jerks," heckling whenever he was so minded, beating out disapproving tattoos on his desk with his fists, taking off a shoe and angrily brandishing it at a speaker. He would show the Communist world, especially his critics in Peking, how a revolutionary leader could take a bourgeois-dominated parliament and convert it into a platform for revolution.

The disorderly scenes on the inside had their mirror image on the outside where behind solid lines of police who gave the UN enclave the look of a beleaguered precinct, demonstrators, many of them the victims and defeated foes of those on the inside, spat, shouted and brawled, as the captains and kings sped from Assembly Hall to more intimate meetings attended by blue-helmeted motorcycle outriders, their progress proclaimed to the city by screaming sirens.

"How do you feel about Hammarskjold?" a newsman shouted up to Khrushchev as he unexpectedly popped out on the balcony of the Soviet delegation offices on Park Avenue for an impromptu press conference. "Just be patient," the shirt-sleeved Khrushchev shouted down to the upturned faces. "I shall talk about it later."

In the Assembly Hall when general debate began he sat silently through the address of Eisenhower whose arrival and departure were elaborately precautioned against an accidental meeting between the two men. He did not react when Eisenhower declared that attacks on the Secretary-General were "nothing less than a direct attack upon the UN itself" and that the fate of the Congo "will determine whether the UN is able to protect not only the new nations of Africa but also other countries against outside pressures."

But Eisenhower, concerned for the Afro-Asian reaction, avoided recriminations. He appealed for a resumption of disarmament negotiations, for generous aid to Africa and for use of the UN to settle world problems. Neutralist spokesmen were delighted that the address was not "cold war" and even Khrushchev at a Togo party called it "conciliatory."

It was another Khrushchev, however, who marched to the rostrum the next day, bowed to the president of the Assembly, put on his rimmed spectacles and began to speak. He had come to attack, not to parley; to shock, not to assuage.

For the first two hours the assault against the West poured forth—for colonial repression, for dragging its heels on disarmament, for the U-2 affair. Then he turned his guns on Hammarskjold. He had "sided with the colonialists" in the carrying out of the Security Council's decisions on the Congo. This had ominous implications in view of the increasing talk about a UN force that would replace national armies after disarmament. The way the UN force had been misused in the Congo to serve the interests of only one group of states "puts us on our guard."

There was a new relationship of forces in the world. There were no longer two camps, as at the beginning of the UN, but three—the socialist, the capitalist and the neutralist.

The Soviet Government had come to the conclusion that "the post of the Secretary-General who alone governs the staff and alone interprets and executes the decisions of the Security Council and sessions of the UN General Assembly should be abolished." It should be replaced by "a collective executive body" of three who would represent the three camps: "the military blocs of the Western Powers, the Socialist states and the neutralist countries."

As he ended his speech, Khrushchev looked up at the Secretary-General seated on the high presidential rostrum behind him, and smiled. Hammarskjold looked straight ahead. The Soviet bloc delegates applauded wildly, the neutralists tepidly. Others looked grim.

As President Boland banged down the adjournment gavel, Secretary Herter hurried to the office behind the rostrum where he found Boland and Hammarskjold talking together. He wanted to move an immediate vote of confidence but learned that under Assembly rules it could not be done. No vote of confidence, moreover, would be more impressive than the 70–0 vote a few days earlier.

The next best thing Herter felt he could do was to present Hammarskjold immediately with a U.S. check for $5,000,000 that was being contributed in response to Hammarskjold's earlier plea for a $100,000,000 Congo Fund. The gesture was well meant, but only provided additional grist for Communist propaganda mills.

Over the weekend, as he relaxed in Glen Cove, Khrushchev in an expansive mood made it clear the triumvirate proposal was designed to give him a veto over the executive operations of the UN. "All three secretaries must be agreed on a concerted decision," he emphasized to newsmen. "I don't know what you call it," he added puckishly. He declared further that there could be no solution of the disarmament problem without reorganization of the Secretary-General's office on a tripartite basis.

On Monday morning when the session resumed Hammarskjold asked Boland's permission to address the Assembly. In a voice totally devoid of dramatics, as if he were reading a lecture on international law, he made his reply.

The issue was not the man but the institution. "Use whatever words you like, independence, impartiality, objectivity—they all describe essential aspects of what, without exception, must be the attitude of the Secretary-General.

"Such an attitude," he went on, "may at any stage become an obstacle for those who work for certain political aims which would be better achieved if the Secretary-General compromised with this attitude. But if he did, how gravely he would then betray the trust of all those for whom the strict maintenance of such an attitude is their best protection in the world-wide fight for power and influence."

He would rather see the office of Secretary-General "break on strict adherence to the principles of independence, impartiality and objectivity than drift on the basis of compromise. That is the choice daily facing the Secretary-General."

It was also the choice now facing the Assembly, he added. As Hammarskjold ended this spirited but impersonally delivered defense of his office, an ovation swept the Assembly Hall. It gathered force and Khrushchev began the first of his deskpounding demonstrations.

Khrushchev's speech, Hammarskjold suggested, perhaps had even raised the "question of confidence." Khrushchev soon removed all ambiguity on the point. Exercising his "right of reply" the Soviet leader made it clear that the Congo was incidental, that he was raising a personal as well as a constitutional issue, and that there had been a major shift in Soviet policy toward the UN reflecting what the Soviet leaders assessed to be the new correlation of forces in the world.

The world situation had been radically altered since the founding of the UN, Khrushchev said. The UN structure was now "out of date." A billion people lived under "socialism." Another billion were to be found living in the neutralist states of Asia and Africa. Neither of these blocs was adequately represented in the organs of the UN, especially the Secretariat.

"Only one man" was the interpreter and executor of the decisions of the Council and Assembly, but there were no "saints on earth" capable of defending the interests of all three groups.

"Is it not clear whose interests he interprets and executes, whose 'Saint' he is? Mr. Hammarskjold has always been biased with regard to the socialist countries, he has always upheld the interests of the U.S. and other countries of monopoly capital." The Congo was only "the last drop" that filled his "cup of patience to overflowing.

"To avoid misinterpretation, I want to reaffirm that we do not trust Mr. Hammarskjold and cannot trust him. If he himself does not muster up enough courage to resign, so to say, in a chivalrous manner, then we shall draw the necessary conclusions from the situation obtaining."

Hammarskjold listened impassively. He knew what he had to do. His reply was clearly blocked out in his mind. As Khrushchev went on to other subjects Hammarskjold leaned over to Boland and said he would like the floor. As they both pressed buttons disconnecting the loud-speakers, Boland suggested, "Perhaps you ought to think it over and do it this afternoon."

Although he knew what he was going to say, Hammarskjold agreed. When the session adjourned he talked briefly with the Ethiopian Foreign Minister and then went up to the thirty-eighth floor where he was soon joined by Cordier, Bunche and Wieschhoff. There was agreement that Khrushchev was trying to drive Hammarskjold into resigning. Hammarskjold quickly dictated his reply, showed it around and sent it off to be mimeographed.

When the session resumed, the Assembly Hall was crowded, the atmosphere electric with tension and all eyes riveted to Hammarskjold. Boland gave him the floor. Again the high-pitched, cool tones rang out. Where Khrushchev had stormed, he understated. His appeal was to men "free of mind" and his faith that "only on a scrutiny of truth can a future of peace be built."

The issue, he repeated, was not "of a man but of an institution. The man does not count, the institution does. A weak or non-existent executive would mean that the UN would no longer be able to serve as an effective instrument for active protection of the interests of those many Members who need such protection. The man holding the responsibility as chief executive should leave if he weakens the executive; he should stay if this is necessary for its maintenance."

This alone should be the controlling consideration.

Khrushchev that morning had said the Soviet Union found it impossible to work with him. "This may seem to provide a strong reason why I should resign." However, the Soviet Union was also insisting that he should be replaced by a triumvirate which "would make it impossible to maintain an effective executive.

"By resigning, I would, therefore, at the present difficult and dangerous juncture throw the Organization to the winds. I have no right to do so. . . ." Here a wave of applause interrupted him. When it died down, he resumed: "I have no right to do so because I have a responsibility to all those states members for which the Organization is of decisive importance, a responsibility which overrides all other considerations."

Trygve Lie, confronted by a comparable Soviet campaign to drive him out, had been kept in office mainly by the U.S. But the UN had changed since 1950. It was now primarily the organization of the small and the weak.

"It is not the Soviet Union or, indeed, any other big powers who need the UN for their protection; it is all the others. In this sense the Organization is first of all *their* Organization, and I deeply believe in the wisdom with which they will be able to use it and guide it.

"I shall remain in my post . . ." Here again Hammarskjold was stopped by a hail of applause as Khrushchev followed by his Communist colleagues futilely pounded their desks. It was minutes before he was allowed to continue. "I shall remain in my post during the term of my office as a servant of the Organization in the interests of all those other nations, as long as *they* wish me to do so."

Khrushchev had spoken of the "courage" to resign. "It is very easy to resign; it is not so easy to stay on. It is very easy to bow to the wish of a big power. It is another matter to resist. As is well known to all members of this Assembly, I have done so before on many occasions and in many directions.

"If it is the wish of those nations who see in the Organization their best protection in the present world, I shall now do so again."

As Hammarskjold finished, Slim was on his feet leading an ovation in which most of the delegates except for the Soviet bloc and a few of the neutrals joined. It was an emotional scene. Hammarskjold later analyzed it quite objectively—what the delegates had responded to was the spectacle of one man standing up to a superpower, he thought.

The next night Khrushchev was host to a party. An invitation had reached Hammarskjold just after Khrushchev's demand that he resign. He called in a Soviet member of the Secretariat and asked him to find out whether the invitation was seriously meant or a technical error. Word came back that it was serious. Hammarskjold decided he had an obligation to attend. As long as it was possible, Hammarskjold wanted to differentiate between Khrushchev on the platform and Khrushchev personally and keep the personal relationship intact. When he arrived at 680 Park Avenue he was welcomed by Khrushchev who embraced him in a boisterous bear hug and banteringly advised him not to "bet on the bad horse of capitalism. Put your bets on the good horse of socialism." He should have more Soviet aides around him, Khrushchev added. He would be happy to, Hammarskjold replied, if Khrushchev supplied him with officials like Madame Mironova, the handsome third-ranking member of the Soviet delegation who had led him to Khrushchev.

Afterwards Janos Kadar, the Hungarian Communist leader was heard to ask Khrushchev why he had been so demonstratively cordial. "Do you know the tradition of the mountain people of the Caucasus in our country?" Khrushchev asked. "When an enemy is inside your house, sharing your bread and salt, you should always treat him with the greatest hospitality.

But as soon as he steps outside your door, it is all right to slit his throat."

Moscow's real attitude to Hammarskjold's defiance of the Soviet goliath was being disclosed in the Soviet press. It spoke of his "pompous" address, of his "delusions of grandeur" and of "megalomania." *Pravda* asked whether he was "really so conceited as to think the UN and mankind cannot exist without him?"

Nonetheless, nine days later Khrushchev, in a farewell statement in the Assembly, insisted: "I am not fighting Mr. Hammarskjold personally. We have met. We have had very courteous and pleasant conversations. In fact, I consider that Mr. Hammarskjold is beholden to me. When he was my guest on the Black Sea, he exploited me; I rowed him around and he has not paid back in kind. So, as representatives will see, this is not a personal matter." Khrushchev then emphasized what he was later to make explicit to Walter Lippmann in the statement that "There are no neutral men." The point is, Khrushchev explained to the Assembly, "I am a Communist, while Mr. Hammarskjold represents large capital."

To which Hammarskjold asked the indulgence of the Assembly to say "just two words to the spokesman of the Soviet Union.

"I was very happy to hear that Mr. Khrushchev has good memories of the time when I had the honor to be rowed by him on the Black Sea. I have not, as he said, been able to reply in kind. But my promise to do so stands, and I hope the day will come when he can avail himself of this offer. For if he did I am sure that he would discover that I know how to row— following only my own compass."

Khrushchev's personal show of cordiality toward Hammarskjold was not just guile. The Communist leaders had maximum and minimum objectives at the Assembly and at this stage were not convinced that a campaign for Hammarskjold's ouster could be combined with their efforts to woo Africa and Asia.

Wladyslaw Gomulka, the Polish party chief, talking with newsmen directly after Khrushchev's you-should-have-the-courage-to-resign speech, blandly asserted that "I cannot share your impression that Mr. Khrushchev asked Mr. Hammarskjold to resign from his post. The fact that there are certain differences of opinion between Mr. Nehru and Mr. Khrushchev shows that study is needed."

Khrushchev was pressing many aims at the General Assembly. Richard Lowenthal, an astute analyst of Soviet affairs, wrote afterwards that Khrushchev's "inconsistencies" at the Assembly are "incomprehensible unless the fact is borne in mind that during all this time Khrushchev was engaged in an effort to prove his revolutionary zeal and international solidarity in preparation for the Moscow conference" at which there was to be a showdown between Moscow and Peking over their ideological differences.

Although Khrushchev on his return to Moscow from New York boasted of the victories he had scored, *Jenmin Jih Pao,* the official organ of the Chinese Communists, complained of the "monstrous insults" hurled at Premier Khrushchev in the Assembly, adding that it remained "a tool of U.S. imperialism, a voting machine for it to pursue its policies of aggression and war."

In the eyes of the Peking dogmatists, the Assembly, like any bourgeois parliament, was a trap and a morass. Khrushchev had to demonstrate that he could convert it to revolutionary purposes, that peaceful coexistence as embodied in the UN could be turned into "the highest form of class struggle." To make this script credible and easily understood it was convenient to cast Hammarskjold in the role of representative of the capitalists and savage him up.

At the same time Khrushchev did not want to disrupt his ties with the left neutralists. None of them had supported his proposal for a triumvirate, but neither had they rushed into a passionate defense of Hammarskjold. They were uneasy over developments in the Congo and embittered by the West's hostile treatment of their bid to bring about a resumption of contacts between Eisenhower and Khrushchev.

Nasser managed to make a major address to the Assembly without mentioning Hammarskjold or Khrushchev's proposals for reorganization. Nkrumah refrained from personal criticism of the Secretary-General but proposed the appointment of three deputies representing the three blocs each invested with "clearly defined authority" of his own. Nehru, while opposed to dilution of the executive powers of Hammarskjold's office, advocated a cabinet of senior advisers. Tito favored doing something to limit or modify the powers of the Secretary-General, although he was averse to any formula which reflected a "bloc" approach to the problem.

Not wanting to get too far out of step with the left neutralists, Khrushchev hinted that his demands for a triumvirate only represented a "maximum" position; at the same time he pressed ahead determinedly with his campaign to obtain a veto over the executive operations of the UN and to weaken Hammarskjold's influence in areas like Africa, the Middle East and Asia.

In the Assembly's Administrative and Budgetary Committee, after Khrushchev left, the Soviet delegate criticized as "improper" Hammarskjold's policy of dispatching special representatives to potential trouble spots, even though he had done so at the invitation of the governments concerned. In sending a technical assistance group to Laos, Hammarskjold had "clearly exceeded his duty." And the Soviet delegate wondered "what administrative problem had impelled the Secretary-General himself to visit Laos in November 1959." Perhaps it was connected with the "political needs" of the U.S., he suggested. "In making a political visit of that nature without the requisite authorization from the Security Council, the Secretary-General had exceeded his competence."

Nor was Laos the only country affected by Hammarskjold's growing practice of sending representatives, on the pretext of the need for urgent economic measures, to various parts of the globe where events took place that caused concern to the U.S. and its allies. Another case in point, the Soviet representative charged, was the assignment of a special representative to Guinea in 1958 at a cost of $39,300.

Such criticism, replied Hammarskjold, ignored "Article 99 and what follows from that Article. If the Secretary-General is entitled to draw the attention of the Security Council to threats to peace and security, has he to rely on reports in the press or from this or that government? Has he to take the word of Moscow or Washington? No, certainly not. He has to find out for himself and that may mean, as in the case of the criticized journey to Laos last November, that he has to go himself. To deny the Secretary-General the right to such personal fact-finding, is in fact to erase from the Charter Article 99."

The technical assistance mission to Laos had been sent "at the request of the Chief of State and his legitimate Government." The Soviet objection would mean that governmental appeals for practical help could not be answered unless approved by the Security Council where it would be subject to the veto or by the Assembly which might not be in session when the need arose.

"Those countries who wish to have the independent assistance of the UN, in the modest forms possible for the Secretary-General and without running into the stormy weather of a major international political debate, will certainly be interested in the attitude of the delegate of the Soviet Union.

"What is true of Laos is true of Guinea. At the moment when that was a most unpopular move in parts of the world which the Soviet delegate alleges that I represent, I offered President Sekou Touré our practical assistance. He and his Government wanted it, accepted it and used it."

His policy of preventive diplomacy had been no secret, he went on. It had been spelled out fully in the Introductions to his Annual Reports. What the Soviet Union now sought was to reduce UN technical assistance to "marginal expert work" and the Secretary-General to "chief administrator of a Secretariat technically assisting a vast conference machinery."

The choice was up to the member governments. "They can choose the line which slowly has been emerging in response to current needs over the last few years, or they can choose to fall back on the pattern of the League of Nations or of the most conservative interpretation of the Charter of the present Organization."

All through the session the Soviet bloc delegates cannonaded away. "No argument has been left untried," Hammarskjold observed just before the Christmas recess. The session had been witness to "a concerted and consistent effort . . . to create conditions for a radical change of the administrative structure of the Organization, and, with that in view, to corrode whatever confidence there may be among members in the integrity of its Secretariat."

The Soviet onslaught against the Secretariat turned into a series of accusations against staff members in which their crimes were not what they had said or done but their nationality. One day a low-ranking official would be pulled out of obscurity and attacked, not for his activities as a UN employee, but because he left Hungary after the war and once worked for Radio Free Europe.

Another day the Legal Office would be pilloried for having obtained the co-operation of the Harvard Law School in drafting a document for the International Law Commission. The merits of the document were not dealt with; instead, the fact that Harvard jurists were asked to do the job automatically rendered it culpable. And could one expect a Legal Office that was 75 per cent staffed by citizens of the U.S. and its "military allies" to go elsewhere than to Harvard?

The Soviet representative in the Second Committee did not like the picture of Soviet economic growth to be found in a 1959 document. By 1960 such "distortion" had become inevitable because "western representatives" ran the Soviet economics section in the Economic Department. Ruefully the U.S. delegate commented that the U.S. did not always like Secretariat analyses either. "But that is not a reason to make war on the UN Secretariat," he added.

Hammarskjold indignantly rejected Soviet accusations that staff members were "the spokesmen of one power bloc or another because of their passports." Men and women who served the Organization "in the true spirit of the Charter, with an integrity beyond praise and a loyalty which does not suffer reservation" deserved "much better."

The Soviet attack on the "bias" of the Secretariat was part of a campaign for larger Communist representation in the Secretariat. There was general agreement the Soviet bloc was under-represented, but it had never before been suggested that Communists had to be employed because there were no neutral men. To accept this thesis would mean abandonment of the Charter concept of an international civil service, independent, impartial, free from national pressures and responsible to the Organization alone.

Nor had it been suggested previously that failure to employ more East Europeans on the Secretariat was a result of Hammarskjold's bias. He had done his best to improve matters as openings presented themselves, but he did not believe people should "be fired for nationality reasons in order to provide possibilities for the UN to arrive at another geographical balance."

But any stick was good enough with which to pound away at Hammarskjold. In January 1961 the Soviet Union even employed an inverted form of racialism in its campaign to drive Hammarskjold out of office. It charged him with greater solicitude for whites than blacks in providing UN protection in the Congo. Finally, in February, after the assassination of Lumumba, the Soviet Government burned its bridges. It accused Hammarskjold of being "a participant in and organizer" of the crime and demanded his dismissal. "The Soviet Government, for its part, will not maintain any relations with Hammarskjold and will not recognize him as an official of the UN."

Gromyko, who returned for the resumed session in March 1961, taunted him with having become "some sort of a UN field-marshal," accused him of usurping the prerogatives of the Assembly and Council, and predicted that if he was allowed to follow this course further "he may assume himself to be the Prime Minister of a world government and, for all we know, may claim that *'les Nations Unies—c'est moi.'* "

The Gromyko performance was outrageous and caused a feeling of revulsion in the Assembly, but Hammarskjold felt that before it adjourned he should keep the record clear, particularly on the issue of usurpation of powers, a charge which had come increasingly to the forefront of the Soviet campaign. He was not hanging on to a job. He would have walked out a long time ago but for a sense of responsibility and duty.

Every member of the Assembly knew why over the years "and again in the Congo crisis, the Security Council and the General Assembly have found it convenient to entrust, in very general terms, executive action on highly explosive problems to the Secretary-General.

"If the Soviet Union regrets its participation in these decisions, it is their right, but is it their opinion now that the Secretary-General, in anticipation of their own afterthoughts, should have refused to respond to requests for which they themselves had voted?"

He reminded the Assembly his fate was in its hands, especially in the hands of the smaller nations. He did not consider himself entitled to resign at the demand of a big power. "On the other hand, I regard the will of the General Assembly in this respect as my law, and the General Assembly may thus consider itself as seized with a standing offer of resignation, were it to find it to be in the best interest of the Organization that I leave."

Soviet withdrawal of confidence had reduced his usefulness, and members of the Assembly would take that into account. But they also had to take into account whether they wanted to extend a big power's right of veto from the election of a Secretary-General to his daily conduct of business. Yielding to the Soviet Union would mean that a big power by withdrawing its co-operation could at any time "break the term of office of the Secretary-General."

The Soviet demand for his dismissal was up to the Assembly and in particular up to "that vast majority of members who have an overriding interest in the proper functioning of the Organization and who cannot be suspected of reflecting any bloc interests."

It was subsequent to this speech that the Assembly gave him the 83–11 (Soviet bloc plus Cuba and Guinea) vote of confidence. There were five abstentions on this vote, curious bedfellows—France, Portugal, Morocco, Mali and Yugoslavia.

Yet the Soviet campaign was not without very serious effects. Hammarskjold's capacity for preventive diplomacy had been restricted, his popular image in Africa, the Middle East and

Asia dimmed and the UN reputation in Africa blackened. General Kettani of Morocco, one of its ablest generals, found himself a stranger in his own country for having upheld the Secretary-General's policies in the Congo. Communist front meetings in Asia and Africa busily were passing resolutions calling for the dismissal of Hammarskjold and denouncing "the treacherous role of the UN" which "has become an instrument of neo-colonialism."

When the next crisis erupts in Africa—be it Angola or South West Africa—will it be possible to use the UN and launch an executive operation of the scope which kept the Congo afloat and the great powers from rushing in?

The Soviet Union does not want an international organization which with a rough approximation to impartiality and independence can serve as a buffer between the great powers in the revolutionary areas of the world and as a force for stability and order.

May the Soviet Union not be making a mistake on the order of its incorrect assessment of Nazism? In the twenties the Communists helped destroy the Weimar Republic, assuming that with the democratic center eliminated, they would, after a brief Nazi interlude, inherit Germany.

It is significant that Khrushchev compares Hammarskjold to Kerensky, the democratic socialist whom the Bolsheviks overthrew in order to come to power in Russia. But can Khrushchev be so certain that with the UN pushed to the sidelines, the Soviet Union will be the main beneficiary of "wars of liberation," revolution and turbulence in the great emergent areas of the world?

20

One-Man Job

Before the Soviet hurricane hit, Hammarskjold had been warned by a high Soviet official it was coming and encouraged to hold tight and ride it out. But the unexpectedly personal nature of the Soviet attack, especially the shocking effort to link him with the assassination of Lumumba, made it highly unlikely that even if before the autumn of 1962 when new elections for the post of Secretary-General will be held, there were a 180-degree shift in Soviet policy, it would encompass a reconciliation between Hammarskjold and the Soviet leaders.

If he refused to resign after the Soviet withdrawal of confidence, it was out of a sense of responsibility to the Organization and a determination to protect and preserve the executive prerogatives of the office which he held and which he had so carefully nurtured.

This, along with carrying the Congo operation through to a

successful conclusion, became his overriding preoccupations after the Soviet storm abated.

There was little support outside of the Soviet bloc for the Khrushchev triumvirate formula. Involving an amendment of the Charter, it was not considered practical politics. But there were other proposals whose consequence would be to weaken and dilute the capacity of the Secretary-General for swift political initiative and efficient executive action. These worried him more.

There was Nkrumah's formula for sharing out the powers of the Secretary-General to three deputies, representing the three blocs, who would not serve "merely as his assistants." Nehru, while opposed to Khrushchev's "three-headed God" idea, urged that Hammarskjold himself consider the creation of a cabinet of senior political advisers representing the different world trends so that he would be able to keep in view all the time the forces pulling in different directions. France, too, favored a variant of the cabinet idea. It had opposed his abolition of the post of Assistant Secretary-General, believing that with the Secretary-General coming from a small nation, it was prudent to surround him with Assistant Secretaries-General from the big powers and blocs who could share with him the policy-making task.

But proposals for reform of the Secretary-General's office ran into three barriers—the Charter, the facts of international life and Hammarskjold's personality.

Under the Charter, the Secretary-General is the only elected official in the Secretariat and is alone vested with explicit political responsibility. He is described further as the Organization's "chief administrative officer" and the executive tasks decided upon by the Council or Assembly are specifically to be entrusted "to him." At San Francisco "the idea of a 'cabinet system' in which responsibility for the administration and political functions would be distributed among several individuals were squarely rejected," Hammarskjold reminded the UN.

Thus the Charter makes the post a one-man job; equally so does the existence of a divided world. Nations otherwise opposed to each other were willing to confide tasks to the UN on the condition that they were personally handled by a Secretary-General whose independence, discretion and competence they trusted.

What was legally stipulated and politically necessary dovetailed with Hammarskjold's strong personal proclivities. Able to do three or four times the work of the average civil servant, a first-rate economist, diplomatist and jurist, with standards "too high, too quick, too critical" to permit delegation of authority, the top-level Secretariat soon after his arrival was reorganized around his extraordinary abilities and enormous capacity for work.

But the crushing burdens of the Congo and the influx of African states made a different allocation of work at the top a necessity. Hammarskjold had begun examining how this might be done even before the Khrushchev attack.

His 1960 Report had called attention to the Organization's lack of highly qualified senior officials. Secretariat organization at the Under-Secretary level which had been adequate for a UN consisting of sixty members would not suit one that was soon to number more than a hundred, with most of the newcomers from Africa.

Congo spurred the reappraisal. More coded cables came in from the Congo in a month requiring his personal attention than from the Suez in a year. Laos except at moments of crisis could be handled by one hour's consideration a day, Suez by a few. But the Congo had meant sixteen, seventeen, eighteen hours' work a day over a period of ten months.

For the first time he began to feel there was a real danger of overburdening the Secretary-General. To deal with the problems that came across his desk—from Africa, the Middle East, Asia—he had to have a fingertip knowledge of the facts, the backgrounds, the personalities. He had to acquire this knowledge without the world-wide diplomatic and intelligence services available to national governments.

"Delegate," both friends and critics, advised him. Yet this was not possible in the UN. In a national government, a chief executive could say, "I myself don't know, but I know my man and I will put my name to his conclusions." That cannot be done in an international organization, Hammarskjold asserts. His collaborators are of different national backgrounds and while he might have complete confidence in them, the outer world does not.

Men like Cordier, Bunche, Wieschhoff did not give a damn what Washington said, if they disagreed with Washington; Hammarskjold knew that, but the outside world says, "We hope so, but . . ." That is what made it so difficult to reduce the one-man aspect. Dayal was a man of high integrity, professional competence, absolutely independent of New Delhi—as much so as Bunche was of Washington. Yet the attack on him, even after Hammarskjold made it clear he fully backed up the decisions made by Dayal, was "but after all, this is Indian policy."

When he went to the Congo at the beginning of 1961 he called to New York Mekki Abbas, the Sudanese executive secretary of the Economic Commission for Africa, and left him in charge of the Congo operation. It had been run very well by a few people, but whatever his confidence in Bunche, Wieschhoff, MacFarquhar, that confidence would not be shared by the outside world because one was British, the other two Americans. So he brought Abbas to New York although he was badly needed in Addis Ababa.

Ambassador and statesmen, when they came in to head-quarters for a tour d'horizon, were not content to see an Under-Secretary; they wanted to talk with the Secretary-General personally so they could cable back to their home capital: "This is the way the SG views the problem."

There were times when the Secretary-General had to say to a delegation, "Sorry, but this is my firm personal conclusion." Such stands would carry less weight if the delegation felt the conclusion was based on secondhand reports and analyses.

Quiet diplomacy would be ruled out if the Secretary-General was obliged to share his political responsibilities. Delegations "can confide in him fully, freely and frankly because they know he will respect their confidence," Narasimhan pointed out in a speech reflecting Hammarskjold's own thinking on the subject.

"If he has to have, say, three advisers sitting with him all the time when he is meeting with either Delegations or visiting world statesmen, it is obvious that such a full and free and frank interchange of views cannot possibly take place."

Charter changes would not solve the problem of devolution of political responsibility. Neither would it be solved by a collegial body or some system of checks and balances. The appearance of objectivity might be achieved, but at the price of efficiency.

He wanted to reduce the one-man aspect, but he had not been able to come up with an alternative, although he was very keen to do so.

The best approach was to put together different task forces for each problem. Just as there were different advisory committees for the Congo and the Suez, so Secretariat groups would be tailored to meet the specific requirements of a crisis. A standing cabinet would introduce an element of rigidity, since the same group would not be the best in all situations.

As for a cabinet's keeping him in touch with the thinking of different regions—Nehru's main argument—he still felt, as he did in 1953, he could get the thinking of countries from the permanent representatives whose advice was available to him at all times.

There were, moreover, great practical difficulties with the concept of a cabinet consisting of regional representatives. Would the countries of Southeast Asia agree to India as the spokesman for all of them? Or would Africa south of the Sahara accept someone from North Africa? What Arab would be authorized to speak for all of Araby? A cabinet assumed that one or two men could speak for a continent; whereas no nation was ever willing to let someone else speak for it—not even in Scandinavia, Hammarskjold noted, despite its homogeneity.

He did see a need for an increased number of senior diplomatic officials, recruited from Asia, Africa and East Europe, to serve as Under-Secretaries for Special Political Affairs, who would travel a good deal as well as be available for operational task forces. And he suspected that in many cases a diplomat from outside the region might have greater access to its capitals than one from the inside.

The Charter, in addition to prescribing paramount standards of integrity and competence, says the composition of the Secretariat should show due regard for geographical representation. Hammarskjold's problem was to meet the claims of representative symbolism without sacrificing internal administrative flexibility and without compromising the concept of an international civil service responsible to the UN alone.

What Khrushchev did in 1960 as part of his drive to secure a veto over the Organization's day-to-day operations was to take the geographical criterion and make it the overriding one. A man's loyalty was determined by his passport. Hammarskjold's colonialist and NATO bias was additionally proved by the nationality of the men he surrounded himself with. The only way to ensure an impartial Secretariat was to give the three blocs equal representation at all levels.

"Geographic distribution means geographic distribution," Hammarskjold insisted, "and nothing but that. The phrase has to be seen in conjunction with the Charter demand for full and exclusive loyalty of the international civil servant to the Organization, the other side of this demand being that UN officials should sever all their ties of interest or loyalty with whatever may be their home country."

Geographic distribution, therefore, could not mean a balanced representation of interests or ideologies. "The Secretariat is international in the way in which it fulfills its functions, not because of its geographic composition but because of the attitudes of the members of the Secretariat and the truly international spirit in which they fulfill their tasks—if that had not been the view, the Charter would certainly have made wide geographic representation a primary consideration, instead of subordinating it to a demand for integrity."

Hammarskjold does not assume that the Soviet approach to service in the Secretariat means that no Soviet national can function as an international civil servant. A man's independence is partly a function of his intelligence. The sophisticated Soviet employee could take the view that he is on the UN staff with the approval of his government, and that if his government approves of his employment by the UN, then it also approves his playing according to the rules.

When Zorin came in during Christmas week 1960 with requests that forty additional Soviet nationals be employed by the UN, including two Under-Secretaries, Hammarskjold immediately called in his top aides to see how much of the request could be accommodated.

His general rule is not to put staff members on assignments where they are likely to come under pressure from their delegations. It would only have embarrassed a Frenchman if he had been put to work on the Suez problem. But it was a question of degree. The concept of an international civil servant unbiased by his nationality is new, not widely understood and less widely accepted. The state ethos in the Soviet Union is such that the area in which a Soviet staff member would not be embarrassed by a UN assignment that ran counter to his country's policy was infinitely smaller than the area in which a Swede or a Swiss would not feel embarrassed.

For Hammarskjold the main criterion in choosing personnel was "integrity." And to him integrity meant that "officials should have only *one* loyalty in the performance of their duties, and that is the one to the UN. Those who do not see their job in that light or who are forced to act on a basis of a different standard, may still be useful in a UN operation, but the difference of the rules of integrity which they apply can never be forgotten by the Chief Executive—and that is true whatever their nationality!"

It was known at UN headquarters during the Suez crisis that top-ranking Englishmen in the Secretariat disagreed with their country's policy, in the Lebanese crisis that Ralph Bunche and Andrew Cordier criticized the U.S. decision to land marines, and that in the Congolese crisis Rajeshwar Dayal took exception to some of the positions taken up by his country.

But such disagreement between Soviet nationals employed on the UN staff and their country's policy are unknown and almost inconceivable given the Soviet view that loyalty to the party is supreme. The Soviet reply to Hammarskjold is that no disjunction can be set up between integrity and geographical representation. "The two considerations were complimentary; they were in no way opposed to each other and could not be separated." Carried to its logical conclusion, Hammarskjold's reasoning, said one Soviet spokesman, implied that "traitors to their country might be considered as the best possible recruits for the UN."

It was not only the Soviet Union which was skeptical of the concept of an international civil service whose members' loyalties would remain with the UN even in a clash with their own governments. Influential voices in the West, notably in France, but with sympathetic echoes in the U.S. and Britain, even argued that an international secretariat reflecting the viewpoint of an alleged international conscience was both unrealistic and an added source of international tension.

An alarmed Hammarskjold called attention to these tendencies in a major address at Oxford University in May 1961. One specific issue was permanent versus limited-term appointments to the staff. The "Realists" were urging emphasis on the latter. This issue had been discussed at the founding of the UN. The London Preparatory Commission had concluded that Secretariat members could not be expected "fully to subordinate the special interests of their countries to the international interest if they are merely detached from national administrations and dependent upon them for their future." He had tried to build a career service that was "politically celibate," if not "politically virgin," he said in Oxford, but recently "assertions have been made that it is necessary to switch from the present system, which makes permanent appointments and career service the rule, to a predominant system of fixed-term appointments to be granted mainly to officials seconded by their governments. This line is prompted by governments which show little enthusiasm for making officials available on a long-term basis, and, moreover, seem to regard—as a matter of principle or, at least, of 'realistic' psychology—the international civil servant primarily as a national official representing his country and its ideology."

Such a line would transform an "international" Secretariat into an "intergovernmental Secretariat, the members of which obviously would not be supposed to work in the direction of an internationalism considered unpalatable to their governments."

Hammarskjold solemnly warned that peace might be the price of abandoning the principles of an international civil service. "Such passive acceptance of a nationalism rendering it necessary to abandon present efforts in the direction of internationalism symbolized by the international civil service—somewhat surprisingly regarded as a cause of tension—might, if accepted by the Member Nations, well prove to be the Munich of international cooperation as conceived after the First World War and further developed under the impression of the tragedy of the Second World War."

The nub of the problem was the assumption stated most explicitly by Khrushchev that there can be no neutral men.

Could the Secretariat, and more particularly, the Secretary-General, implement controversial political decisions in a manner fully consistent with an exclusively international responsibility? Much of Hammarskjold's Oxford address was devoted to answering this key question.

If the answer were in the negative some form of plural executive would have to be instituted. And a plural executive has traditionally been the prescription for executive inaction and impotence.

He did not dispute that he frequently had to exercise his own political judgment, since he had been handed mandates "of a highly general character, expressing the bare minimum of agreement attainable" in the Council or Assembly. That had been the case in Palestine, Lebanon and the Congo. The execution of vague mandates in highly charged situations was bound to create controversy. Conflicting interpretations could be referred back to the Council or Assembly but often it was not possible for them to agree on more explicit instructions to the executive.

Should he then have refused to implement the resolution, as some had urged, "since implementation would offend one or another group of Member States and open him to the charge that he has abandoned the political neutrality and impartiality essential to his office?" Such a refuge "may be tempting" but would it be "compatible with the responsibility placed upon the Secretary-General by the Charter?"

The answer to him seemed "clear enough in law; the responsibilities of the Secretary-General under the Charter cannot be laid aside merely because the execution of decisions by him is likely to be politically controversial."

This brought Hammarskjold to the "crucial issue: Is it possible for the Secretary-General to resolve controversial issues on a truly international basis without obtaining the formal decision of the organs" and to do so "without subservience to a particular national or ideological attitude?"

If he answered affirmatively it was not because he considered himself "a kind of Delphic oracle who alone speaks for the international community." There were various signs and markers to keep him from going off the path of independence and impartiality. There were the principles and purposes of the Charter which though "general and comprehensive" were "specific enough to have practical significance in concrete cases." These were "supplemented by the body of legal doctrines and precepts that have been accepted by States generally, and particularly as manifested in the resolutions of UN organs."

But principle and law could not decide all questions confronting the Secretary-General. "Problems of political judgment still remain." Here there were other techniques that could help him reduce "the element of purely personal judgment." Frequent consultation with the Permanent Missions to the UN was one. Another was the advisory committee which in the case of UNEF and the Congo "provided an essential link between the judgment of the executive and the consensus of the political bodies."

Despite all such safeguards there would still remain an "area of discretion" which though reduced would be "large enough to expose the international Secretariat to heated political controversy and to accusations of a lack of neutrality."

Here one entered the realm of integrity and conscience. "The international civil servant must keep himself under the strictest observation." He will have his likes and dislikes, his ideals and "interests which are close to him in a personal capacity." His obligation is "to be fully aware of those human reactions and meticulously check himself so that they are not permitted to influence his actions. This is nothing unique. Is not every judge professionally under the same obligation?

"If the international civil servant knows himself to be free from such personal influences in his actions and guided solely by the common aims and rules laid down for, and by the Organization he serves and by recognized legal principles, then he has done his duty, and then he can face the criticism which even so, will be unavoidable."

As the author was bringing his book to a close, changes were taking place on the thirty-eighth floor. The group that went out to lunch with Hammarskjold and reviewed the day's events at sundown was changing complexion. It was acquiring an Afro-Asian cast. Andy Cordier as a final earnest of service and devotion to Hammarskjold was retiring. Other changes were under way designed to make the executive arm of the UN representative of the enlarged organization without impairing its operational effectiveness.

The issues had been squarely drawn and were now in the hands of the member states of the UN. They have to decide between Khrushchev's view that there are no neutral men and Hammarskjold's faith in an integrity and impartiality that can rise above national loyalties.

They have to decide between the demands for a collegial body despite its potentialities for paralysis and Hammarskjold's concept of a strong executive serving the needs particularly of the small and the weak in the international community.

They have to decide whether the UN's capacity to undertake executive operations such as those in the Middle East and the Congo should be ended, its ability to help emergent countries curtailed, its role as a custodian of the brushfire peace annulled.

Whatever the fate of Dag Hammarskjold, even if he should be succeeded by a "clerk" and the UN pushed to the margin of international activity, that will not be the end of the story.

We are, as Hammarskjold has so often said, only in the

embryonic stage of international co-operation and integration. In future decades, unless complete disaster brings the human story to an end, there will be strong Secretaries-General and weak ones. The strong ones will seek to advance the frontier of international co-operation and they will find their model and inspiration in the way this reserved Swedish aristocrat discharged his duties.

Working at the edge of the development of human society is to work on the brink of the unknown. Much of what is done will one day prove to have been of little avail. That is no excuse for the failure to act in accordance with our best understanding, in recognition of its limits but with faith in the ultimate result of the creative evolution in which it is our privilege to cooperate.

Speech at the University of Chicago Law School, 1960.

Epilogue

"... but he would have wanted every living person to do something now—at once—to establish and ratify the pure ideas for which he lived. Can you tell me what we must do for UN?"

An artist friend of Hammarskjold's on hearing of his death, September 18, 1961

The early months of 1961 were among the most difficult of Dag Hammarskjold's incumbency. The Soviet attack on him reached levels of brutality and vituperation that shocked the world. The long hours that he had worked without a break since the beginning of the Congo crisis began to exact a toll. He became edgy and moody.

"For God's sake, get the meeting adjourned," he begged a friendly delegate in a note as the speeches droned on one night in the Congo Advisory Committee. He told a Middle East diplomat, with whom he had often crossed swords, that he could stand up against the political cannonading of the Russians, but he didn't know whether he had enough strength to stand up against their vulgarity. A worried Andy Cordier signaled Per Lind in Stockholm that he hoped he was coming over as a member of the Swedish delegation to the resumed session of the Assembly and would stay with Dag as he always did when he was in New York. As a particularly interminable and squalid procedural wrangle drew to a close in the First

Committee in the early hours of the morning, Hammarskjold penciled a note: "This end (if end it is) is nightmarish." The atmosphere was becoming hateful to him, he added. He hoped his feeling was "temporary."

It was. Within a few weeks he had bounced back. The 83–11 vote of confidence, the turn for the better in the Congo, the end of the speechmaking with the adjournment of the Assembly all helped his natural buoyancy to reassert itself. He found a line from Shelley to give expression to the mending of his spirits: one should "hope 'til Hope creates from its own wreck the thing it contemplates."

"Let's have a fun party," he said to Freddie Boland of Ireland, who as President of the Fifteenth Session had gone through the ordeal of the shoe-banging Assembly with him and to whom he had become quite attached. The "fun party" was an evening of high intellectual talk at his apartment. The other guests were the John Steinbecks, the Wieschhoffs and Lotte Lenya. There were many toasts—to Steinbeck's new book and another by Hammarskjold to his "gray eminence" Heinz Wieschhoff.

In London, on his way back from Oxford, where he had received an honorary degree and in a combative speech defended his concept of an independent and impartial international civil service, he browsed in the bookstores and delightedly picked up a first edition of Forster's *Passage to India*. He dropped in at an exhibition of paintings and sculptures of Barbara Hepworth to whom he had been introduced by George Ivan Smith. She had done something especially for him, she told Hammarskjold. Don't point it out, he begged her. He wanted to see whether he could pick it out by himself. He looked around and unerringly headed for it.

By the time the Bizerte crisis came into the Security Council in July he was back to his old form, moving deftly and confidently behind the scenes to assert the powers of his office to help bring about a solution. The French rebuff did not deter him. He took it for granted that as the executive arm of the UN asserted leadership and the General Assembly took on the aspects of a parliament a right- as well as a left-wing opposition would develop.

He would have appreciated stronger U.S. backing on the Bizerte mission but did not complain of this when the U.S. at a later stage sounded him out on sending a UN force to Bizerte. This was after the failure of efforts by Secretary Rusk and Ambassador Stevenson to budge President de Gaulle aroused fears that fighting might be renewed. He was as ready as ever to let them "give it to Dag," but where was his authorization to send troops? he asked. And where would he get them?

He was critical, too, of U.S. and British reluctance to take the offensive against de Gaulle on the issue of the UN's future. He could understand why Soviet Russia's East European allies did not dare speak out against the *troika*, although some of their diplomats let him know privately that they did not agree with Soviet UN policy, but why should the U.S. and Britain hide their views?

During the summer Andy Cordier resigned as his executive aide to make it easier for him to reshuffle the top-level Secretariat in order to provide greater representation for Africa and Asia. It was hoped others would follow Andy's self-denying example, but none did, and Andy was the only one to be reorganized, Narasimhan taking on the job of Hammarskjold's *chef du cabinet*. But there was no change in their personal relationship. Hammarskjold would still come into Andy's office to exchange ideas, announce a policy, share a joke.

Did he have a premonition of death? Some of his closest friends think so. Toward the end of the summer he wrote a will. When he left for the Congo, his normally orderly apartment was in a condition of superior orderliness. He presented a draft of the Introduction to his Annual Report to Cordier with the words, "I don't see what I can write after this one." It was his testament, he indicated, the way he construed the Charter.

In it he warned again, as he had in his Oxford speech, that the Organization was at a turning point: it could be set back not simply to the ineffectiveness of the League of Nations but to the almost total lawlessness and anarchy which preceded the

League. Members had to choose between two concepts of the UN—as a "static conference machinery" or as a "dynamic instrument" by which nations could shape "an organized world community."

The UN intervention in the Congo, an international operation which he considered unique in its magnitude and complexity, was illustrative of the growth of the UN out of the conference pattern. If the hopeful developments of the summer, the reconvening of Parliament, and the progress toward national reconciliation represented in the government of Cyrille Adoula were to provide a basis finally for the peace, unity, and independence of the country, that would "definitely confirm the correctness of the line pursued by the UN in the Congo."

As his Report circulated among delegations and the 16th Session of the Assembly neared, only Katanga remained outside of the new consensus, its resistance to UN decisions instigated, emboldened, and stiffened by several hundred foreign mercenaries. In the staff dining room on the thirty-eighth floor there hung an enlargement of his Anapurna photograph. He would refer to it often when the Congo Club ate together to show where he thought the UN operation was in relation to achieving its aims. They were close to the crest now. To make it easier for Tshombe to come to terms with the Central Government and the UN he accepted Adoula's invitation to fly to Leopoldville.

Cordier, Bunche, General Rikhye, Sir Alexander were at the airport to bid farewell to the SG, Heinz, and Bill Ranallo. "As far as Leo is concerned this will be the most pleasant of your trips there," Cordier observed.

"Yes, I hope," was Hammarskjold's cautious reply.

He exchanged a few words about Djuna Barnes with Mrs. Wieschhoff, how much he admired her writing. She asked him how he was coming along with his translation of Martin Buber from the German into the Swedish. He had frequently sought Heinz's advice on this project. The question started some unexplained train of thought. He fell silent and turned to the plane.

The only book he took with him this time was the devotional

work from his bedside table, his seventeenth-century Brussels edition of *Imitatio Christi*. In it was found after his death the Secretary-General's oath of office.

"I, Dag Hammarskjold, solemnly swear to exercise in all loyalty, discretion and conscience the functions entrusted to me as Secretary-General of the United Nations, to discharge these functions and regulate my conduct with the interests of the UN only in view and not to seek or accept instructions in regard to the performance of my duties from any government or other authority external to the Organization."

Index

H. refers to Dag Hammarskjold

Abbas, Mekki, 284
Acheson, Dean, 72
Adenauer, Konrad, 170
Africa, 6, 176, 178; economic aid to, 185–88; H. awareness of, 223–24; independence movement, 224 ff.; new states, 5; pan-Africanism, 251–52, 253; solidarity, 253–54; and UN, 262; UNEF, 179, 180; UN "presence," 184, 186–88; UN reputation in, 280
Afro-Asian bloc, 84, 85, 102, 124, 170–71
Aggression, 86, 114, 120
Almquist, Carl Jonas Love, 19
Alphand, Hervé, 74, 107, 160
Anderson, Robert, 75
Anglo-French-Egypt war, 82, 84, 85, 90
Aquaba, 104, 106; gulf of, 101, 103; issue, 101–11
Arab "good neighbor" resolution, 125
Arab-Israeli Armistice Agreements of 1949, 66–67, 69, 70, 71, 72, 75, 86, 104, 105, 109, 129, 133
Arab-Israeli war, 66 ff., 129
Arab refugees, 67, 69, 75, 133–34
Arab states, 66. *See also under* name of state
Arkadyev, Georgi P., 4–5
Arms race. *See* Disarmament
Asia, 178; economic aid to, 185; new states, 5; UNEF, 179, 180; UN "presence," 184
as-Said, Nuri, 113, 116
Aström, Sverker, 43
Aswan High Dam, 76
Atoms-for-peace Conference, 1955, 152–53
Austria, neutralization, 3

Backlund, Sven, 11, 43, 215
Baghdad Pact, 113
Baltika, 243, 264, 265
Bandung Treaty Powers, 97, 228
Bang-Jensen, Povl, 196–97
Barco, James W., 80–82; Suez crisis, 85
Beck-Friis, Ambassador, 139
Beer, Max, 194
Belfrage, Lief, 41, 89, 219, 221
Belgium, 2, 4, 5, 6, 97, 226 ff., 245–46, 250, 259; H. and, 245–46
Ben-Gurion, David, 67, 68, 69, 72–73, 75, 76, 89, 129; H. and, 215, 219
Ben-Gurion, Paula, 73, 219
Berlin, 157, 178, 181; Foreign ministers meeting, 159; UN in, 161; UN "presence," 183
Bernadotte, Count Folke, 130
Beskow, Bo, 11–12, 13, 64, 217, 220, 221, 222
Beskow, Greta, 64
Bjorklund, Andreas, 213
Black, Eugene, 96
Boheman, Erik, 11, 13
Bohlen, Charles ("Chip"), 248, 256
Bokhari, Dr. Ahmed, 12, 54, 60, 61, 173
Boland, Frederick, 268, 269, 270
Bomboko, Justin, 237
Bourguiba, President, 240, 262
Buber, Professor Martin, 149–50, 215
Bulganin, Nikolai, 74, 89, 161
Bull, Odd, 115
Bunche, Dr. Ralph, 1, 2, 54, 60, 87, 95, 188, 220, 270, 284, 287; Congo crisis, 226 ff., 239, 249; UNEF, 88
Burns, Gen. E. L. M., 68, 72, 77, 87, 88, 95

Cambodia, 139
Camerouns, French, 131
Canada, 83, 90, 140, 174
Castro, Fidel, 266
Cease-fire: Arab-Israeli Armistice Agreements, 71–76; Suez Canal crisis, 81, 83, 90–91, 94
Charter, UN, 8, 61, 62, 70, 81, 84, 117, 139–40, 165, 179, 184; Articles: *II (7)*, 225, *VII*, 203, *28 (2)*, 159, 161, *29 (2)*, 142, *51*, 71, *97*, 203–4, *98*, 203–4, *99*, 160, 203–4, *100*, 47, 50, *101*, 47, 50; Chapter VII, 102, 158, 173; geographic representation, 286; legal interpretations, 203 ff.; provisions, unused, 79; Secretary-General position, 53
Chamoun, Camille, 113, 114, 115, 116, 126
Chehab, Fuad, 117, 120, 126
China. *See* Nationalist China *and* Red China
China Lobby, 57, 58
Chou En-lai, 10, 58–59, 60 ff., 64–65, 207
Churchill, Winston, 174
Clay, Lucius, 96
Cleveland, Harlan, 169, 178
Coexistence, 147–48, 151, 176, 274
Cold war, 178; new nations and, 262; UN and, 147–63
"Collective colonialism," 77
Comay, Michael, 108
Congo, 1, 2, 4, 5, 6, 188, 223–62, 287; Advisory Committee, 259, 260; crisis, 174–182; delegation, 237; *force publique*, 254; Fund, 268; Lebanese precedent, 238; ONUC, 230 ff., 241, 247, 248, 249, 252, 255, 262; request for military aid, 227 ff.; UN: Command, 252, 254, intervention, reason for, 243, nonintervention in internal affairs, 261–62
Congo Club, 1, 182, 259; Afro-Asians in, 260–61
Constantinople Convention, 100
Cook, Charles, 209
Cordier, Andrew, 1, 2, 54, 55, 85, 96, 108, 220, 226, 229, 230, 241, 247, 270, 284, 287, 291
Corea, Sir Claude, 236, 240, 257
Coulter, General, 88–89
Council of Europe, 43
Crowe, Eyre, 170
Cuba, 4–5, 264

Dayal, Rajeshwar, 4, 115, 246, 247, 249, 254, 256, 259, 284, 287
Dean, Sir Patrick, 177, 256
Decolonization, 5, 183, 186
De Gaulle, Charles, 162, 164–65, 166, 170, 171, 210, 266
Denmark, 36, 37, 90, 97
De Seynes, Philippe, 54, 223
Diefenbaker, John, 266
Diplomacy, 209; Chinese, subtlety of, 61; of conciliation, 150; conference, 151; preventive, 137–46, 166, 276, 279–80; public debate, 151; of reconciliation, 159, 211
Disarmament, 154–58
Dixon, Sir Pierson, 74, 80, 82, 83, 116, 160; on H., 82; Suez Canal crisis, 83, 85, 88
Dobrynin, Anatoly, 54–55, 143, 220
Drummond, Sir Eric, 8, 46, 47
Dulles, John Foster, 7, 8, 62, 63, 76–78, 80 ff., 99, 109, 114 ff., 120, 125, 148–49, 194, 207; Suez Canal crisis, 76, 83, 84, 100, 106

Eban, Abba, 70, 74–75, 76, 90, 102, 106–7, 128, 171–72
Economic and Social Council (ECOSOC), 184, 187, 203
Economic Cooperation Administration (ECA), 40
Eden, Sir Anthony, 9, 60, 67, 68, 76, 79, 89, 91, 99, 110
Egypt, 68 ff., 76, 81, 85, 112, 265; -Israeli Armistice Agreements. *See* Arab-Israeli Armistice Agreements; Suez Canel crisis, 91. *See also* United Arab Republic
Eisenhower, Dwight D., 57, 59, 68, 75, 77, 82, 83, 119, 120, 122, 131, 157, 169, 180, 207–8, 227, 243, 266, 267; "Doctrine," 113, 114; Suez Canal crisis, 77, 84, 90
El-Auja, 68, 73
Elizabeth II, Queen, of England, 219
Engen, Hans, 57, 58, 84, 85, 88, 123, 124, 174, 180, 229; UNEF, 89

Faisal, King, 113, 116
Faura, Oscar, 3
Fawzi, Dr. Mahmoud, 73, 76, 77, 78, 86, 87, 97, 101 ff., 106, 123 ff., 130, 131
Fedayeen groups, 69, 110
Federation of Rhodesia and Nyasaland, 234

Finland, 44, 90; neutralization, 3
Formosa, 59, 63
Formin, Andre, 242
France, 210; Congo, 258; Egypt, 82, 84; Guinea, 139; H. and, 9; Israel, 81; Middle East, 67 ff.; Secretary-General formula, 282; Suez Canal crisis, 76–79, 81, 84, 90–91, 99, 100; Tripartite Declaration of 1950, 67; UNEF, 98; UN estrangement, 164–65, 170. *See also* De Gaulle, Charles

Gaitskell, Hugh, 9, 206
Gardiner, Robert, 259
Gaza, 104, 106, 108, 109, 177; Strip issue, 101–11
General Assembly (UN), 137, 203 ff., 216; 1958, 156; 1959, 152, H. report, 139; 1960; 172, 263 ff., annual report, 177–78; center party shift, 174; December 1954 resolution, 57–58, 61; eighth, 53; first, 47; Hungarian Revolution, 87; Lebanese crisis, 120; operation methods, 172–73; Suez Canal crisis, 82 ff., 87, 91, 108; UNEF, 98
Geneva, 60, 64, 78; Agreements (Indochina war), 140, 141, 145; Big Four meeting, 157, 161; Committee of Ten, 157–58; summit meeting, 1955, 159; test ban, 156; UN staff, 50, 147
"Gentleman's agreement," 109
Germany, 96; Federal Republic of, 97
Ghana, 227–28, 236, 252–53, 254
Gierow, Karl Ragnar, 216, 218, 220
Gizenga, Antoine, 227, 234, 235, 237, 239, 250, 257, 259
Goldmann, Nahum, 72–73, 209
Gomulka, Wladyslaw, 273–74
Great Britain, 210; Egypt, 82, 84; and H., 9, 67, 165–66; Israel, 81; Laos, 141; Lebanon crisis, 116; Middle East, 67 ff., 74; state service, philosophy of, 32; Suez Canal clearing, 96, 97; Suez Canal crisis, 76–79, 81, 84, 90–91, 99, 100; Tripartite Declaration of, 1950, 67; and UN, 165–66; UNEF, 98
Great Depression, 27, 184
Gromyko, Andrei, 9, 121 ff., 156, 157, 166, 167, 258, 278
Guinea, 139, 188, 236, 242, 257

Hagerstrom, Adel, 22, 27–28
Hailsham, Viscount, 97
Hammarskjold, Agnes Almquist (mother), 19, 20, 21, 23, 24, 33, 35, 41
Hammarskjold, Ake (brother), 20
Hammarskjold, Bo (brother), 20, 25, 32, 33, 221
Hammarskjold, Dag: Africa trip, 184; ambition, 29–30; Ben-Gurion, 72–73, 129, 215, 219, 261; birth, 18; Bohlen, 248; Chou En-lai, 60–61, 207; de Gaulle, 210; diplomacy, 69, 71, 137–46, 148, 151, 166, 209; doctoral dissertation, 28–29, 30, 198; Dulles, 148–49, 169; economist, 28–30, 33; on equality, 33–34; family background, 17 ff.; "fire brigades," 123; Foreign Office, 41, 42–44; government service, 32; Gromyko, 127; growth in, 137 ff.; interests, 14, 24–25, 35–36, 89, 198, 213–22; Kennedy, 207; Khrushchev, 167, 207, 215, 272–73; language, 39, 197–98, 200; Laos, 140–46; Lodge, 49–50, 82, 168; Lumumba, 261; marriage, 36, 42, 219; Middle East, 66–79, 134–37; as moralist, 149; mother's influence, 19–20; Nasser, 73, 81, 261; on national maturity, 165; OEEC, 39–41; Oxford address, 288–89; Peking mission, 56–65, 137, 207; personal characteristics, 31, 34, 87, 190, 198–99, 206–12; philosophy, 17, 149, 199, 200; Pineau, 99; press conferences, 191 ff.; private life, 13, 190, 213–22; pronunciation of name, 13; religion, 24; Riksbank, 37, 38–39; Secretary-General. *See* Secretary-General (UN); Social Democrats, 32–34; special abilities, 30, 31, 32, 33, 35, 37–38, 40, 60, 167, 198, 200, 206, 207, 208, 209, 283; student, 21–23; Suez Canal crisis, 76–79, 98–99; Sweden, love of, 26, 200, 220–21; Swedish Academy, 17, 19; Swedish neutrality, 43–44; Syngman Rhee, 193; tradition of service, 32–33; Under-Secretary of Finance, 31 ff., 34–39; Unemployment Commission, 28, 30; UN: concept of, 175, 178–79, 271; personnel policies, 49–55, small powers, 171, 271–72

Hammarskjold, Hjalmar (father), 13, 17, 18–19, 20–21, 22, 23, 24, 26, 31, 32, 33, 35, 36, 42, 222

Hammarskjold, Landhovding Bo, 18–19

Hammarskjold, Sten (brother), 20, 21

Herter, Christian, 131, 187, 227, 256, 268

Hickenlooper, Senator, 172

Hoffman, Paul, 40, 185

Holmes, John, 179–80, 211–12, 261

Hoover, Jr., Herbert, 80

Hoppenot, Henri, 8

Hungarian Revolution, 87, 89, 92, 168, 173

Hussein, King, 113, 116, 126, 171

Imperialism, 66

India, 51, 100, 110, 124, 140, 152, 174; UNEF, 181

Indochina war, 140

International Bank, 96, 100

International civil service, 47, 48, 50–51, 53; nationality and, 287–89, 291; personal requirements, 207

International Control Commission, 140, 141

International Court, 20, 100, 101

Intervention. *See* UN, "presence" concept

Iraq, 113, 118; revolt, 121

Israel, 66 ff., 100, 128, 198, 210, 265; cargo question, 130–32; -Egypt Armistice Agreement, 68–76, 83, 86; -Egypt Suez war, 80–82; -Egyptian border clashes, 132–33; establishment of, 66; reprisal and retaliation policy, 67; Sinai invasion, 80, 81, 82; Suez Canal crisis, 80, 91, 101 ff.; UNEF, 102–3

Italy, 97, 142

Jamali, Fadhil, 113–14

Japan, 142

Jawad, Hashim, 85

Jebb, Sir Gladwyn, 8, 12, 67

Johansson, Alf, 27, 28, 29, 35

Jordan, 113, 116, 151, 177, 180; UN "presence," 182–83, 188

Kadar, Janos, 272

Kasavubu, 226–27, 228, 234, 236, 245, 247, 249–50, 255–56, 260

Katanga, 234, 236, 245; secession, 228

Kennan, George, 218

Kennedy, John F., 145, 158, 178, 207, 251, 256; Administration and UN, 169–70

Kerensky, Alexander, 280

Kettani, General, 237–38, 280

Keynes, John M., 27, 33

Knowland, Senator, 57, 148

Kock, Karin, 29, 41

Korean War, 9, 10, 56, 57, 60, 88; armistice, 57, 148; UN Command, 88–89; UN formula, 252

Khrushchev, Nikita S., 74, 113, 117, 119, 120, 156, 161, 166, 207, 208, 241, 243, 244, 258, 263–80; General Assembly (1960), 263–74; on H., 215, 272–73, 280; neutral men, 289, 291; troika formula, 274–75, 282

Kuznetsov, 237, 240, 244

Lall, Arthur, 85, 88, 89

Laos, 2–3, 5, 140–46, 160, 177, 178, 204, 265, 275–76; UN technical assistance mission, 3

Lebanon, 72, 113, 145, 151, 177, 178, 180, 182, 205–6, 229, 287; civil war, 112–27; UN operation in, 137

League of Nations, 8, 47, 276

Leopoldville, 224, 226, 234 ff.

Lie, Trygve, 8–10, 13, 14, 46, 48, 49, 51–53, 190, 271; on H., 10–11; *In the cause of Peace,* 11; Soviet boycott of, 11

Lind, Per, 13, 54, 220

Linnaeus, 165, 216

Lippmann, Walter, 273

Lloyd, Selwyn, 76, 77, 78, 79, 96, 109, 123, 125, 198

Lodge, Henry Cabot, 7, 8, 10, 48, 49, 59, 80, 81, 82, 85, 120–21, 150, 169, 170, 211, 218; H. and, 49–50, 82, 168; Lebanon crisis, 118; Suez Canal crisis, 80, 85, 99, 101

Loridan, Walter, 229

Loutfi, Omar, 4, 114

Louw, Foreign Minister, 225

Lowenthal, Richard, 274

Lumumba, Patrice, 2, 4, 226–28, 233–36, 238–39, 245–47, 249, 253, 255, 257, 261, 278

Lundberg, Erik, 27, 28, 29, 34, 35, 37

McCarthy, Joseph, 48, 49, 58

McCloy, John J., 96

Macmillan, Harold, 119, 120, 161, 266
Malik, Charles, 113, 114, 115
Mansfield, Senator Mike, 172, 195
Mao Tse-tung, 120
Marjolin, Robert, 40
Marshall Plan, 8, 38, 39–40; U.S. requirements, 39
Marx, Karl, 27–28
Matsudaira, Ambassador, 118
Matthews, H. Freeman ("Doc"), 7
Mendès-France, M., 60
Menon, Krishna, 10, 103, 174, 179, 215, 261–62
Menzies, Robert, 266
Middle East, 66–79; 137; Arab-Israeli war, 66; Armistice Agreements. *See* Arab-Israeli Armistice Agreements; Lebanese civil war, 112–27; "quiet diplomacy," 69; Suez crisis, 76–111; UN "presence," 183–84
Mikoyan, Anastas, 167, 215
Miller, Dorothy, 216–17
Mobutu, Colonel, 2, 4, 244, 246, 254
Mollet, Guy, 89, 90, 110
Mrydal, Gunnar, 27, 28, 29, 34
Murray, Geoffrey, 55
Murrow, Edward R., 24

Narasimhan, C. V., 54, 55, 259, 284
Nasser, Gamal A., 68–69, 72, 73, 75, 76, 79, 80, 81, 96, 97, 100, 113, 115, 117, 125, 126, 130, 180, 193, 196, 266, 274; Suez Canal crisis, 81, 90, 95, 108; UNEF, 88, 97–98, 103
Nasserism, 112, 113; rise of, 67
Nationalism, 66, 118; African, 224 ff.; Arab, 112–13, 116, 127
Nationalist China, 59
NATO, 43, 88, 155, 157, 249, 286
Nehru, Jawaharlal, 85, 180, 258, 266, 274, 285; Secretary-General formula, 282
Netherlands, 96, 97
Neustadt, Richard E., 192
Neutralists, 266, 268, 274–75
Neutrality, 289
Neutralization, 3
New nations, UN and, 230, 264
Nigeria, 174
Nitze, Paul H., 7
Nkrumah, Dr. Kwame, 187, 251–55

Nkrumah, Premier, 227, 237, 258, 266, 274–75; Secretary-General formula, 282
North Vietnam, 140, 141
Norway, 18, 36–37, 90, 100, 174; OEEC delegation, 40; UN delegation, 57
November 2 cease-fire resolution, 83, 86, 90, 91
Nuclear testing, 154, 155; ban, 119
Nwokedi, Francis C., 259

Ohlin, Bertil, 28
Olympio, Sylvanus, 188
"Operation momentum," 74
Organization for European Economic Cooperation (OEEC), 9, 39, 40, 41, 43; Swedish delegation to, 41
Outer Space: Committee, 197–98; UN and, 151–54

Pakistan, 90
Palestine partition, 66, 72, 133
Paris summit meeting, 158, 162, 176, 263
Pasternak, Boris, 149, 215
Pathet Lao (Communist), 140, 144, 145
Pearson, Lester ("Mike"), 9, 10, 13, 14, 83–84, 85, 86, 91, 103, 106, 108, 174, 181, 185, 229; resolution, 83; UNEF, 83, 87, 88, 89
Peking: "formula," 61, 225; H. mission to, 56–65, 66, 137, 207. *See also* Red China
Perse, Saint-John, 216, 218
Phoui Sananikone, 144
Phouma, Souvanna, 140, 143, 145
Piao, General Keng, 59, 63
Pineau, M., 76, 77, 78, 79, 86, 106, 110; Suez Canal crisis, 86
Poland, 140, 236
Police force, international. *See* United Nations Emergency Force (UNEF)

Rabi, I. I., 153
Ranallo, Bill, 219, 221, 224
Red China, 10, 120, 274; American airmen prisoners, 57 ff.; diplomacy, 61; entry into UN, 58; H. mission to Peking, 56–65; Laos, 140, 143; US recognition of, 59
Rhee, Syngman, 193
Rikhye, General, 182, 259
Roosevelt, Franklin D., 174, 235

Rooth, Ivar, 39
Rudzinski, Dr. Aleksander, 9
Rusk, Dean, 169
Russia, 44. *See* Soviet Union

Sabry, Ali, 131
Sanctions, 99, 106
Schweitzer, Albert, 34, 214
SEATO, 2, 140
Secretariat (UN), 203; dispersion of posts, 51–52; independence of, 46, 48–51; reorganization plan, 53. *See also* International civil service
Secretary-General (UN): authority of, 61–62, 65, 70, 81–82, 138, 139–40, 143, 160; dimensions of job, 201–2; H. and, 7–15, 46–55, 67, anti-resignation speech, 271–72, concept of job, 14, 81–82, 283–92, legalism, 98, 109, 110, 133, reappointment, 137, techniques, 109–10, top-level staff, 53–54, use of personal representatives, 275–76; oath of office, 14; one-man job, 281–92; political potentialities of office, 5; powers, 9, 70, 92, 118–19. *See also* authority; role of, 81; sources of "power," 203–12; Soviet attacks on post, 268; and U. S. Presidency, 143; *vox populorum* concept of, 201
Security Council (UN), 81, 137, 203 ff., 211, 212, 224; agenda, 67; Armistice Agreements, 70; and Cold War, 158–63; Congo, 228 ff.; on H., 82; Hungarian Revolution, 87; impotence of, 65; Lebanon, 113, 115; Middle East, 67, 70; "operation momentum," 74; role, 173–74; Secretary-General obligation to, 5; Suez crisis, 76–79, 81, 90, 101
Shepilov, Dmitri, 76, 78
Sinai Peninsula, 80, 82
Sisco, Joseph, 168
Skang, Arne, 40, 41
Slim, Mongi, 174, 229, 230, 231, 236, 240, 250, 257, 272
Smith, George I., 72
Snow, Edgar, 64
Sobolev, Arkady, 70, 82, 85, 90, 114, 118, 144, 155, 160, 184, 187, 241; on H., 82
Söderblom, Archbishop Nathan, 23
Souvannavong, Prince, 140, 143, 144
Soviet Union: Africa, 224, "plan,"
187–88; Congo, 236, 241–46, 249, 250, 252, 253–55, 257, 258; disarmament, 154–58; General Assembly (1960), 263–80; Hungarian Revolution, 87, 89, 92; Laos, 140–43, 145–46; H., 82, 145, 155, 166–68, attacks on, 178, 257, 258, 265, 267, 269–73, 278–80, knowledge of, 9–10, Peking mission, 60; Lebanon, 117, 118; Lie, 9–10; Middle East, 67 ff., 113, 132–33; on negotiation, 150; outer space, 151–54, 197–98; propaganda, 151; state ethos, 287–88; Suez Canal crisis, 84, 89, 90, 95; Swedish plane incident, 42–43; three-bloc secretariat, 51; Tripartite Declaration of 1950, 67–68; troika proposal, 268; and UN, 166–68; UNEF, 98, 102, 179, 180, 181; UN posts, 52. *See also* Khrushchev
Spaak, Henri, 99; "amendment," 99, 100
Spinelli, Pier Pasquale, 188
Stalin, Joseph, 10, 42, 67, 148, 174
Stavropoulos, Constantin A., 188
Stevenson, Adlai, 169, 256–58
Stockholm, 16, 59; Movement, 23; "School," 27–28, 29, 37
Stolpe, Sven, 26, 29, 34, 35
Subversion, 114. *See also* Aggression
Suez Canal, 76, 80, 86, 94, 95–96, 100, 101, 110; crisis, 76–111, 117, 168, 173, 177, 205, 208, 210, 229; nationalization of, 76, 193–94
Sukarno, 266
Summit meetings, 119, 120, 161; Geneva, 159; Paris, 158, 162, 176, 263; periodic, 161
Swartling, Eric, 36
Sweden, 7–8, 89, 97, 114; anonymity policy, 190; civil service aristocracy, 17–18; foreign affairs approach, 43–44; Lutheranism, 23; neutrality, 36, 44; state service, philosophy of, 32; welfare state, 32
Swedish Academy, 16–17, 24, 25, 35, 63, 213, 214, 221
Swedish Tourist Association, 25–26, 220
Syria, 72, 112. *See also* United Arab Republic

Tchernyshev, Ilya, 60
Thailand, 108, 139
Timberlake, Clare, 227

Tito, Marshal, 217, 266, 275
Touré, Sekon, 276
Trevelyan, Sir Humphrey, 55, 210
Tripartite Declaration of 1950, 67–68
Tshombe, Moise, 234, 235, 236, 238, 242, 259
Tunisia, 113, 142, 174, 229
Tuomioja, Sakari, 143–44

UN (United Nations): Arab-Israeli war, 67 ff.; balance of power shift, 170–71; change in, 271; Cold War, 147–63; diplomacy, 56 ff., 162–63; disarmament, 154–58; Economic Commission for Europe, 143; economic thinking, 184–85; Emergency Force (UNEF), 93–95, 101–3, 123, 178–82, 184, 229, 262, 265, Armistice Committee, 181; employment criteria, 47, 48–49; European office, 188; executive arm, 253, 291. *See also* Secretary-General; FBI check, 48–49; force, 83–84, 87, 141, 179. *See also* UNEF; great powers and, 171–74; indispensability of, 78–79; Israel, 66; Korea, 88–89; legislative process, 151; London Preparatory Commission, 288; Meditation Room, 222; military aid, request for, 227; new nations, 174; Nov. 2 cease-fire resolution, 83, 84, 86; Observation Group in Lebanon (UNOGIL), 115–17, 181, 182, 238, 253; observers, 75; outer space, 151–54; Palestine partition, 66; police force. *See* UNEF; Preparatory Commission, 47; preparedness, 182; "presence" concept, 177–88, 224; press corps, 192, 194–95; propaganda potentials, 150–51; public information, 189; Red China admission, 58; Relief and Works Agency (UNRWA), 133, 184; role, 6, 78–79, 230; salvage fleet, 96–97; Scientific Advisory Committee, 152, 153; small nations, 264; Special Fund, 185, 187; staff members. *See* International civil service; technical assistance, 3, 184, 185, 187; as third force, 164–76, 201; Truce Supervisory Organization (UNTSO), 68; U.S. relationship, 48–49
Unden, Osten, 9, 41, 42
Union of South Africa, H. mission, 224–26

U.S.S.R. *See* Soviet Union
United Arab Republic, 4, 112, 113, 130, 152; in Congo, 255
U.S. (United States): Africa, 224, "plan," 187; Central Intelligence Agency (CIA), 116, 145; -Chinese relations, 59, 61, recognition of Red China, 59; communism and neutralism, 145; in Congo, 246, 248–49, 251, 253, 256–57, 259–60; disarmament, 154–58; and H., 168–70; Hungarian Revolution, 87; Israel, 81; Laos, 140, 141–42, 145–46; Lebanon, 115–16; loyalty investigations, 47, 48; Middle East, 67 ff.; on negotiation, 150; outer space, 151–54; Presidency, 143, 192, 200; Sixth Fleet, 85; State Department, 7, 10, 62, 168; Strategic Air Command, 155; Suez Canal, 80, 88, 99–100; Tripartite Declaration of 1950, 67–68; UN, 48–49, 168–70, 172, delegation, 58, 82; UNEF, 85, 88, 98, 180
Urquhart, Brian, 255
Urrutia, Dr. Francisco, 85, 88, 206

Vaughan, David, 230
Virally, Michel, 206
Vishinsky, Andrei, 7, 8, 10, 14, 67
von Horn, General, 247

Wachtmeister, Wilhelm, 224
Wadsworth, James J., 157, 248, 256
Warsaw Pact, 157
Wheeler, Raymond A. (Jack), 96, 97
Wicksell, Knut, 27, 33
Wieschhoff, Heinz, 2, 4, 54, 224, 229, 234, 270, 284
Wigforss, Ernst, 30–32, 37, 38–39, 41
Willers, Uno, 59–60, 63, 65, 216, 220
Wold, Knut Getz, 36
World Jewish Congress, 72
World War I, 19, 222
World War II, 36

Yalta concept, 174
Yugoslavia, 82, 97, 174, 217

Zeineddine, Farid, 131
Zellweger, Edouard, 2, 144
Zorin, Valerian A., 4, 244, 249, 258, 287